# Early Burial Customs in Northern Egypt

## Evidence from the Pre-, Proto-, and Early Dynastic Periods

Joanna Dębowska-Ludwin

BAR International Series 2571

2013

Published in 2016 by
BAR Publishing, Oxford

BAR International Series 2571


*Early Burial Customs in Northern Egypt*

ISBN 978 1 4073 1192 0

© J Dębowska-Ludwin and the Publisher 2013

COVER IMAGE *Digital reconstruction of enclosure no. 55 from Tell el-Farkha by Karolina Rosińska-Balik*

BAR Publishing is the trading name of British Archaeological Reports (Oxford) Ltd.
British Archaeological Reports was first incorporated in 1974 to publish the BAR
Series, International and British. In 1992 Hadrian Books Ltd became part of the BAR
group. This volume was originally published by Archaeopress in conjunction with
British Archaeological Reports (Oxford) Ltd / Hadrian Books Ltd, the Series principal
publisher, in 2013. This present volume is published by BAR Publishing, 2016.

Printed in England

# BAR
PUBLISHING

BAR titles are available from:

BAR Publishing
122 Banbury Rd, Oxford, OX2 7BP, UK
EMAIL    info@barpublishing.com
PHONE   +44 (0)1865 310431
FAX    +44 (0)1865 316916
www.barpublishing.com

# LIST OF CONTENTS:

# 1. INTRODUCTION

The issue of burial customs practiced in the formative period of pharaonic civilization belongs to the most important and interesting in the archeology of ancient Egypt. Although many pages have been written on burial customs themselves and objects offered to the deceased in those early days, it would be mistaken to think the topic is exhausted. In a closer look, a clear disproportion in the state of research on Upper and Lower Egypt is striking. Whereas the situation in the South is fairly well-known, the North remains hardly recognized. Following seasons of works, new and highly significant discoveries are being made in the field, which may be exemplified by Polish excavations at the site of Tell el-Farkha or French works in Kom el-Khilgan. Each year fresh field reports, studies and monographs on particular sites are published, but there is still no general synthesis of sepulchral traditions typical of the northern part of Egypt. It mainly concerns the time of full blossom of the Lower Egyptian culture, the period of the so-called Naqadan expansion or even the earlier epoch when Lower Egypt was encompassed by the emerging Egypt-wide monarchy. Without such a synthesis, any comparison of the cultural situation in these two major Egyptian areas, or pointing out the source of many characteristic features of pharaonic Egypt (dualistic monarchy, beginnings of religion, development of administration and bureaucracy or burial customs typical in later periods) become impossible. We do know that ancient Egyptians equipped their deceased with the objects they regarded as essential to provide them with the same social and material status in the afterlife. Still, there remain numerous questions we need to answer. We do not know, for instance, to what extent relatively simple burial goods in the North reflect the actual economic condition of the region, customs connected with some unrevealed cult, or whether they are derived from other ethnic roots and differences between typically agricultural and pastoral people. It is worth pondering on whether the reality preserved in ancient burials mirrors historical traditions of the unification of two independent kingdoms. Therefore, any generalization on the beginnings of the pharaonic state cannot be treated as binding without proper attention paid to burial customs.

## 1.1. STATE OF RESEARCH

Specificity of archeological sources explains – in a way – the ensuing state of unbalance: in the South, as early as since the late 19th century archaeologists have been discovering mainly cemeteries, also the royal ones. Intensification of field research in the Nile Delta observed from the early 1980s resulted in the discovery of numerous settlements and cemeteries and forced scholars to pose new questions on the Egyptian past. Answering them will give us more information that could prove vital to reconstruct the beginnings of the unified Egyptian state. Unfortunately, the Delta still does not deserve the title of thoroughly examined, since excavations have been focused on its eastern part with almost complete omitting of its central and western areas.

A study which undertook the systematization of data connected with early Egyptian burial customs is *The Development of the Egyptian Tomb down to the Accession of Cheops* by G.A. Reisner (1936). However, the work is over 70 years old now and needs major supplements. A lot has also changed since *Brick Architecture in Ancient Egypt* by A.J. Spencer (1979) was published. Thus, there seems to be no up-to-date general synthesis of sepulchral traditions of Northern Egypt in the Pre- and Early Dynastic periods, which is probably partially due to diversified state of publications of field works results. Only a part of excavated sites has been exemplarily published in a form of an extensive monograph. Particularly worth mentioning is Minshat Abu Omar, where each tomb was presented with its full documentation and details of offerings, and Wadi Digla, Maadi or Heliopolis with complete discussion on material collected from graves, as well as results of physical anthropological, archeozoological and paleobotanical analyses. Apart from the just quoted studies, there are numerous publications which date back to the early 20th century (e.g. Turah, Tarkhan, Gerzeh, Abusir el-Meleq) but do not meet present standards, or excavations published partially, in nothing but preliminary field reports (e.g. Zawiyet el-Arian). Since the late 20th century a new trend has been observed which leads to the reassessment of materials acquired in the course of earlier excavations by applying modern techniques. The approach was initiated by J.J. Castillos (1982; 1983) and followed, among others, by T.A.H. Wilkinson (1996), who established many new facts resulting from field activity of W.M.F. Petrie in Tarkhan (1913; 1914) and of H. Junker (1912) in Turah; or by A. Stevenson (2009), who republished the results of works at Gerzeh. Another novelty introduced at the end of the last century was re-excavation of sites where field research was interrupted without publishing any final report, as was the case with e.g. Helwan or Kafr Hassan Dawood.

And finally, modern surveys and regular excavations should also be kept in mind as they set new standards for studies in co-operation between archeologists and specialists in various other fields. This modern and multi-scientific approach proves especially fruitful as it provides plenty of new data, which is absolutely priceless for further development of early Egyptian archeology and changes the modern way of thinking about an idea archaeological publication.

## 1.2. AIMS AND LIMITATIONS OF THE STUDY

On account of the above reviewed state of research, the presented study was meant to at least partially cover the existing gap, which is the lack of a general synthesis of

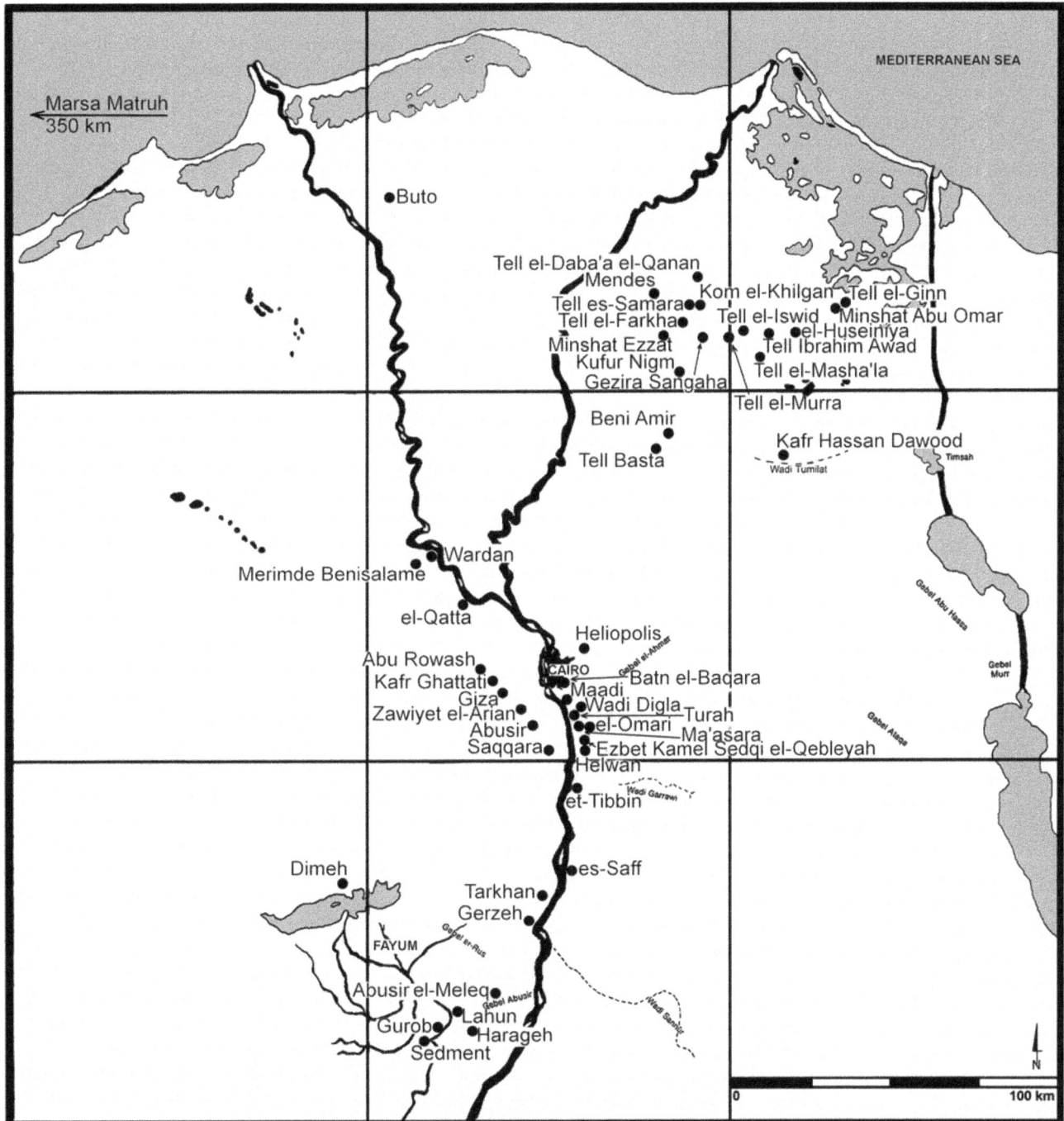

*Map no. 1. Position of all sites quoted in the study*

early burial traditions in Northern Egypt. That is why Appendix no. 1 comprises a large table with detailed enumeration of all, at least partially published sites from the area and time of interest which brought any burial discovery, together with a list of major publications on the finds. The presented study aims to systematize numerous data on burial customs in the scope of widely understood sepulchral architecture, offering goods, ways in which the deceased were buried and various side elements which emerged in some periods and were undoubtedly connected with burial practices. Another goal was to create a synthesis of sepulchral traditions and trace their development typical of particular epochs. Since Lower Egypt in various moments of its history was dominated by various cultural units, an attempt was also

made to isolate elements which were handed over from older units to their successors, to finally raise the issue of so-called Naqadan expansion in the light of changes visible in burial customs.

The lower chronological frame of the following study is determined by the oldest recorded and relatively few burials linked with the activity of the Merimde and Omari cultures, which was registered only at their eponymy sites. Definitely more representative is a group of settlements and cemeteries with graves of the Lower Egyptian culture, while the most abundant are necropolises from the epoch after Naqadan expansion to the North. The studied period is closed by cemeteries of people with diversified social status (including kings) dating back to/from the times of Dynasties 1 and 2. The geographical area of interest constitutes the Nile Delta and the lower part of the Nile Valley down to the region of the Fayum Oasis. Whereas the Delta represents a zone of clearly distinguished borders which do not need any further definition, delimitation of the southern boundary of the author's research is more problematic. The limit was accepted a little south from the Fayum Oasis and was marked by the southernmost located site of Northern Egyptian features and supported by the presence of still unexplained settlement vacuum between Harageh and Matmar. Therefore, the term *Lower Egypt,* which runs through the study, concerns the whole mentioned area. The author is aware of the fact that from the historical point of view, such a definition is not completely accurate, but, in contrast to the term *Upper Egypt,* it emphasizes cultural diversity shown also in the presented study.

There are two major theories to explain the puzzling "vacuum" situation. The first of them (Kaiser 1985a: 70) assumes the presence of the Lower Egyptian people much farther to the South than its actually documented range. The lack of settlement remains is explained by erosion and later human activity in the area, however, it does not clarify very limited contacts with Upper Egypt. According to the second theory (Seeher 1990: 151), the discussed region was inhabited by a more or less independent group of people who remained under the Lower Egyptian influence and who in the period of Naqada I acted as a kind of cultural stopper. It would have enabled to penetrate only particular and filtered elements. Unfortunately, the lack of traces of the enigmatic unit's existence makes it difficult to accept the theory, even if one assumes the group was completely destroyed in the course of Gerzaen expansion to the North. It seems possible, then, that a suitable solution lay in the over 250 km long distance which separated both inhabited areas of Egypt, too significant and thus difficult

| Period | Culture | | Relative chronology | | Ruler's name | BC dates |
|---|---|---|---|---|---|---|
| | Lower Egyptian | Naqada | by Kaiser | by Hendrickx | | |
| Predynastic | | Naqada I | N Ia | NIA | | 3900-3600 |
| | early | | N Ib | NIB | | |
| | | | N Ic | | | |
| | | | N IIa | NIC | | |
| | | Naqada II | N IIb | NIIA | | 3600-3500 |
| | | | | NIIB | | |
| | classic | | N IIc | NIIC | | 3500-3400 |
| | | | N IId1 | NIID1 | | 3400-3300 |
| | transitional | | N IId2 | NIID2 | | |
| | | | N IIIa1 | | | |
| Protodynastic | | Naqada III | N IIIa2 | NIIIA1 | unknown rulers | 3300-3200 |
| | | | | NIIIA2 | | |
| | | | N IIIb1 | NIIIA2/NIIIB | | 3200-3100 |
| | | Dynasty 0 | N IIIb2 | NIIIB (I part) | ? | 3150-3100 |
| | | | N IIIc1 | NIIIB/NIIIC1 | Iry-Hor<br>Ka<br>king Scorpio | |
| Early Dynastic | | Dynasty 1 | N IIIc2 | NIIIC1 | Narmer<br>Aha<br>Djer<br>Djet | 3100-3000 |
| | | | | NIIIC2 | Den<br>Anjeeb | 3000-2890 |
| | | | N IIIc3 | NIIID (early) | Semerkhet<br>Qa'a | |
| | | Dynasty 2 | | NIIID | Hetepsekhemwy<br>Raneb/Nebra<br>Ninetjer<br>*Weneg*<br>*Nebunefer*<br>*Sened*<br>*Seneferka*<br>*Sekhmib*<br>Peribsen<br>Khasekhem/wy | 2890-2686 |

*Table no. 1. Correlation of early Egyptian chronology*

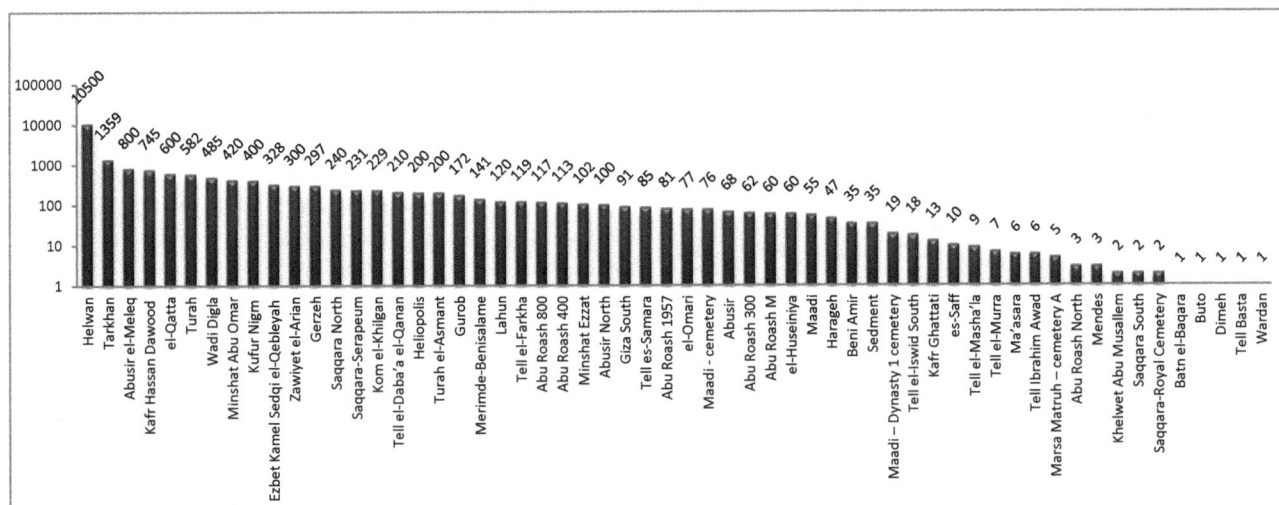

*Chart no. 1. Disproportion in the number of graves registered at particular sites*

to be regularly covered.

The main reason why the following study was focused on data exclusively from the limited geographical area is the bulk of material from the South, while not numerous analogies from the neighbouring region were quoted only in short mentions. That is why, all conclusions and generalizations in the work concern solely Lower Egypt.

## 1.3. REMARKS

For the purpose of the presented study the author uses the system of relative chronology by S. Hendrickx (1996; 2006), but in Table no. 1 it is presented in correlation with an older proposition by W. Kaiser (1985a; 1990) and presently accepted absolute BC dates.

Sources for the discussed issue appeared to be very vast and diversified. Chart no. 1 illustrates huge size differentiation of 58 sites with published numbers of graves from all 64 archaeological sites (registered in 48 locations, see Appendix no. 1) mentioned in the text. The numbers vary from over 10.000 (in the case of Helwan) to single burials. Unfortunately, systematization of these materials caused numerous technical problems, mostly because there is no standardized system of publication, which often makes it impossible to draw proper comparisons. One of these difficulties is establishing of the actual number of graves connected with specific periods and sometimes even particular sites. Therefore, some quoted numbers are nothing but estimation, in case of long used necropolises arithmetically divided into particular phases, and in instances of small and imprecisely dated sites the numbers were repeated for every sub-period. Imprecise dates of many sites do not facilitate the reconstruction of the picture of changes in burial practices and its clarification often becomes impossible due to the scarcity of accessible data.

Similarly, precise location of numerous sites which were quoted in the work is presently impossible. And since there is no possibility to return to them, also plans for their re-assessment had to be abandoned. It results partially from the aggressive expansion of modern settlement and devastation of archeological areas, and partially also from the multitude of names under which a particular site appears in publications. Many of them do not match modern maps of the area or are too vague for local people to help localize them. Map no. 1 comprises the closest possible reconstruction of 47 locations where almost all of the sites[1] quoted in the study were registered.

The presented generalization is based on all published results of works from the Nile Delta and the northern part of the Valley, where any remains of burial activity dated to the Pre-, Proto- and Early Dynastic periods were registered. The juxtaposition comprises typical extramural cemeteries of various size, settlements with graves discovered within its borders or sites of a questionable character, recognized by some scholars as devastated cemeteries. And finally, Appendix no. 2 organizes the list of sites in chronological order with marked possibly detailed periods of particular cemeteries' use.

---

[1] The only location missing in the map is the site of Khelwet Abu Musallem imprecisely described as located in Markaz Abu Hammad, the Sharqiya province (Leclant 1973: 396), that is ca. 20 km from the modern city of Zagazig.

9

# 2. CULTURAL BACKGROUND

## 2.1. THE EARLIEST CULTURES IN LOWER EGYPT

It is customary for this kind of study to refer to cultural background of the discussed phenomena. And thus, in the following chapter the reader will find the most important information on subsequent cultural units such as their chronological position, archeological evaluation, typical objects, settlement pattern or history of research, however, in a much compressed form. Since the objective of the work is to analyze rich archeological data of sepulchral significance, such a compact background description seems justified, especially in the situation when many general studies on early Egypt have recently been published – to mention just a few: *Ancient Egypt. Foundations of a Civilization* by D.J. Brewer (2005), *La naissance d'un royaume. L' Égypte dès la période prédynastique à la fin de la I^ère dynastie* by K.M. Ciałowicz (2001), *Aux origins de l' Égypte. Du Néolothique à l'émergence de l'Etat* by B. Midant-Reynes (2003) or *The Archaeology of Early Egypt. Social Transformations in North–East Africa, 10,000–2,650 BC.* by D. Wengrow (2006). Moreover, the most characteristic shapes of pottery of particular periods were catalogued by A. Wodzińska (2009; 2009a) in her *Manual of Egyptian Pottery*. The exception was made only for the Lower Egyptian culture because it is the fastest changing issue and discoveries of recent years have completely transformed the state of our current knowledge.

### THE MERIMDE CULTURE

It was distinguished on the basis of materials recovered from the site of Merimde-Benisalame, located in the south-eastern part of the Nile Delta base ca. 60km north-east from Cairo. The first excavations were carried out there in 1928-1939 by H. Junker, who divided the history of the site into two settlement phases separated by a transitional layer. In 1976 excavation works were shortly undertaken by Z. Hawass, who represented the Supreme Council of Antiquities (SCA) and established radiocarbon chronology of the site (Hawass et al. 1988: 32). Then, after fieldworks carried out in 1977-1980 J. Eiwanger (1984; 1988; 1992) proposed a new stratigraphic division into three phases within five layers and paid attention to unclear continuity of the settlement use. Basing on calibrated $C_{14}$ dates received from layers I and V, it was generally accepted that the Merimde culture closes within the chronological frames as follows: ca. 5000/4900–4500/4400 (Ciałowicz 1999: 44).

In various periods the settlement covered the total area of ca. 20ha and thus it belongs to the largest sites known from prehistoric Egypt, being smaller only than Hierakonpolis. Supposing, the whole settlement had been inhabited simultaneously, its population would have come to 16 000 people however, on the basis of ethno-anthropological analogies the initial estimation is being reduced to 5 000, which still in the environmental conditions of the time remains a huge number (Hoffman 1991: 169). Nevertheless, it is worth mentioning that the significant differences are derived from the actual state of research on the site, which was never inhabited on the whole vast area in one time.

The settlement in Merimde from its very beginning demonstrated Neolithic type of economy (for a short review of Egyptian Neolithic see Köhler 2011). The people generally made a living by the husbandry of sheep, pig, goat and cattle, which was becoming increasingly important, as well as the cultivation of wheat and possibly also barley and sorghum. The diet was supplemented by gathering and hunting for hippopotamus, tortoise, crocodile, birds and ruminants (Ciałowicz 1999: 101).

Material culture of Merimde (which was presented in detail in the three volumes of final publication from the site – Eiwanger 1984; 1988; 1992) shows its unquestionable identity on the one hand, but on the other hand there is numerous evidence in favour of the fact that people from the site did not live in isolation. Contacts with Upper Egypt remain unconfirmed, however, Levantine elements observed in lithic industry and also Levantine origin of wheat cultivation or sheep and goat husbandry speak for Merimde's connection with the Levant.

### THE OMARI CULTURE

It is called after a young Egyptian geologist – Amin el-Omari. In 1924, he localized a Neolithic settlement a few kilometers North from Helwan at the mouth of Wadi Hof, in a desert area at the foot of Gebel Turah, known from the pharaonic period as the source of excellent limestone. First works in the area were carried out in 1925 by P. Bovier-Lapierre who represented Egyptian SCA. Twenty years later, research was resumed by F. Debono, who spent at the site three digging seasons: 1943-1944, 1948 and 1952 (Hoffman 1991: 192). Unfortunately, the final report was published as late as 50 years after the fieldworks (Debono, Mortensen 1990). The publication shows that the division into Omari A and B, which was propagated in older literature, is irrelevant and three sites previously described as separate should be regarded as unequally excavated parts of the same settlement. Researchers have distinguished nine occupational phases during which the settlement was developing from sector B.III towards sectors A and B.I to finally create a single and vast estate (Ciałowicz 1999: 102). Dating of the culture is problematic – calibrated carbon dates suggest years 4700/4600-4400, and thus a 300 to 200-year-period of the site occupation contemporary to the last phases of Merimde and the youngest Neolithic settlements from the Fayum Oasis (Ciałowicz 1999: 44). It is questioned by B.

*Fig. 1. Lower Egyptian building from the Western Kom, Tell el-Farkha*

Mortensen (1992: 173), who despite the late $C_{14}$ dates compares Omari to koms W and K – the sites of the Fayum A culture and to phase II of Merimde.

The settlement in Omari spreads over the area of ca. 750 x 500m. It is composed of over 100 round, oval or irregular cottages and of numerous oval pits of economic use. The whole unit and its material culture was discussed by numerous authors (see e.g. Ciałowicz 1999: 101-103; Midant-Reynes 2000: 118-123) and since no more recent discoveries have been made, in the present study the subject will not be explored in further detail.

The culture of Omari appears to be an original unit which is hardly comparable to other Neolithic communities that inhabited Lower Egypt. It is characterized by unexpectedly high technical achievements like pottery of very fine quality in forms differing from those popular in Lower Egypt but, on the other hand, definitely unrelated to the South, and lithic industry resembling rather Levantine products. The fact stands in clear contrast to relatively low level of social organization revealed by random location of housing structures and the lack of artistic craft. Omari, however, was not a group that lived in isolation – external influences are disclosed by Near Eastern origins of crops cultivation and husbandry of crops cultivation and husbandry, which could have come via Merimde, Fayum A or – what is the most probable – appeared independently.

## 2.2. THE LOWER EGYPTIAN CULTURE – THE FIRST PAN-LOWER EGYPTIAN UNIT

The presence of a new cultural unit was noticed thanks to discoveries made in Maadi and thus, for a long time the name of the site was used for the culture. In mid 1990s the results of works in Buto/Tell el-Farain provoked K. Schmidt (1993: 267) to propose an updated term *the Buto-Maadi culture*. However, numerous important and recent discoveries mainly from the area of the Eastern Nile Delta (e.g. Tell Ibrahim Awad, Tell el-Iswid or Tell el-Farkha) have proved another change is essential, namely the introduction of term *the Lower Egyptian culture*, which slowly, though rather reluctantly, is becoming more and more popular (see Ciałowicz 2001; Mączyńska 2011; Tristant, Midant-Reynes 2011[2]).

The Lower Egyptian culture covered the area of the whole Nile Delta and the northern part of the Nile Valley, which is evidenced by the findings from remote Sedment located 500km away from the Mediterranean Sea. A survey of the Eastern Delta carried out by the University of Amsterdam in 1984-1987 revealed a puzzling linear concentration of younger sites. The phenomenon was interpreted as a proof for Predynastic inhabitation along permanent river flows. According to this assumption, the settlements of Tell el-Farkha, Tell el-Iswid and Tell Ibrahim Awad would have been situated at the banks of presently inexisting Nile drain almost perpendicular to the course of the Tanitic Nile branch (van den Brink

---

[2] These authors actually use the term "cultures of Lower Egypt".

1993: 296). It is possible, however, that the line of sites reflects the course of a trade route which connected the Nile Valley with the Near East, or both hypotheses should be combined when the presence of a river based trade route is considered. Verification of these theories should wait for further results of field works carried out in the region.

The most difficult problem connected with the Lower Egyptian culture is its dating. Development of the unit is divided into three phases: early, middle/classical and late/transitional. And this division is well consolidated, however, recently some important changes to the system have been proposed (Mączyńska 2011: tabl. 2). The division is as follows:

- the early phase is represented by the settlements in Maadi, Buto Ia-b and beginnings of Tell el-Farkha (TF 1a) as well as cemeteries: Wadi Digla I-II, Heliopolis and Kom el-Khilgan 1;
- middle/classical phase is attested in Buto II, Tell el-Farkha 1b, Tell el-Iswid A, Tell Ibrahim Awad 7, Mendes B3 ?, Kom el-Khilgan 2 and Minshat Abu Omar 1;
- while the late/transitional phase was discovered in Buto IIIa, Tell el-Farkha 2, Mendes B2 and Minshat Abu Omar 1.

The above list enumerates only a part of sites recognized as Lower Egyptian, however, precise dating of the remaining localities is rather difficult and thus, they are treated as rather supplementary. Numerous imports enabled to establish relative chronology of particular phases of the Lower Egyptian culture and according to it, phase 1 is dated to the period of Naqada IA/IB-IIB, which is contemporary to the Palestinian complex of Ghassul-Beersheba, phase 2 to Naqada IIC – Naqada IID1, while phase 3 to Naqada IID2, which is contemporary to Early Bronze Ia in Palestine. $C_{14}$ dates (Seeher 1990: 155) do not solve the problem of absolute chronology definitively. Those from the older field research in Maadi (5055±55 to 4730±60 BP) after calibration give ca. 3900-3600, which corroborates the simultaneity of the site mainly with the period of Naqada I; however, those from latest works in a younger zone of the site (4900±70 BP and 4680±70 BP) calibrated are ca. 3650, which means a simultaneity to Naqada II. More difficult for interpretation are dates from cemeteries – relatively early from Wadi Digla: 4830±120 BP and 4800±140 BP, late from Maadi: 4540±140 BP and 4380±120 BP. In conclusion, it is believed that the beginnings of the Lower Egyptian culture fall on ca. 3900 BC and its end, basing on gradual disappearance of its elements in transitional layers in Buto, Mendes and Tell el-Farkha, to 3300/3200 BC (Ciałowicz 2001: 38, tabl. 3). Particular sites represent regional variants of the culture's general model, which reflects chronological differences and the large size of the occupied territory. Studies on the issue induced even L. Watrin and O. Blin (2003) to conjecture

*Fig. 2. Lower Egyptian settlement divided by a mud brick wall from the Central Kom, Tell el-Farkha*

that after Maadi was abandoned and before the next stage of Lower Egyptian habitation represented by Buto II, Tell el-Iswid III-I, Tell el-Farcha 1 and Tell Ibrahim Awad 7, comes a hiatus in the continuity of the unit, followed by the appearance of characteristic pottery decorated with zig-zags – probably the proof for the introduction of a new technology and that Buto I (Watrin 2003) should be regarded as even older than the beginnings of the settlement in Maadi. However, it seems that these theories have few followers.

Until very recently, it was believed that people of the Lower Egyptian culture did not know any solid architecture, but discoveries from the lowest strata at Tell el-Farkha proved the opinion has to be changed. However, the most popular housing structures were oval huts (Rizkana, Seeher 1989: 39-43) with plaited walls plastered with mud, which were supported by posts and with entrances open to the south. Close to the huts were usually located hearths surrounded by stones – with possible additional use as a pottery kiln – and storage jars dug into the ground. Apart from these simple shacks, there are also attested remains of rectangular or oval constructions, which needed to be supported by foundations. They were preserved as narrow channels and accompanied by numerous mud pits or conical features made of silt with crushed pottery and calcite. Most commonly they were interpreted as pens for domestic animals in the *zeriba* type (Rizkana, Seeher 1989: 43-49). Nevertheless, the already signaled results of excavations at Tell el-Farkha finally show that at least some of them were of habitation use. One of these examples is a large building composed of numerous rather small rooms with three constructional phases, which was unearthed at the Western Kom (Fig. 1) and related to the oldest activity phase at the site (Ciałowicz 2012a). The structure was preserved as similar furrows, thus the applied materials were organic, but the complicated layout – probably reflecting its internal division into housing and economical parts – proves the building was certainly not a pen. More similarly constructed habitation structures were discovered at the Central Kom still at Tell el-Farkha (Nowak 2011; Chłodnicki, Geming 2012). The entire settlement composed of such rectangular houses was divided into zones. One of them was surrounded by a double fence, which measured at least 20 x 10m and in the subsequent phase was replaced by a massive mud-brick wall (Fig. 2) built certainly before 3350 BC within the Lower Egyptian context (Chłodnicki 2011: 43-45; Chłodnicki, Geming 2012: 95). This part of the settlement had a very complicated layout and was identified as a Lower Egyptian "residence", which is also confirmed by discoveries of the most precious artifacts there, such as: golden and semiprecious stones beads, a copper knife, a Hammamiya flint knife, a stone vessel and two piriform mace-heads. The mentioned pits and conical features of various size were abundantly found in this part of the settlement in Tell el-Farkha as well (Chłodnicki, Geming 2012: 91-92, Figs 5, 6), but they are also known from Maadi (Rizkana, Seeher 1989: 33-47, 57-64), Buto (von der Way 1997: 61-76), Tell el-Iswid (van den Brink 1989:62) and Tell el-Masha'la

(Rampersad 2006: 792-797). Their function is currently under discussion as it seems they could be used – probably depending on their dimensions – as storage containers, post holes or cooking installations. Nevertheless, they belong to the repertoire of typical Lower Egyptian settlement structures (Ciałowicz 2001: 68; Cichowski 2001). The third type of visibly housing structures known only from Maadi are subterranean dwellings (Rizkana, Seeher 1989: 49-55; Hartung 2003; Hartung et al. 2003) discovered in the western zone of the site. They had the form of oval pits, which measured 3 x 5m and were 3m deep. Their entrances were accessible through a staircase hewn in bedrock. Additional post holes suggest the presence of a wooden roof, while their floors were paved with tamped mud, and their walls – with stones and in one case even with archaic mud-bricks. A rectangular structure which measured 10.5 x 5.5m preserved to the height of 2m diverges from the scheme since it was probably a semi-subterranean dwelling (Badawi 2003) but finished in the same way as it was in the previous case. Numerous every-day-objects found inside prove these structures were in fact human residences and/or storage facilities (Hartung 2004: 347), not cult objects as it was suggested before. Buildings of this type find their counterparts in the culture of Ghassul-Beersheba and, what is more, J. Seeher (1990: 129) thinks they were inhabited by representatives of the cultural unit settled in Maadi. The site of Tell el-Farkha also provides strong arguments for further introduction of mud-brick, which is visible with the example of mud-bricked walls found in the neighbourhood of typical row structures or breweries (Ciałowicz 2001: 66-77; 2012: 157-159; Cichowski 2006; Chłodnicki 2011; Nowak 2011).

A so far unique discovery (Fig. 3) in Northern Egypt are specific constructions of production use interpreted as breweries and found in Tell el-Farkha (Cichowski 2008: 35-37). The oldest complex of such structures (W201, W201A, W192, W200) functioned from NIIB to NIIC in two phases of its rebuilding. The oldest breweries in the sequence were much destroyed by overlapping younger ones, however, it was determined that all of them were constructed in a more or less similar way. The outer walls were made of secondarily fired (as a result of using the structure they were found in) and unfired D-shaped bricks forming circles with a large vat for brewed beer in their centres. One of the vats was even found *in situ*. Within the whole installation the circles with vats were arranged in two rows. The successively flooded breweries were rather large constructions which measured 10 x 17m (Ciałowicz 2012a: 149-159). Another rather badly preserved breweries' remains are structures C485 and 490 (Chłodnicki 2010: 108; Chłodnicki, Geming 2012: 99-100, Figs 22, 24, 25). They were in form of three intersecting circles – ca. 1.5 m in diameter – or hexagonal with a diameter of ca. 1.15m respectively, both constructed of characteristic D-shape bricks. Contemporary to them is the youngest structure of the type from the Western Kom (W47), which had the shape of three connected ovals – ca. 3.6 x 4m in size – surrounded by radiating bricks and it is relevant to the

*Fig. 3. Brewery complex from the Western Kom, Tell el-Farkha*

period of NIID1-2 (Cichowski 2008: 34-35). Paleobotanic analyses indicate two phases of the brewing process (Chłodnicki, Ciałowicz 2005: 132-134; Kubiak-Martens, Langer 2008).

A combined – local and imported – character of pottery discovered at Lower Egyptian sites simply imposes "natural" division into typical objects made of local silt, which realize local tradition and technological achievements, and foreign products that were made of marl clay, as well as tightly connected with them local imitations. Also characteristic of local pottery production is the common use of rough organic temper, most often in the form of chaff as well as – in a very limited range – mineral temper.

Lower Egyptian pottery production is represented by functional objects, even items registered in graves have no special features, which would suggest they were intentionally made for burial use. Pottery was produced in households, probably by female hands and for household needs. This probably explains rather low standardization of shapes, predominance of thick forms, as well as the common use of manual and hardly careful pots' shaping – more often from lumps of plastic clay fabric. Jars built of clay slabs were much less popular and even unknown at the very beginning of the culture's development. Precision in surface treatment was probably of little importance – outer surfaces were usually wet smoothed was rare and limited to the workout of rims and bases of jars representing only one early type. The presence of slip was acknowledged, however, it is often difficult to distinguish it from the so-called self-slip (Matson 1969: 564), that is a thin layer of the smallest elements of rough material concentrated in the upper zone of a pot's walls created as a result of very intensive polishing.

A Lower Egyptian potter fired its wares relatively short in open bonfires under cover of burning fuel. In such primitive conditions only low temperatures were possible to maintain – mainly 600-650C – and the atmosphere, mostly oxidation, was difficult to control, since oxygen-free conditions were only rarely kept for a longer time (Nørdström 1972: 37). All of these had a very important impact on the final product, which was rather soft and often unintentionally spotted. In general, it may be accepted that the colour of finished pots fluctuates from reddish-brown to almost black, which from the technological point of view was more difficult to attain. This is probably why, in the culture's beginnings the most popular were reddish-brown wares, which were later replaced by black items, while the return of lighter wares in the late phase seems to reflect changes in aesthetic tastes. Practically, however, the wide range of shades often makes it impossible to name them accurately, thus the pottery colour cannot be regarded as a significant classification criterion.

The corpus of pottery shapes (Jucha, Mączyńska 2011) in the oldest phase is characterized by jars on a raised base and ovoid jars with a pointed base, elongated barrel-shaped jars, ovoid and globular jars, bowls with a T-shaped profile and large storage jars. In the middle phase, the most representative are lemon-jars that became an important cultural marker of the unit (Buchez, Midant-Reynes 2007), along with rounded jars with a rim slightly inverted to the exterior, small bowls with a simple rim, a rounded rim or formed into a small external lip. Typical for the last phase are still lemon-jars, as well as small bag-shaped jars with a rounded or slightly pointed body and an increasing number of Naqadan pottery. Lower Egyptian pots were rarely decorated. Decoration occurs in a few types: dark painted against a light background, plastic in form of various applications and knobs or impressed – among them the most characteristic zig-zags. A separate kind of decoration are the so-called potter's marks registered at pottery objects.

Flint industry was based on blade tools. It clearly combines foreign influences with local tradition represented by arrowheads with concave base, knives and sickle bladelets. Upper Egyptian features are visible in daggers and *fish-tails*, however, their one side remained unretouched, which suggests we deal here with an imitation, not an authentic import. Massive blades were used for production of Hammamiya type knives, which are typical of the NIIC-D period and were discovered in Buto, Tell el-Farkha, Tell el-Iswid and Tell Ibrahim Awad (Schmidt 1992a: 32-34; 1992b: 85; Kabaciński 2003: 201-202). Palestinian impact on the flint industry is represented by so-called Canaanite blades (Rizkana, Seeher 1988), that is sickle blades with double rectilinear ribbing commonly discovered with sickle gloss, as well as large scrapers of layer flint known from Maadi and Buto (von der Way 1989: 300-307).

Among the findings there are no stone axes. The tool's type is known thanks to copper examples and points to the growing significance of the material brought in the form of almost standardized ingots, probably from Wadi Araba. It seems that the import of relatively poor copper ore was not regarded as cost-effective, since it was found only as a few small lumps interpreted as a natural dye rather than the actual source of copper. Also some bone artifacts (Rizkana, Seeher 1989) were gradually being replaced by small copper tools such as: bars, spatulas, hooks and personal adornments. A unique discovery consists of golden beads found in the Lower Egyptian "residence" at Tell el-Farkha (Chłodnicki 2011: 43), showing a great level of craftsmanship and that also this precious metal was known by the people. Quite popular were also stone vessels (Seeher 1990: 141-143) made of basalt and other softer metamorphic rocks. They were cylindrical and ovoid in their shape and especially the latter strongly resemble forms typical for pottery repertoire, and thus, they are regarded as Lower Egyptian objects exported to the South, not the other way round.

However, even presently there are no attested remains of any workshop that would produce this kind of vessels. Other categories of objects like: a few examples of combs made of bone or horn, rhomboid palettes of greywacke and conical mace-heads (Ciałowicz 1987: 17) have typically Upper Egyptian character and are rarely represented. A unique find is also a pottery figurine showing human head (Seeher 1990: 144).

The economy of Lower Egyptian societies was based on agriculture and animal husbandry. The cultivated plants were wheat, barley, flax and vetch, while domestic animals were cattle, sheep, goats, pigs and dogs. For the first time in Egyptian history also donkeys were bred, mostly as transportation animals, which was proved by bone remains analyses. Hunting played a secondary role for the Lower Egyptian economy – only 2.3% of identified bone material belonged to wild animals like: hippopotamus, tortoise, waterfowl and deer (Seeher 1990: 128). Till recently it was believed that similarly fish were not popular (in Maadi only 10% of animal remains belonged to fish), but research in Tell el-Farkha shows the statement must be revised and although the number of fish bones at the site is visibly increasing in succeeding periods, it is still ca. 20% of the material (Abłamowicz 2002: 113; 2004: 72; 2006: 110-114).

Also trade turned towards the Levant was of great significance for the Lower Egyptian economy. J. Seeher (1990: 151) made a long list of products that could be the objects of exchange, such as: pottery, basalt vessels, copper, flint nodules, Canaan knives, Red Sea shells, pigments, resins, oils, cedar wood and bitumen. The objects exported to the Levant could be: pottery, basalt vessels, flint tools, shells, Nilothic fish. E Oren (1989) recreated even the way of the trade route between Egypt and Canaan which ran along the Sinai. Discovering the remains of domesticated donkey, as well as subterranean dwellings from Maadi, corroborate the theory about the existence of caravan trade. Especially the latter finds (Faltings 1998) were popularly interpreted as traces of Palestine settlement, a kind of trading factory located within regular Lower Egyptian site. However, evolution of dwellings' form and the fact that only few imported objects were registered in and around them, in the opinion of U. Hartung (2004: 351-353) point to the fact that the presence of Canaanite settlers was not necessarily connected with their commercial activity and thus, complete understanding of the different aspects of the Egyptian-Levantine interconnections remains obscure. But the Levantine contacts would probably had no larger importance without the existence of exchange with Upper Egypt. Recent discoveries at Tell el-Farkha, located in a naturally favourable position to be involved in this kind of activity, show that the connections were far more intense than it was assumed.

Just like the beginnings of the Lower Egyptian culture are not explained, the problem of its disappearance in around NIID2 is still being discussed. There are three major and very recent propositions (Köhler 2008b; Buchez, Midant-Reynes 2011; Mączyńska 2011). The first of them focuses on multi-layer interaction between Lower and Upper Egypt facilitated by the Nile River, which produced uniformity in material cultures in both regions, without losing cultural identity of northern people even after they received southern technologies or ideas. The two latter models use the terms "assimilation" and "integration" to describe cultural transformation that took place in the period previously referred to as "Naqadan expansion". All the theories are based on the assumption that Lower and Upper Egypt were inhabited by two independent cultural complexes/facies best adapted to their native environments and drawing extensively on their locally available resources. The most controversial issue concerns the final "product" of the transformation, which is the Egyptian society of the NIIIA period. The term "assimilation" stresses the situation in which the Lower Egyptian culture was absorbed by the dominant southern unit, while "integration" or "uniformity" place them both side by side as equally important partners. Detailed studies on pottery assemblages, in particular from phases 1 (NIIB-C), 2 (NIID1 – the transitional layer) and 3 (NIID2/NIIIA1) from Tell el-Farkha suggest rather the second option (Mączyńska 2011: 889-898). The only fact that presently remains certain is that there was no traditionally seen Naqadan conquest of the North in the early period.

The significance of the Lower Egyptian culture is not fully appreciated. It is still not treated as an equal of the Naqada culture. However, with its diversity, widespread range, copper processing, animated contacts with the Levant – Lower Egyptian involvement in long distance trade and Canaanite populations settled in Buto (Faltings, Köhler 1996: 106-107; Faltings 2002) and Maadi (Hartung 2004: 353-354) – or much advanced social complexity – proved by discoveries of prestigious goods and organization of the settlement in Tell el-Farkha (Chłodnicki 2011; Nowak 2011) and Maadi (Hartung 2004) – the Lower Egyptian culture surely made an important contribution to the Egyptian civilization. It seems that the major problem with common understanding of the unit is the history of Egyptian archaeology, which accustomed us to looking at the Delta from the southern Egyptian perspective.

## 2.3. THE GERZAEN CULTURE AND THE PROBLEM OF NAQADAN EXPANSION TO THE NORTH

The name of the Gerzean culture comes from the cemetery of Gerzeh registered in the Fayum area, however, the whole unit is usually called Naqada II – sometimes even restricted to NIIC-NIID2 (see Stevenson 2006: 2) – mainly in favour of stressing its position in the development cycle of the Naqadan cultural complex. The most important Gerzean sites were discovered in Upper Egypt, especially in the area of Naqada-Matmar and Hierakonpolis, nevertheless, sites located further north should also be regarded as very significant since they represent diffusion of the Naqada culture from the region inhabited in former periods.

Crafts in the period benefited a lot from the introduction of many important technological improvements. It was also related to progressing craft specialization resulting from gradually increasing need for luxurious objects desired by a small group of the society. Thus, on the one hand, we can observe full bloom of new technologies and, on the other hand, changes within social structure and the emergence of privileged classes.

Characteristic of the Gerzean period is pottery which – basing on technological reasons – J.C. Payne (1993) has classified into categories C and D. According to W.M.F. Petrie (1921) pottery was described as R (Rough) and L (Late), as well as classes D (Decorated) and W (Wavy-handled). Jars of class D were probably produced for burial use and they were decorated with geometric and zoomorphic motives, extended scenes with human representations involved in some rituals, or combinations of signs interpreted as elements of Upper Egyptian landscape – presumably marking the beginnings of documentation of every-day-life for the purpose of its continuation in the beyond, so popular in later times (Ciałowicz 2001: 104-106). Figural decoration known from the pottery was sometimes repeated in the form of anthropomorphic figurines with arms stretched over the head. The actual meaning of these objects remains undefined, although quite often they are seen as linked with the cult of fertility or some ritual scenes (Hendrickx 1995; 2002).

Also, the production of stone vessels developed in the period. As a result, numerous accessible raw materials were used, including: limestones, calcites, basalt, breccia, diorite, granite. Moreover, various stones were sometimes combined in a single object. The most popular forms were jars with a conical ring base, cylindrical jars, jars with a distinguished neck and flat or rounded base, beakers and atypically shaped vessels, e.g. zoomorphic (Payne 1993: 133-144).

Among cosmetic palettes (Ciałowicz 1991), rhomboid palettes, known in previous period, lost their popularity and appear only sporadically. The most common became shield palettes with plastically shaped tops and zoomorphic palettes. There were also registered examples in a boat-styled form. Most of these objects were used for blending of dyes, which left typical depressions in their central part, however, with the end of the period some palettes were also decorated in relief.

Also typical of the period are piriform mace-heads (Ciałowicz 1987: 22-26), which replaced previously popular conical examples. Mace-heads were made mostly of limestone, calcite or marble. They were initially used as a kind of weapon but by the end of the period they also gained importance as symbols of power and thus, they are less common in archaeological materials than when they actually played a functional role.

*Fig. 4. Eastern part of the Naqadan residence at the Western Kom, Tell el-Farkha*

Lithic industry of the Gerzean period was at the highest level of craftsmanship (Ciałowicz 2001: 108) and among its numerous achievements the most spectacular is the *ripple-flake* technique, used for producing beautiful knives of probably ritual and ceremonial significance as most of the known examples come from graves where they were deposited, having been previously intentionally broken. The commonly used raw material was flint, while obsidian is rarely attested. Apart from obvious similarities, detailed studies on lithics, derived from particular sites, revealed (Holmes 1989) that industry of the Naqada II period had also local variants, different in the areas of Badari, Naqada and Hierakonpolis.

Although little is known about metallurgy of the time, copper objects became more and more popular, together with a few items of gold and silver (Baumgartel 1960: 10). Unfortunately, precious metals are preserved very rarely as they were repeatedly processed or stolen on a large scale. Much more examples represent objects of personal adornment (Ciałowicz 2001: 109) such as: beads, pendants and amulets in various shapes made of a wide range of organic materials (bone, ivory, shell), pottery, faience, multicolour stones and, sporadically, also of metal. Amulets in the shape of a bull's head, which were worn as the central element of necklaces composed of small beads, are especially worth the attention. A few/not numerous bracelets and rings usually made of bone and some also of metal were also found.

Gerzean buildings are rather badly preserved. Until recently, in their major part they were reconstructed on

the basis of models known from graves, especially the pottery object found in el-Amrah (Randal-MacIver, Mace 1902: 42; pl. X, 1-2), representing a rectangular house with a wooden lintel over a door, which was placed in one of the shorter walls, and with small windows opposite the entrance. Walls of the building (the model measures 45 x 27.5 x 20cm) tapper towards the top. However, the largest discovered construction connected with the Gerzean period is a vast mud-bricked structure (Fig. 4), excavated at the Western Kom in Tell el-Farkha, which was built in NIID2 (Chłodnicki, Ciałowicz et al. 2002a, 2004; Ciałowicz 2012b). The structure was a few times rebuilt, finally, in its last phase it was burnt down (NIIIA1) and the ruins were flooded with a layer of Nile mud. In its older phase, the building was composed of numerous little rooms preserved to the level of their foundations, which were arranged around an open courtyard and encompassed by a massive external wall 1.4-1.6m thick. The edifice was quickly rebuilt into a monumental structure with two large rooms (7 x 2m) and a courtyard encircled with smaller quarters. The large wall was reinforced with an extension also constructed of mud-bricks arranged in rounded corners with total thickness of 2.5m (Fig. 5). At the same time, smaller storage compartments were built adjacent to the main structure, moreover, storage jars were found *in situ* there. The whole construction was consistently oriented along the NE-SW axis. Another buildings' remains of the period were also excavated in Elephantine (Lindermann 1988), el-Tarif (Ginter et al. 1982, 1998), Abydos (Peet 1914: 7-10), el-Adaïma (Midant-Reynes et al. 1996) and Mahasna (Garstang 1903: 6-7), where in their majority they were represented by simple post structures made of

*Fig. 5. Rounded corner of the Naqadan residence from the Western Kom, Tell el-Farkha*

perishable materials, although examples of the use of stone for foundations were registered.

Fieldworks in Hierakonpolis in locality 29A (Hoffman 1987; Friedman 1996, 2009) shed new light on the issue of the presence of cult places in the Gerzean period, since till then they were only reconstructed on the basis of imprecise representations in art. A large complex dated to NIIB-NIID, and preliminarily called ceremonial centre, was discovered at the site. It was composed of an oval courtyard (33 x 14m) paved with four or five layers of mud and surrounded by a fence and extensions. The structure was shortly reused in NIIIA and NIIIB. According to R.F. Friedman (1996: 33), the structure from Hierakonpolis 29A proves that it was the place where later Upper Egyptian tradition of *per-wer* chapel was born. However, it remains an open question whether the complex played the role of an actual temple or, instead of being related to a deity's cult, it was important for ceremonies in honour of leading individuals (Adams 1999a).

Changes within the society had their impact also on the character of the settlement, as in the Gerzean period appeared first towns which played the role of the elite residences and – since they gathered specialized craftsmen as well – centres of art, culture and trade. Such centres were identified in the South in Hierakonpolis, Naqada and Abydos, where they emerged as a result of coincidence of numerous factors, like e.g. favourable geographic position. In changing climatic conditions all of these enabled the introduction of irrigation agriculture, which was of crucial importance for demographic peak, accumulation of goods and crafts development (Bard 1987: 90-91). The first of the centres is Egyptian Nekhen, which ancient people considered to be the capital town of the Upper Egyptian state. The third phase in the development of the settlement, the so-called centralization phase (Hoffman et al. 1986: 183), dates to the Gerzean period and, to be more precise, NIIB-D, when as a result of important environmental and social transformations, a village metamorphosed into the capital city with monumental architecture (the cult complex mentioned above). Significantly, excavations at the site brought evidence for continuity and originality of the Egyptian civilization, which despite documented contacts with the Near East and Nubia kept its own character. At about the same time, Naqada became the centre of copper and gold trade, for which it was known in the later period under the Egyptian name of Nubt. Whereas the significance of Abydos, on account of the fact that the location of its settlement was not identified, has not been determined satisfactorily, although graves registered in the area point to its high position (Ciałowicz 2001: 93-94).

Another – apart from the development of crafts specialization and towns – and the strongest evidence of the presence of social stratification are elite tombs and separated cemeteries composed only of such rich burials. The most important among them are necropoles B, G and T in Naqada (Petrie, Quibell 1896; Davis 1983) – each of them counted less than 100 graves, cemeteries in Diospolis Parva (Petrie 1901a), Hierakonpolis (Quibell, Green 1902; Friedman 2008) and, finally, the most important cemetery U in Abydos (Hartung 1998) – all of them, on the grounds of a vast repertoire of luxurious equipment defined as belonging to the class of leaders or princes of the late Gerzean period.

An example of such an early burial is the best known and the most significant tomb from locality 33 in Hierakonpolis labeled no. 100 (Quibell, Green 1902: 20-21) and dated to NIIC (Kaiser, Dreyer 1982: 242). It was a rectangular single-chambered structure (4.5 x 2 x 1.5m) with slightly inside sloping walls. Mud-bricks used for the construction were of various size and were bound by mud-and-sand mortar. The burial chamber was to the half of its width divided into two parts by a low wall. Both, the mud-bricked floor and the walls were covered with a kind of mud plaster and part of their surface was painted white. The oldest preserved Egyptian wall painting was discovered in the very tomb and was located on the longest wall in the grave, in front of the small partition wall. Representations on the painting were discussed by numerous scholars, just to name some of them: J. Capart (1905: 211-215), J. Vandier (1952: 561-570), H. Case and J.C. Payne (1962), W. Helck (1987: 88), J. Monet-Saleh (1987), B. Williams and T. Logan (1987: 253-265), B. Kemp (1989: 47), B. Adams (1990) or K.M. Ciałowicz (1993, 1998a). To outline the issue briefly, the painting shows four main motives probably connected with the grave owner: fight and triumph, hunt and two boat "journeys", with elements of an early ruler's ritual (Ciałowicz 2001: 163-166). The tomb was plundered already in the antiquity, however, even faint remains of its original equipment form an interesting set. It was composed mostly of pottery jars, two stone vessels and a fragment of a V-shaped *fish-tail* knife. Remains of the grave's owner him/herself were incomplete and very badly preserved.

The Naqada culture in its second phase intensified its contacts with Nubia at the south and, in particular, with

18

the Lower Egyptian culture in the north. The phase of these increasingly close relations is well attested in many Lower Egyptian sites and dated to NIIC-D. Although the moment was interpreted as the one when the process of Naqadan expansion covered the whole Nile Delta (Kaiser 1990: 288-289), nowadays it appears to be a much more complex case. The period is marked by exchange of goods and ideas, peaceful cooperation of people and slowly progressing uniformity of material culture typical of both major Egyptian areas, probably resulting from virtual Naqadan presence in Lower Egypt. However, it seems that Naqadan settlers were not in such a privileged position as it was commonly believed. Evidence comes from the site of Gerzeh which is quite popularly accepted to be an early Naqadan intruder (Wenke 1999a: 316) in Lower Egypt. Recently, there have been new proposals which suggest mixed (von der Way 1993: 91) or somehow transitional (Buchez, Midant-Reynes 2007; 2011) character of the cemetery, but A. Stevenson (2006; 2009) in her revised publication of Gerzeh disagrees with the point of view. She keeps stressing that the site is the earliest known in Lower Egypt with fully Upper Egyptian cultural assemblage. Leaving aside the vivid discussion, it does not seem improbable that the settlers from Gerzeh had to cooperate with the Lower Egyptians and thus, the former could be in a way influenced by the latter ones. Also of great interest is the situation in Tell el-Farkha, where the first Naqadan residence was constructed in the place of earlier brewery complex, while local people continued their uninterrupted habitation at the Central Kom. The newcomers, then, had to settle in the less convenient location. Finally, one should expect the example of Minshat Abu Omar as a proof for early Naqadan presence in the far Eastern Delta. Nothing could be more misleading since very recently it was convincingly pointed out (Buchez, Midant-Reynes 2007; 2011) that MAO I in fact represents the activity related to the Lower Egyptian culture.

To summarize, at the present stage of our knowledge the term "expansion" should rather be replaced with "transformation". Transitional layers at Lower Egyptian sites corroborate peaceful face of the change and even the example of Buto, with a level of burning just before stratum IIIa, is interpreted (von der Way 1991: 422-423) as traces of a local disaster, especially because it is not followed by visible differences in settlement character at the site.

## 2.4. CULTURAL UNIFICATION OF UPPER AND LOWER EGYPT – BUILDING FOUNDATION OF PHARAONIC STATE IN THE PROTO- AND EARLY DYNASTIC PERIODS

The third phase of Naqada culture stands out mostly because of important changes in its social and political structure, while its material culture constitutes direct continuation of the Gerzean period. From the chronological point of view, Naqada III was divided into three sections which include so-called Late Predynastic,

Protodynastic and Early Dynastic periods. It was during the development of the Naqadan unit that cultural and political unification of Upper and Lower Egypt under the supervision of a centralized power took place. The beginnings of political history of the newly emerged state are connected with so-called Dynasty 0 and are rather well-known, however the situation prior to its reign is still widely discussed (Wilkinson 1999: 52-54). One of the proposals explaining this part of Egyptian history is the introduction of the term "Dynasty 00" as a sequence of rulers with only local impact, yet with a high royal status (van den Brink 1992a), but it should be kept in mind that the dynastic history of Egypt cannot be extended back ad infinitum. For the first time in the Egyptian history we deal not only with archeological but also with written sources. Among them there are inscriptions found on particular objects, e.g. so-called potmarks engraved on pottery, cylindrical seals and their impressions, especially those with royal names, or plaques of ivory and ebony, which determined the content of the jar they were attached to but also included a description of events from a particular year of a king's reign. Useful for the reconstruction of the sequence of particular kings are also the Stone of Palermo, the Canon of Turin and the chronicle of Manetho.

Probably after some Late Predynastic rulers of unknown names, whose influence covered at least a large part of Egypt, the reign was taken over by monarchs representing the Thinite line, Iry-Hor and Ka. Then the power went into the hands of king Scorpio originating from Hierakonpolis (it is possible as well that his reign was contemporary to that of king Ka), finally there came the times of Narmer, creator of the first historic dynasty of Egyptian kings. However, the blood relationship between him and Ka is rather doubtful. It also remains uncertain if kings ascribed to Dynasty 1 represent a single line of rulers, though, it seems they should be treated as members of the Thinite dynasty – a family related line of sovereigns consequently buried in Umm el-Qaab. An exception is king Scorpio, who – according to our present state of knowledge – was related with Hierakonpolis (Ciałowicz 1996).

The number of Dynasty 1 kings and order of their reigns is the best known during the whole Early Dynastic period. It is commonly agreed (Wilkinson 1999: 66-67) that Dynasty 1 consisted of eight kings, the first being Narmer, identified with Menes. But also in this case there are some exceptions as German scholars, in general, start the dynasty with Aha. The reign of Aha saw the introduction of numerous essential innovations. Also queen Merneith, the regent of Den, was mentioned among other rulers. Assessing the reign length of Dynasty 1 is possible on the basis of the Palermo Stone, and on the assumption that a generation was estimated at 25-30 years.

Regardless of the discussion on identification of Narmer with Menes, the figure of the first of them must have played a very significant role in the formation of pharaonic monarchy in its typical shape. The name of

Narmer is the one which for the first time was registered all over the new state's territory, although – what is presently commonly accepted – he was not the great conqueror of Lower Egypt. Nevertheless, during his reign, the foundations of state administration and central reorganization of long-range trade took place, especially at the line Egypt-Palestine. Ancient sources (see Ciałowicz 2001: 29) attribute to Narmer a number of significant actions, such as regulation of the Lower Nile, construction of a dam in the Memphite area, foundation of the first temple of Ptah in Memphis, as well as putting into circulation luxurious objects. As far as archaeological data enable to agree with the last information, the remaining ones are much more difficult to be proven, although in the light of recent studies (Jeffreys, Tavares 1994), it may be assumed that construction of weirs is probable and the oldest part of Memphis was founded at the Western river bank. The successor and possibly even a son of Narmer, Aha left traces of his activity mainly in Saqqara North, where during his reign, a rich necropolis of the highest state officials was started to corroborate the transfer of central power to a new capital, and in Abydos, which through the whole length of Dynasty 1 was regarded as the traditional royal burial ground (Kaiser, Dreyer 1982). Most probably Aha established Egyptian control in the area of the First Cataract, was in constant trade contacts with Palestine, claimed supremacy over the Libyans and Nubians, and started construction of fortresses (Emery 1961: 51). The following king was Djer, visibly focused on dualistic form of his monarchy and reinforcing of its unification. He presumably strengthened Egyptian power over Nubia and periodically controlled terrains between the First and Second Nile Cataract (Ciałowicz 2001: 31). Ancient sources from the reign of Djet registered a mention of great hunger, which could have resulted from various causes, such as years of neglect in administration of the state or insufficiently low or too high Nile flooding level. Unfortunately, the relevant part of the Palermo Stone is damaged. Apart from that, construction of the Kokhome pyramid, identified with a structure from Saqqara, as well as an expedition to the Eastern Desert, are usually placed during the time of Djet (Ciałowicz 2001: 32). The long reign of Den was an advantageous period for further development of the state. Numerous notes, which concern many war expeditions against the Asians, nomads from the Sinai and an undefined people called Tesemtiu, as well as a vast irrigation action, have been preserved. Worth a mention is also a clearly noticeable increase in the number of rich burials founded at necropoles in the Memphite area, which may also prove deeper changes within social structure (Wilkinson 1999: 76). The reign of Andjeeb was probably relatively short and only few sources have been preserved from the time, moreover, it seems significant that his Abydene tomb was small and impoverished (Ciałowicz 2001: 35). Also the time of Semerkhet, the penultimate king of Dynasty 1, appears to be unfavourable for the country. Such information is provided in the chronicle of Manetho and, what is more, archaeological data indicate that Near Eastern trade was very limited then. It is worth stressing that during his reign no structure was built in Saqqara North, which until

the time had been a regular practice, and his tomb in Abydos was equipped with objects containing names of his predecessors, with the names of Merneith and Anjeeb intentionally destroyed. Thus, it can be concluded that Semerkhet could have been a son of Den and a stepbrother of Anjeeb. Semerkhet decided to erase the memory of his both predecessors but later he was regarded by his own successor as an usurper (Wikinson 1999: 79-80; Ciałowicz 2001: 35-36). The king who closes the history of Dynasty 1 is Qa'a (Wilkinson 1999: 80-81). His reign was marked by visible development of sepulchral architecture, which is best illustrated by his highly constructional advanced royal tomb in Abydos, as well as great mastabas built during the time in Saqqara North.

In contrast with Dynasty 1, the succeeding one remains largely obscure. Inscriptions and artifacts of the period bring lists of kings that do not supplement each other, thus, the actual order of particular kings, except for three of them, is hardly established. Internal tension within Dynasty 2 is suggested by the appearance of Seth in the titles of Peribsen and mentions of battles against enemies from the North during the reign of Khasekhem (Wilkinson 1999: 82-83). It is possible then that in the middle of Dynasty 2 the control over the country was divided between kings from the South and North. Simultaneously, in accordance to the Palermo Stone after the reign of Dynasty 1 the average level of the Nile's flood was visibly lower, thus, political unrest could have its origin in some environmental changes (Hoffman 1991: 312). The large number of imponderables in the history of Dynasty 2 makes the proper assessment of its duration is practically impossible.

We do not know the reasons for which Hetepsekhemwy belongs to the second dynasty of Egyptian kings (Wilkinson 1999: 83-84). We know, however, that he acknowledged and appreciated his predecessor by continuing his funerary cult. On the other hand, he was the first to break the long-term tradition according to which royal burials were located in Abydos, and built his own tomb – in a very innovative form – in Saqqara. The change might possibly reflect the reinforcing position of Memphis as the centre of the whole state. Little is known about the following king named Raneb. There was even a discussion concerning the proper way in which his name should be read. As a result, the reading of Raneb "Ra is my lord" is sometimes reversed to obtain Nebra "Lord of the Sun" (Wilkinson 1999: 84). Much more information relates to Raneb/Nebra's heir, Ninetjer, mostly thanks to preserved parts of the Palermo Stone. The king was visibly connected with the Memphite area and he remains fairly unattested beyond the Delta. (Wilkinson 1999: 85-87). This may indicate that his rule was particularly strong in Lower Egypt, while the remaining part of the country was affected if not by war, at least by some grave social unrest, or was reigned by another ruler. The internal authorities' upset is also reflected by a list of ephemeral kings mentioned about the end of Dynasty 2. Although the actual sequence of particular rulers remains blurred, there are a few names that belonged to leaders who probably, at least for a while, maintained royal power. Among these quite numerous names are Weneg (Kahl 2006: 102), Nebunefer (von Beckerath 1984: 43), Sened (Kaiser 1991), Seneferka (Ryholt 2008), Sekhemib (Kahl 2006: 105) and Peribsen (Kaiser 1991; Wilkinson 1999: 90-91). It is suggested that some of the names belonged in fact to a smaller number of rulers and thus, Weneg is identified as Raneb, Ninetjer as Ren, Sekhemib as Peribsen (Kahl 2006: 103-106). The latter king is quite well attested as the one who built his tomb in the old necropolis in Abydos but his funeral cult was practiced in Saqqara, which may prove a new concept of the central power or Upper Egyptian origin of the ruler. Finally, the last king of Dynasty 2 was Khasekhem, who primarily ruled only in Upper Egypt and after his reign covered the whole country. Probably in order to commemorate the event he changed his name into Khasekhemwy. The name was found (Wilkinson 1999: 92-94) in the area of the whole early Egyptian state but also in regions clearly influenced by the Egyptians like Byblos. Worth a mention are structures built during his reign and, in particular, his burial enclosure in Abydos – a gigantic brick construction with important additional use of stone (Petrie 1901; Ayrton et al. 1904), or even – tentatively attributed to him – the stone Gisr el-Mudir in Saqqara (see Regulski 2011: 305), which is sometimes considered (Mathieson et al. 1997: 53) to be a counterpart of the Abydene enclosures. Thus, the reign of Khasekhemwy presents itself as a turning point in the history of Egypt, combining the achievements of his predecessors of Dynasties 1 and 2, and preparing the base for the full bloom of Egyptian civilization at the beginnings of Dynasty 3.

Doubtlessly, during the reign of the first dynasties, the formation process of highly stratified society came to its end. In archaeologically accessible materials, it finds its strongest reflection in changes observed in burial customs. Particularly important for the issue are the Upper Egyptian necropolises in Hierakonpolis and Abydos, together with Lower Egyptian cemeteries discussed in Chapter 3. However, the former two sites deserve special attention as they were places of royal burials, to mention only Hierakonpolis (Adams 1996a; Hoffman 1982; 1983) as one of rival centres with long sequences of impressive tombs, among which tomb no. 16 (Friedman et al. 2011) with its enclosure and fence superstructure proves that as early as the period of Naqada II Egyptian society new strong leaders of an outstanding position, while tomb no. 1 is ascribed to king Scorpio (Hoffman 1982: 45). Also Abydos should not be underestimated with a series of closely located prestigious cemeteries: U (Dreyer 1990; Dreyer et al. 1993; 1996), the location of the vast and magnificently equipped tomb U-j (Dreyer 1998), so-called B, believed to be a burial place of the earliest Egyptian rulers (Kaiser, Dreyer 1982; Dreyer et al. 1996), and finally, the main part of Umm el-Qaab with remaining tombs of the Dynasty 1 kings (Petrie 1902; 1903; Kaiser, Dreyer 1982; Dreyer 1990; Dreyer et al. 1998). With their variety of architectural forms these burials represent evolution of a royal tomb and with their diverse equipment, impressive

dimensions, and the presence of the most numerous sets of subsidiary burials or funerary boats, they exceed all other necropoles of the period.

An issue worth raising is also the presence of enclosures surrounded with massive walls and rows of subsidiary burials, related to a king's burial ceremonies (Kaiser 1969; Kaiser, Dreyer 1982: 253-255; O'Connor 1989; Bestock 2008). The oldest of eight discovered structures (six dated to Dynasty 1 and two to Dynasty 2 – among them the monumental enclosure in Shunet el-Zebib) is connected with Aha (O'Connor 1989: 54-55). A massive wall encircling the enclosure of Djer proves that at least from the time of his reign such structures, which played a role in royal mortuary cult or were used during a royal funeral, were built for dead kings. Solid walls built around some mastaba tombs in Saqqara North could reflect the royal tradition from Abydos and according to W. Kaiser (1969), may have contributed to the emergence of the complex of Netjerikhet (Djoser). Moreover, W. Kaiser (1985) postulates that the cemetery in Saqqara-Serapeum excavated by R. Macramallah (1940) belongs in fact to an unpreserved cult enclosure of king Den.

Worth a mention is also high position of women in early Egyptian society proved by all the titles and impressive burials of the wife or mother of Aha, Neithotep as well as Merytneith most probably a daughter of Djer, wife of Djet and, mother and regent of Den (Ciałowicz 2001: 33).

The most popular and change-prone type of objects is still pottery. From the technological point of view, jars were made of silt with admixture of chaff or calcium carbonate, marl clay with mud or sand. Characteristic of the period are storage jars of various size with a distinct neck or ledge rim, slandering towards the bottom or barrel-shaped and ovoid, cylindrical vessels, bowls and jars with red surface that were emulations of older red-polished and black-topped pottery, as well as reddish-orange strap polished bowls (Adams, Ciałowicz 1997: 24-26). W.M.F. Petrie gathered the above mentioned products into class L with more chronological than typological significance. At the same time, disappeared previously popular painted pottery, which had been commonly used only in the first part of the period in a form of net pattern registered on cylindrical jars with a vestigial *wavy-handles*.

Stone vessels manufacturing flourished during the period of Naqada III with clearly increasing number of discovered objects (their straight majority comes from richly equipped tombs) made of various stones (Ciałowicz 2001: 107). Popular shapes were: jars with a distinct neck and flat base, sometimes with additional *lug-handles*; jars with a distinct neck and rounded base, short to oval, all with *lug-handles*; bowls with flat base; cylindrical jars often decorated with *lug-* and *wavy-handles*; flat bowls and plates sometimes with a tall conical ring base, as well as unusual shapes e.g. zoomorphic.

Quite often discovered were elements of personal adornments and jewellery such as: various beads of colourful raw materials, mostly of stone and more and more popular amulets in new shapes – serpent's heads, geometric pendants, stylized objects like *fish-tails*, phallic symbols of Min, combs with short teeth, pilar *djed* connected with the cult of Osiris or so-called Isis' knot (Ciałowicz 1999: 196). The most beautiful examples of bracelets known from the period are those discovered in the tomb of Djer in Abydos, which in a stunning way combined parts made of colour stones, bone and gold. Other finds, however, are more simple: usually composed of beads or in a form of hoop with a flat-and-concave section – made of bone, greywacke or less frequently of flint, shell, limestone, calcite and sporadically of gold or copper. Finger-rings were seldom registered in a shape of very simple circles. The number of bone finds (spoons, few pins and combs, jars in forms imitating pottery and stone items, boxes, pawns and gaming pieces) visibly decreased in the context of graves which belonged to ordinary members of the society, but increased in elite tombs. The great popularity of various types of games is especially worth stressing. They included simple conical pawns, cuboids, balls (in some field reports described as marbles) and sticks or canine and feline figurines, which are most commonly believed to be gaming pieces[3]. Gaming boards were made of ivory, marble, or wood, and were often furnished with beautifully shaped bulls' legs. Game elements were probably also discs found in the tomb attributed to Hemaka, decorated with figural scenes, pierced and sealed with numerous sticks in a single box (Ciałowicz 1999: 206). Such boxes, as well as pieces of furniture increasing in number (beds, chairs, tables and head-rests) were often richly incrusted, decorated with combinations of geometric patterns, representations of niche facades (an example comes from tomb 1050 in Minshat Abu Omar – Kroeper, Krzyżaniak 1992) or figural e.g. with a row of captives. Cosmetic palettes in the period are divided into practically used, that is geometric – rectangular, square and oval decorated at the most with a simple geometric design by their edges, and ceremonial, that is shield-shaped with extended figural scenes, which played the role of ideas' carriers (Ciałowicz 1991). In general, during the period of Naqada III spiritual culture developed greatly, which in archaeological material is reflected by changes in functions of particular types of objects like palettes and mace-heads from previously clearly practical into ritual, cult and symbolic.

A change is visible in utilization of raw materials for tools production. Thus, the number of flint objects decreased such as: sickle inserts, knives, scrapers, crescent borers which were gradually being replaced with metal tools – axes, chisels, knives. Characteristic of the Naqada III period are high-quality flint knives with a distinct handle in their straight majority found in burials (mainly Abydos, Saqqara, Tarkhan, Helwan), often intentionally broken. They were bifacially manufactured with surface retouch by pressure or produced as models and then, they were rough and large, while their handles were straight or hooked, always short. Most of registered examples come from the period of Dynasty 1, one of them was even partially covered with a golden foil with the name of Djer (Ciałowicz 1999: 221). Metal knives were made mostly of copper but sometimes also of silver. There were registered some double knives with tangs for attaching hilts and rounded points as well as knives with pointed blades with straight edges and without tangs made of a very thin metal sheet, which were rather models produced for burial use.

---

[3] Small pottery objects in the shapes of balls, cones and discs have recently become an object of reinterpretation as tokens used in an early pre-writing counting system connected mostly with trade activities. Such an interpretation was first suggested for similar early Mesopotamian objects by D. Schmandt-Besserat (1992), in Egypt the phenomenon is currently being studied by P. Kołodziejczyk (2012).

# 3. EVOLUTION OF BURIAL CUSTOMS

## 3.1. THE EARLIEST BURIAL CUSTOMS REMAINS IN NORTHERN EGYPT

### THE MERIMDE CULTURE

The oldest burials known from Northern Egypt are connected with the Merimde culture, which – at least in the present state of research – is attested only on a single site. Therefore, it is obvious that all the graves that will be discussed below come from the solitary location. Surprisingly, it does not mean that the definition of general burial custom rules followed by the people of Merimde is easy to be given. The main question is whether graves registered in Merimde were intentionally placed below houses' floors and in their immediate vicinity (as H. Junker states – after: Kemp 1968: 23 – for the living did not parted their dead), or in a separated cemetery, which, as the settlement was growing, was later reoccupied (Kemp 1968: 28).

The additional difficulty in interpretation of the Merimde burial custom is formed by the visible predomination in the number of graves that comprised children (55.5% of the thorough 134 number of all Merimde burials ever registered) and female remains, while only 6% of burials were identified as male skeletons (Castillos 1982c: 171-172). This fact indicates – what raises no doubt – a very high children mortality rate, but the almost complete lack of male burials may also suggest that there existed another separated and still undiscovered cemetery for men only. This hypothesis is easily acceptable when the earlier phase of the settlement occupation is considered, while in the younger period all community members might have been interred in abandoned settlement areas at once.

Regardless of specific rules governing graves location, the remaining burial customs elements are visible in archaeological material which was acquired at the site. Therefore, we deal with simple customs that do not disclose social differentiation or significant care of burial forms. Only simple, shallow and oval pit graves were registered with average dimensions ca. 1m in length and ca. 0.5m in width. The deceased were usually wrapped up in mats or leather and buried in a tightly contracted position. The most popular was the right-sided position (84%) with the head turned south (57%) or eastwards (34%). Burials oriented to west and north were also attested, however, they are of marginal importance, similarly as multiple inhumations. These simple and small graves were only exceptionally equipped and when a case like this occurs it was nothing but very few objects, like food offerings (grains, animal bones) or few pottery vessels.

### THE OMARI CULTURE

Like in the case of Merimde, burial customs practiced by the people of Omari are quite obscure. Here also, the issue of burials and settlement simultanity remains an unanswered question, since part of graves was discovered in the site housing area. The dominant view (Ciałowicz 1999: 231) is that the deceased were buried in the vicinity of their houses, however, only in the already abandoned zones. This theory is supported by the reusage of pits which had previously played storage or dwelling functions. The Omari graves do not reveal any concentration and seem to be spread rather randomly all over the site.

Bodies were interred in simple, structurally uncomplicated, shallow and oval pits that measured on average 0.9-1.2m x 0.7-1.1m. Their original depth remains undefined due to damages of the upper layers of the site (Debono, Mortensen 1990: 74). The straight majority of burials was put into pits intentionally prepared for the purpose (ca. 58% of the whole registered number), although it was not an absolute rule since graves were also found in pits of primarily clearly housing use or in close relation to them. In general, burials related to the Omari culture may be divided into the simplest ones, that is devoid of any superstructure remains, and those which were provided with a kind of over-ground structures made of perishable materials or marked with stone circles.

In the light of archaeological data, the Omari burial customs appear to be uncomplicated and really homogenous. The deceased were buried in a contracted position on their side with their hands on the chest or in front of the face. In the majority of cases (ca. 84%) the left side was chosen and bodies were oriented with their heads south and faces west (ca. 72%), other directions were of meager popularity (Debono, Mortensen 1990: 74). Bodies were usually wrapped in or covered with mats (their traces were discovered in ca. 63% of burials) and sporadically, even with hair leather (only ca. 7% of the graves total number). Wooden sticks found in one burial which were arranged around the deceased in a rectangular shape might have been a kind of a light bed or a bier. Definitely little is known about infant burials, since nothing but a single grave was discovered. The infant was interred in a bag made of brown plant fibres.

Among the unexplained elements of the Omari burial customs there are also stones registered in almost a half of graves (ca. 46%). They were mainly small slabs of limestone laid in two or three behind the deceased back and sometimes over the bodies. A little mud wall found in one of graves was presumably of the same function (Debono, Mortensen 1990: 74). It is an interesting detail that a few burials were provided with stone "head rests" or "pillows" found below the deceased heads.

Offerings were registered in ca. 74% of graves, nevertheless, poor preservation state of numerous remaining burials enable researchers to state that it is not the complete number. In the case, burials which were doubtlessly devoid of equipment form as little as 7% of the whole cemetery. Despite the high popularity of grave furnishing, the offerings themselves belong to definitively poor as they were composed of singular small pottery vessels or few wooden objects. Pottery represented two types – a beaker-like one with a rough surface and a vase-like one covered with polished slip. Regrettably, these types do not provide any dating hints. Among the offerings an oblong object with worked-out edges deserves a mention, since it was widely interpreted as a kind of a scepter or a wand. Other interesting items found in burials are: shells, beads and flowers registered in one grave. Pots were placed in front of the upper body part or, in much fewer cases, between the legs. Infant burials were probably left unfurnished (Debono, Mortensen 1990: 74-75).

The discovered archaeological material, although connected with two separated settlement phases (4 and 7), does not suggest a development of burial customs, except for a slight tendency towards gradual reduction in the number of stones found within graves (Debono, Mortensen 1990: 75). Similarly, there are no hints concerning the presence of possible social stratification since all graves were following the same uncomplicated equipment scheme and the so-called "scepter" seems to be an overinterpretation. No data point to the emotional attitude of the Omari people to the afterlife question. The fact that the majority of the deceased was offered at least a small object proves an unknown afterlife concept. The bunch of flowers found in one grave expresses even more personal interest in the deceased fate, nevertheless, as a unique case it does not allow to draw general conclusions. On the other hand, the simultaneous practice of burying human bodies in pits which were previously used in the normal everyday life of the settlement suggests that the construction effort was being minimized by reusing the ground that was already loosened instead of hewing in an untouched bedrock. Therefore, the lesser effort could be the actual reason of the reuse of abandoned domestic structures rather than the desire for intentional keeping of the dead near inhabited houses. Any grave distribution pattern cannot be presently reconstructed, although a kind of sector system probably existed, since children burials were more frequent in the eastern part of regions A and B, and in region A male burials occupied the zone located farther to the west.

## 3.2. THE LOWER EGYPTIAN CULTURE

The Lower Egyptian culture expanded over a vast area and thus, the number of sites connected with the culture is far more significant, at least in comparison to earlier periods. Burials attributed to the culture were registered at 17 archaeological sites (see Map no. 2), nine of which are clearly separated cemeteries. A long period of activity brought gradual changes into burial customs of the Lower Egyptian culture but till the very end of their history the people preferred to bury their dead in an uncomplicated

way and did not reveal strong aspiration for the customs' standardization. That is why, every generalization allowed by the present archaeology should be regarded as an indication of a tendency, rather than an absolute rule.

Bodies were interred in simple oval pits, almost completely devoid of any interesting structural features. The pits were small in size and grew only slightly in subsequent phases. Grave goods offered to the deceased were found in every second grave on average, unavoidably few and poor. What is significant, the most popular category of goods was formed by pottery vessels represented only in functional types well attested in settlement strata and commonly deposited in a highly worn out state, even incomplete. The undeniable novelty which was introduced to the Northern Egyptian tradition at the earliest stage of the Lower Egyptian culture was clearly extra-mural burial custom. However, it should be stressed here that apart from quite numerous cemeteries which had up to 100 graves (only Wadi Digla and probably Heliopolis exceeded the number) a common tradition were infant burials in large pots placed within a settlement area. Adults were also buried in settlements, but since only two examples are known (one in Maadi – Rizkana, Seeher 1989: 65; and one in Buto – von der Way 1997: 74-75) they do not enable any further conclusions as they could be enclosed into a settlement as a result of later relocation of inhabitants activity. These two unique examples are even more difficult for interpretation in the light of discoveries of loose human bones in Lower Egyptian culture settlements. The latter are explained as remains of those exceptional adult graves damaged by relocated younger activity at a settlement or – as it is suggested in relation to a human skull probably intentionally placed on the top of a mound of ashes in Maadi (Rizkana, Seeher 1989: 67) – they contain a proof for presently unknown and archaeologically imperceptible burial practices.

Tradition of this kind is well attested in Upper Egypt, to quote only el-Adaïma (Crubézy, Midant-Reynes 2000), Hierakonpolis (Dougherty, Friedman 2008) or Naqada (Petrie, Quibell 1896). Multiple burials were registered there, presumably secondary or connected with human sacrifice, as well as traces of mutilated human bones which were interpreted as (Petrie, Quibell 1896: 19) related to cannibalism. This assumption, however, is presently regarded as highly unlikely. Nevertheless, the category of discoveries points to the fact that some individuals or even groups of the early Egyptian society deserved special treatment.

## THE EARLY PHASE

Burial customs of the Lower Egyptian culture, however simple, evolved together with the whole development of the unit. According to the latest proposals, the early phase is the longest part in the culture's history. Such a division is fairly justified when discussing the culture's pottery

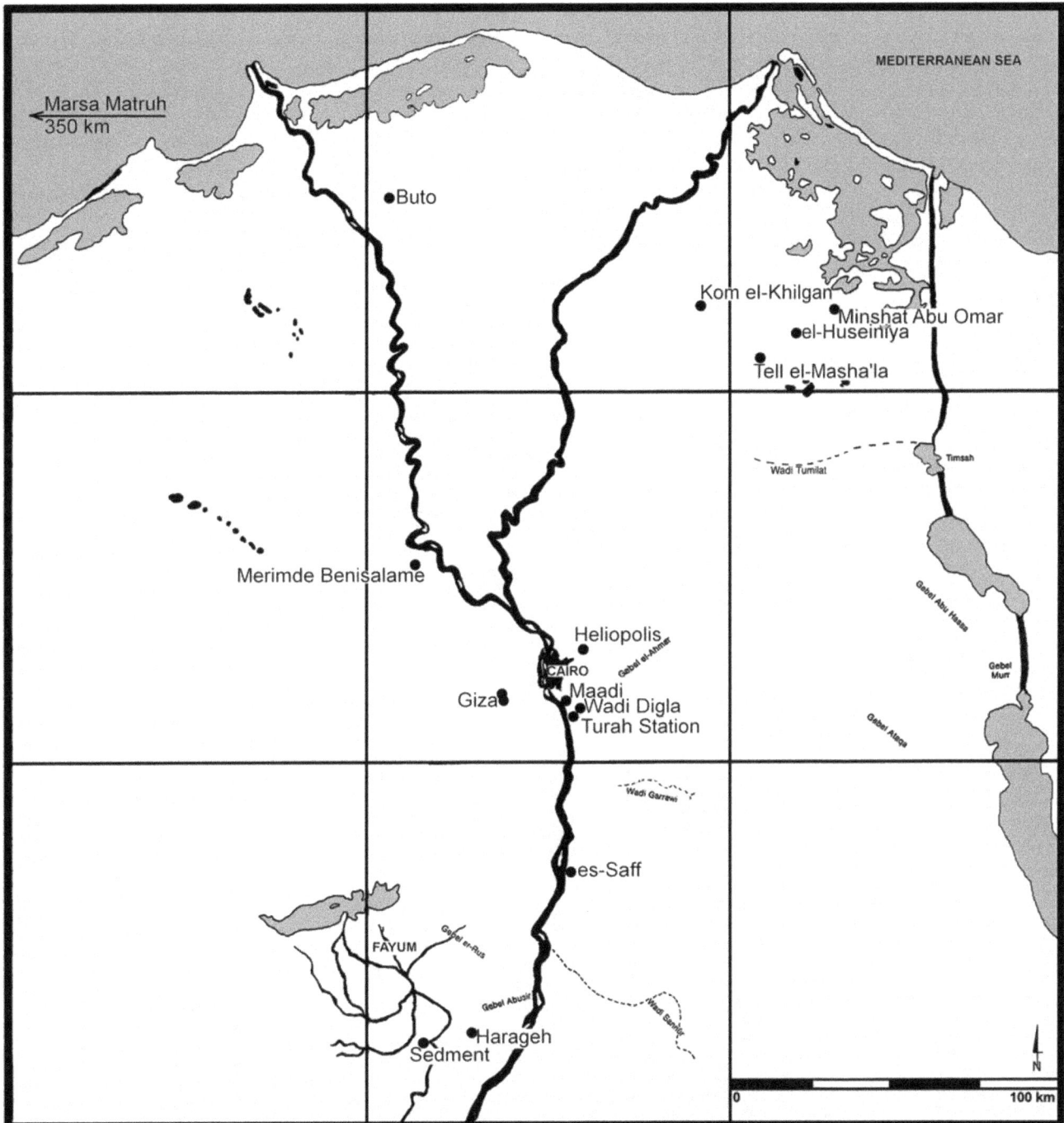

*Map no. 2. Cemeteries connected with the Lower Egyptian culture*

and flint industry but in case of its burial tradition the situation seems to be more complex. It obviously shows the subject needs more profound studies and, preferably, new discoveries.

Five burial related sites are dated to the early phase of the Lower Egyptian culture and there is a significant difference visible between a group of older and younger sites dated to the phase. The older group is composed of graves from cemeteries in Maadi (Rizkana, Seeher 1990: 23) and Wadi Digla, phase I (Rizkana, Seeher 1990: 65) and from the settlement in Maadi (Rizkana, Seeher 1989: 67). The archaeological material collected there proves that a popular custom was to bury adults in single graves (double ones are extremely rare) in separated cemeteries

(the unique burial of an adult female registered in an unclearly explained context in the settlement in Maadi seems to confirm this assumption), while infants were interred both in settlement areas (also examples from Maadi) and in regular cemeteries in selected sectors (Maadi). Hence, in Lower Egypt the tradition was to bury infants in pots in typical functional forms and the rest of population in shallow pits (0.4-0.7m of depth on average) of rather small size (0.6-0.8 x 0.75-1.1m in average), mostly oval in shape (only few round examples are known from Wadi Digla). There was no sophisticated structural solutions of any kind – all graves were inevitably simple pits. Particular burials, although they were quite densely located in cemetery areas, did not intersect each other and, what is even more puzzling, no traces of marking burial places on the surface were found. Remains of mats and plaiting were attested at some graves' bottoms, so the custom of inlaying graves before the actual burial was interred was known and rather popular. Regrettably, the very perishable character of those materials does not enable an appropriate assessment of the actual scale of the phenomenon.

Another interesting burial customs element was noticed in 50 graves of Wadi Digla (Rizkana, Seeher 1990: 69). It is the presence of stones within grave pits, which is characteristic exclusively for the first part of the early Lower Egyptian culture phase. The stones appeared singularly (they are interpreted then as of pillow use, although only five attested examples form a number too insignificant for further analysis) or from few to a dozen or so of them, in most cases then they were arranged in a row. Their location within a grave pit itself near one of its edges and their rather little stable form as for an eventual wall do not allow interpreting them as of structural function. Interestingly, the presence of stones in graves was also quite popular in the Omari culture burial customs (Debono, Mortensen 1990: 74), where – as a matter of fact – it falls outside any clear definition, too. It is difficult to judge, however, if it was an element inherited by the Lower Egyptian culture since both cultural units are separated by a long and unrecognized period of time.

A grave's simple shape and form seem quite a justified solution in comparison to the preferable contracted body position on a side. At the development stage of the culture burial customs no clear preference for body arrangement was registered, although right-sided burials were more popular. The deceased were in about a half of graves oriented their heads southwards, nevertheless, even in the case it is not a strict rule as all other orientations were reflected in the archaeological data. The issue may be perfectly illustrated by two burials from the cemetery in Maadi, where the deceased was pushed into a too little grave pit (MA39) or was laid on his/her back with feet sticking out of the pit (MA60). Both examples stress the obvious lack of special care concerning the dead. Another element which probably had an impact on the simple burial form were poor and rarely attested grave goods. Few, in the majority of cases appearing singularly, pottery vessels represented types perfectly well known from settlement strata (in particular pots on a raised base of the red polished ware), often worn out or even crushed into pieces. The remaining goods categories were singular pottery fragments of an unknown purpose, simple flint tools, very few stone vessels, Nilotic mollusk shells, most probably of a container use, grey mangan ore used as a cosmetic dye, cosmetic palettes, cosmetic bone objects and beads – all of local production. In the light of collected data, grave goods were not regarded as a compulsory burial custom element, since they were found in less than a half of registered burials. Moreover, they were always simple sets devoid of valuable objects.

The younger group of early phase graves was discovered in the cemeteries in Wadi Digla, phase II (Rizkana,

Seeher 1990: 76), Heliopolis (Debono, Mortensen 1988) and Kom el-Khilgan 1 (Buchez, Midant-Reynes 2011). It is worth stressing that in the second part of the early phase we deal with the largest cemeteries of the culture (the burial number in Wadi Digla II is estimated to have been ca. 200 and in Heliopolis probably ca. 200).

Still, graves were simple pits of a round, oval or ellipsoid shape and of average dimensions (0.5-1.1 x 0.9-1.5m) slightly larger than previously. The average depth of grave pits was permanently insignificant – ca. 0.4-0.8m. The only structural variety registered in two burials in Heliopolis was a kind of steps that led to a grave bottom. The rules of burial customs were slowly becoming standardized, although graves were still left unmarked on the ground surface or all traces of marking practices were unpreserved. Mats that inlayed grave pits' bottoms became more popular and the previously attested stones of insufficiently interpreted purpose almost completely vanished (the only registered example comes from Heliopolis). The clearly preferable body position became the contracted on the right side one, the head to south, and the face to east. Even in this case, however, regional differentiation existed and the rule was applied to burials in Wadi Digla and Heliopolis, while in Kom el-Khilgan the preference is not so clear. Both left-sided position and other orientation variants were represented in the archaeological material and since they were relatively common they were still outnumbered by the first rule. The more and more significant burial element was wrapping bodies in mats and leather before the actual interment, which is a proof for growing care of the dead. Moreover, the increasing interest in the afterlife and thus in the burial quality is reflected by a general tendency toward more generous offerings. Among the growing repertoire of objects pottery, the black and brown-black wares in particular with the most popular ovoid barrel-shaped pot, still reigned. Other registered categories of objects were: copper ore, flint knives, flint row material, Nilotic and sea mollusks' shells, basalt and limestone vessels, necklaces of shells and beads, bracelets, malachite, very rarely preserved cloths and a few food offerings in form of animal bones remains. Also, singularly represented objects were discovered, for example an eroded copper object or a rhomboid palette. Goods other than pottery were in every case rare findings clearly dominated in quantity by many pots in popular, functional types, often severely damaged. However, the total number of graves with equipment of any kind increased to over 60% of the whole registered group of burials connected with the second part of the phase. Still, the standard was to furnish the dead in a single and simple pottery vessel of local production, but – it should be stressed – the majority of graves which are regarded as rich belong to the same phase. Infants were continually buried without offerings, still in specific sectors of regular cemeteries (Heliopolis).

A novelty introduced into the Northern Egyptian burial customs in the early period of the Lower Egyptian culture were animal burials located within regular cemeteries among regular human graves and organized according to the same burial rules as in the case of humans. They became an almost characteristic element of burial customs connected with the second part of the early phase of the Lower Egyptian culture. Unfortunately, this interesting issue has been up till now left without any proper explanation, what is more, there is not enough data which would allow further progress in the case. The oldest example is represented by a single dog burial from the cemetery in Maadi (Rizkana, Seeher 1990: 27), then in the second part of the phase come further 13 lamb, six dog and six goat burials, which were registered at the sites of Wadi Digla (Rizkana, Seeher 1990: 93-94) and Heliopolis (Debono, Mortensen 1988: 39-40). All the animals were buried in grave pits of the same type as in the case of adult human burials and – what surprises the most – animal burials belonged to richer graves as their smaller dimensions reflected rather smaller size of the interred animals. Every goat was equipped and oriented its head southwards, a half of lambs was furnished with a single pot and one of them even with a stone bead and probably copper ore. Dogs, however, were buried without offerings and any clear orientation pattern. The distribution of animal burials displayed concentration in certain sectors within regular cemeteries meant for humans.

Similarly unexplained remains the function of the so-called pottery pits registered in cemeteries of Wadi Digla (Rizkana, Seeher 1990: 95) and Heliopolis (Debono, Mortensen 1988: 38). These were invariably simple pits, from the structural point of view, identical with those of grave function. The only feature that distinguished them were different contents, that is exclusively typically functional complete and broken pots. In Wadi Digla pottery pits were concentrated in the central part of the cemetery, in four cases in the very vicinity of animal burials; however, the remaining ones did not reveal this coincidence. It cannot be decided then whether the pottery pits were a sort of supplementary equipment for one specific burial or if they played the role of a sacrificial place in relation to burial practices in general. It is possible that they were connected with few hearths found in the Lower Egyptian culture cemeteries of the period but their function also remains undefined.

**THE MIDDLE PHASE**

Along with the growing number of sites of the Lower Egyptian culture in the Nile Delta, the middle phase burial customs were represented in more numerous sites. The phase opens a group of sites with rather imprecise dates which makes them seem to be dated on the turn of phases 1 and 2, according to the recent shifts in the internal chronology of the culture. However, in the author's opinion they represent rather the classical phase. Among the group composed of five sites, two – that is Giza "at the foot of the Great Pyramid" (Kamal 1911: 116-117; Mortensen 1985; el-Sanussi, Jones 1997) and Giza-Tramway (Mortensen 1985; Rizkana, Seeher 1987: 61; el-Sanussi, Jones 1997) brought only conjectures

about their character, while the remaining ones with their small number of burials also offer little possibilities for interpretation. The latter sites are Merimde (Badawi 1980: 70-74) – six burials, es-Saff (Habachi, Kaiser 1985: 43-44) – 10 burials and Tell el-Masha'la (Rampersad 2006) – 7 burials[4].

Sites which fully represent the classical phase of the Lower Egyptian culture are: Kom el-Khilgan 2 (Buchez, Midant-Reynes 2011), Marsa Matruh (Bates 1927: 137), the settlement in Buto (von der Way 1997: 74-75), el-Huseiniya (Kroeper 1988: 18; Mostafa 1988, 1988a), Turah Station (Kaiser, Zaugg 1988; Mortensen 1999: 851; Scharff 1931: 122), Harageh (Engelbach 1923; Kaiser 1987a; Williams 1982), Sedment J and K (Petrie, Brunton 1924a; 1924b; Williams 1982), Minshat Abu Omar I (Wildung, Kroeper 1985; 1994; 2000) and also the end of use of the cemeteries in Wadi Digla II and Heliopolis, as well as the settlement of Maadi, all of which overlap with the beginning of the phase. The number of sites is quite significant, regrettably, materials collected there are rather disappointing. The character of the site in Turah Station is highly disputable, in Buto only a single inhumation was registered within regular settlement strata, el-Huseiniya is hardly partially published and the only hint that connects the site with the Lower Egyptian culture is the opinion of K. Kroeper (1988: 18), who compares pottery from the graves to MAO I and II, and since MAO I (see below) is recently recognized as Lower Egyptian, it may be assumed that the same is true in the case of el-Huseiniya. The opinion is also shared by S. Hendrickx and E. van den Brink (2002: 348, tabl. 23.1). Unfortunately, the presently known data do not allow any statement on the character of possible continuation of the cemetery use in following periods.

Marsa Matruh is another small (five burials) cemetery of a very distant location, which probably explains its specific features. There are even suggestions the site should be connected with the Merimde culture (Hendrickx, van den Brink 2002: 348, tabl. 23.1) but the author of the study concurs with the opinion of Lower Egyptian links of people buried there.

The remaining sites are Harageh, Sedment, Kom el-Khilgan and Minshat Abu Omar. In Harageh 47 early burials were registered, while at Sedment there were no human bones at all but only pottery pits, however both sites brought very similar pottery. It is generally accepted they are dated to NIIC, however, there are proposals which shift this dating to NIA (Williams 1982). It is especially tempting as it offers the possibility to place the sites in the cultural sequence as a link between the cultures of Omari or Merimde, but in present days it

---

[4] The case of Tell el-Masha'la is interesting, as the quoted publication only mentions that the discovered burials may have belonged in fact to a larger, though presently destroyed cemetery and only tentatively suggests that the site is connected with the Lower Egyptian culture. The published material is scarce, however, it actually seems to fit the Lower Egyptian culture, especially in the light of recent research at other settlement sites of the cultural unit.

seems to be rejected (see Buchez, Midant-Reynes 2011). The situation in Kom el-Khilgan 2 is also difficult as to the phase were ascribed 30 burials with offerings, while the cemetery was surely composed of some poor burials, too, but their number remains imprecise. Nevertheless, all graves show low effort investment into their construction and present the cemetery as belonging to a relatively poor and provincial community.

Finally, there is Minshat Abu Omar, which until very recently seemed to be clear and obvious, but reexamination of the materials proves that phase I and possibly II belong to the Lower Egyptian culture. The reappraisal is based mostly on the interpretation of lemon-shaped pottery jars characteristic especially of group Ib dated to NIID. Thus, the material is hardly consistent or sufficient. What can be drawn out of it is that typical were simple pit graves, mostly oval, but in Harageh, Tell el-Masha'la and Minshat Abu Omar also rectangular. Their average dimensions seem to be larger than in the previous phase (1.1-2.1 x 1-1.3m and up to 3.2m deep in MAO), their bottoms were inlayed with mats, moreover, Harageh preserved some wood remains and at Tell el-Masha'la traces of fabric around human bones were discovered. The preferable position of the deceased was the contracted on a side one, with heads turned usually northwards, the rest was changing according to a particular site (Buto – left side, head to north; Harageh – left side, head to south; Kom el-Khilgan – right and left side, head to north; Marsa Matruh – left and right side, head to east; Merimde – right side, head to north; Minshat Abu Omar – right side, head to north; es-Saff – right side, head to south; Tell el-Masha'la – left side, head north). All these differences show there was no a commonly followed rule and thus, it is justified to state that the actual body orientation was not of the highest importance for the people of that time, but, on the other hand, the larger or lesser degree of variations within a single cemetery indicates that the custom was just during its formation.

Typical offerings were obviously not regarded as obligatory but if they appeared, they were usually single pottery vessels. However, some cemeteries (Harageh, Merimde, Minshat Abu Omar) were visibly richer with graves equipped even with 32 items. Apart from pottery also other categories of objects were sometimes deposited within graves such as: mollusk shells, beads, flints, malachite, lumps of clay, dyes, copper, ivories, cosmetic pallets, vessels of basalt, travertine, limestone, breccia or greywacke and some imported objects (MAO I).

A continuation of customs introduced during the early phase of the Lower Egyptian culture are pottery pits in the classical phase known from Sedment J (175), a few from Sedment K (Petrie, Brunton 1924a; 1924b; Williams 1982) and only one from es-Saff (Habachi, Kaiser 1985: 43). Still, these puzzling features fall outside our present understanding.

## THE LATE PHASE

Burial customs of the late phase of the Lower Egyptian culture are hardly recognized, although the phase is well attested at numerous settlement sites, where slowly but gradually local Lower Egyptian traditions were blurred and melted into the new cultural picture of the Delta in the period of NIIIA. The only cemetery site attributed to the phase is Minshat Abu Omar Ib and, very tentatively, also II.[5] As MAO Ib is generally dated to NIID, only a part of these burials (ca. 56% of early graves at the site) actually represent the late phase of the Lower Egyptian culture (for the needs of the study their number is simplisticly estimated as ca. 117). Unfortunately, to precisely mark them off more studies have to be completed. The situation does not become clearer when the presence of other neighbouring cemeteries is considered, such as: the above mentioned el-Huseiniya with its unclarified Lower Egyptian-Naqadan sequence, as well as Kafr Hassan Dawood, Minshat Ezzat or Beni Amir (see below) which seem to be Naqadan sites coexisting with the last Lower Egyptian phase.

Typical graves discovered in MAO Ib followed the same rules that existed in its previous phase – MAO Ia – that is contracted right side position of the deceased, with their heads turned northwards. The offerings were composed mostly of locally made pottery and some imported Upper Egyptian and Levantine wares, as well as limestone and travertine vessels, flints, cosmetic pallets, beads, bone spoons, harpoons and other, though not numerous, objects of bone and copper. Burials were deposited in simple oval or rectangular (1-1.5m in average length) and rather deep (from 0.6 to 3.2m) pits, described even as "shaft pits" (Kroeper 1988: 14).

It remains obscure, though, how far the Minshat Abu Omar data may be representative of the whole cultural unit since the site is the only Lower Egyptian cemetery dated to the late phase and the only one whose use was incessantly continued in the following period. It should also be considered that MAO II represents the actual cultural transition with continuation of major Lower Egyptian burial traditions and typically Naqadan pottery grave offerings.

## THE LOWER EGYPTIAN SUMMARY

The burial customs of the Lower Egyptian culture appear to be simple, only creating its clear rules which were never fully followed. Among these "rules" are:
- the preferable contracted body position on its right side with its head mostly oriented southwards;
- the graves' role was played by structurally simple pits of insignificant size (with a slight tendency

---

[5] MAO II is hardly recognized (only ca. 2% of early graves at the site) and the major argument in favour of the suggestion is the continuing tradition of unchanged burials' form and bodies' position in comparison to MAO I.

toward growing in time) with bottoms inlayed with mats as the maximum of care;

- the obvious preference of the Lower Egyptian people was for the extra-mural burial custom, although even in this case numerous exceptions were registered, like: rather common infant burials within settlement areas and two known examples of adults buried there, as well as discoveries of loose human bones in settlement strata – probably remains of damaged graves or some unexplained burial practices;
- children were buried together with other community members – in Maadi and Heliopolis in separated sectors – after they reached the "proper" age[6], while infants were consequently "kept" within or close to settlement borders. In many cases infants were hidden inside large pots or simple pits;
- the straight majority of burials was registered in separated cemeteries, which were composed of rather few burials (only Wadi Digla and probably Heliopolis exceeded the number of 100 graves) of more family character.

Grave offerings were a practice known by the people of the Lower Egyptian culture but not always present. Generally, only ca. a half of the culture burials was equipped with any object, however, there is an observed tendency toward increasing popularity of the tradition together with the whole unit development. Apart from that, rich offerings seem to be a practice borrowed from other areas since it appeared as late as in the period of intensified Lower Egyptian-Naqadan contacts. Before, typical offerings had comprised a single pottery vessel from the commonly attested functional repertoire, frequently severely worn out. Objects of other categories also appeared in graves sporadically, however, they constituted rare discoveries, moreover, they were rarely of any significant value. A general rule seems to be local origin of all items accompanying burials. The small number of grave goods does not allow to capture social stratification and forms a proof that the society functioned according to simple rules, without division into material groups. The assumption may be supported – in a way – by the fact that infant burials were commonly left unfurnished. However, it cannot be forgotten that the data collected in the settlement in Tell el-Farkha (Chłodnicki, Ciałowicz et al. 2002: 60-70, 2004: 50; Chłodnicki, Geming 2012) seem to suggest the beginning of social differentiation with the moment when the "Lower Egyptian residence" was built, shortly followed by first mud brick structures. As burial customs are popularly regarded as very conservative and change-proof, the evolution of social situation could not find its reflection in the grave tradition.

The archaeological material does not reveal any particular care of the afterlife. Neither sophisticated architectural constructions nor significant number of grave goods were registered. The dead were buried directly in ground pits without care of any protection or tight body cover. Still, some issues are far from being explained, which may add some individual colour to the uncomplicated burial customs. One of these unanswered questions is the tradition of animal burials. All of them belonged only to three species (goat, lamb and dog), consequently buried according to rules applied to human burials, moreover, often better equipped and inevitably within regular cemeteries (e.g. Heliopolis grave no. 37, where a goat was furnished with six undamaged pottery vessels or grave no. 24 with eight jars). Similarly obscure remains the purpose of the so-called pottery pits which were attested in cemeteries but cannot be directly attributed to any of the surrounding graves and therefore they are treated as independent structures. Presumably, both animal burials and loose human bones registered in settlement strata (e.g. on the top of a mound of ashes in Maadi), the so-called pottery pits and the presence of hearths in cemeteries compose particular elements of the Lower Egyptian tradition and enriched the burial customs as a whole. However, the actual importance of these elements is presently undefined and we must await future discoveries before they are eventually explained. It is likely that intensification of field research in previously archaeologically untouched areas would bring new comparative material.

The last but not least issue to discuss is the distribution of sites reflecting directions of expansion of the whole unit (Map no. 2). The oldest cemeteries from the formative period were registered by the Nile Delta base in the area of present Cairo, while the most numerous sites (both settlements and cemeteries) are connected with the middle phase and were discovered around the previously occupied area and in much vaster territories in the Delta. Unfortunately, in the late phase the situation is unclear since only a single cemetery is attributed to the period. However, looking at the map, it should be kept in mind that it shows only a part of Lower Egyptian sites, those related to burial activity of the people. In the context, the juxtaposition of the number of sites with the quantity of graves dated to particular phases of the culture (Table no. 2) appears to be interesting, although it does not reflect perfectly changes within the whole cultural unit. Quite

|  | Phase 1 | Phase 2 | Phase 3 |
|---|---|---|---|
| Number of sites | 5 | 14 | 1 |
| Number of burials | 692 | 262 | ca. 117 |

*Table no. 2. Number of registered burial related sites of the Lower Egyptian culture in comparison to the number of burials in particular phases of the unit*

surprisingly, the largest number of graves is dated to the early phase, but when we consider this phase is the longest one in the history of the culture and that Heliopolis, Wadi Digla II and the settlement in Maadi slightly overlap with the beginning of the classical phase, the predomination does not seem to be so overwhelming

---

[6] The excavated material is really diverse and does not allow to specify the age limit between the infants kept within settlements and children buried at regular cemeteries. The author suggests then that the actual threshold condition was the ability of speaking, walking etc. important from the social point of view but unrecognizable in skeletal remains.

any more. The highest number of sites dated to the middle phase correlates well with growing geographical range of the culture and the relatively small group of burials suggests rather what should be still hidden in the ground. The late phase remains archaeologically unrecognized, which is also reflected by the numbers.

## 3.3. THE NAQADAN EXPANSION INTO NORTHERN EGYPT

### THE EARLIEST NAQADAN SETTLEMENT

The earliest cemetery in Northern Egypt attributed to the Gerzean period is commonly accepted to be the eponymy site of Gerzeh (Petrie et al. 1912: 1-24). Although there are some discrepancies among scholars in the understanding of the site (see Buchez, Midant-Reynes 2011), it is generally believed the cemetery does not display features that could link it to any older type of human activity in the area of the Fayum oasis, so it is regarded (Wenke 1999a: 316) as an early Naqadan intruder in the region.

All graves registered in the cemetery of Gerzeh represented the simple pit type. They were divided according to their shape into: large and oblong (1.25 x 0.75m in average), and small and oval (0.62 x 0.37m in average), which were the most popular. All of them had been dug in sandy ground to the level of hard gravel which formed bottoms of the deepest burial pits, reaching up to 0.75m of depth. No remains of any actual grave roofing or strengthening other than mud plaster were registered. The deceased were eventually secured with a kind of coffin which was plastered with mud and filled in with earth and then covered with another layer of mud.

Every burial but three belonged to a single deceased, the exceptions were adults buried with infants and one grave with three adult skeletons. G.A. Wainwright (Petrie et al. 1912: 5) suggested in the final publication of the site that the majority of these cases had been mothers with their offspring, however, no detailed studies on the bone material were undertaken, therefore the sex of the deceased was left undetermined. Moreover, there are also doubts concerning age distinction, most probably done on the ground of simplistic size criteria of skeletal remains. We should keep in mind that if the term "infant" is fairly clear, more problematic is talking about "children". The beginning of childhood does not need explaining but its end is dependent on cultural phenomena. That is why we can only tentatively accept the number of 51 as burials belonging to small children. Even in such a case, Wainwright's assessment of infant mortality rate was surprisingly low. It has been estimated (Stevenson 2006: 14) that the typical childhood mortality rate was ca. 50%, that is much higher than 20.5% of burials from Gerzeh. Children were interred in pottery jars, in most cases devoid of offerings. There are, however, exceptions from the rule as grave no. 70 comprised a tiny child buried in a large pit furnished with 11 pottery jars, one stone vessel

and a shell pendant. To explain the differences and the significantly low number of child graves, a selective burial practice is proposed (Stevenson 2006: 15).

Adults were buried in the contracted mostly left-sided position, the head turned northwards (of course, numerous exceptions were present) while for children the preferable position was also the left-sided one, however their heads were pointing south and north with almost the same frequency. A practice which was quite common was wrapping bodies in reed mats or eventually in cloths, no leather in this function was recorded. Wood was rarely preserved, in majority as a single stick placed along walls of a grave pit or beneath the deceased.

Among objects registered in graves of Gerzeh were: pottery vessels; stone vessels made of colour limestone, granite and basalt, porphyry, brown alabaster/travertine and dark serpentine; model vessels made of stone and pottery; beads and pendants from necklaces made of iron (probably of meteoric origin), gold, carnelian, agate, chalcedony, sard, steatite, calcite, limestone, lapis lazuli, turquoise and onyx; zoomorphic, shield-shaped and round cosmetic palettes sometimes decorated as it was with the so-called "Hathor-palette" (see Stevenson 2006: 41-42); very few flint knives also ripple-flaked and a single fish-tail; ivory spoons and pins; a pottery cow horn model, stone balls (so-called "marbles", which may possibly be tokens) of granite and limestone; a copper bowl and finally a pottery rattle. Green ore malachite probably used as green dye was also quite popular in the Gerzeh graves, other colours obtained thanks to galena and kohl were registered in a part of richer burials, therefore it seems possible they might have been regarded as having underlined some specific status. The richest grave (no. 67) in the cemetery belonged to a young individual who was equipped with unique iron beads, the only registered pieces of weapon (a pear-shaped mace head of limestone and a copper harpoon), one cosmetic palette of greywacke and the only ivory vessel known from the site (Petrie et al. 1912: 5).

281 graves from the site comprise material wide enough to preserve some ritual activity remains. The most imagination firing are those examples associated with body mutilation practices (Stevenson 2006: 58-63). In the above-mentioned grave no. 67, the deceased's head had been parted from the rest of the body and left on its base, while quite an impressive necklace with golden beads was found still on the neck. Grave no. 251 belonged to an adult devoid of the head and offerings. The owner of grave no. 260 had been buried on the back, but the head was lying face down to the ground. In graves nos 123, 137, 138, 142, 187 and 284 absence or rearrangement of some body parts as feet, hands or pelvis was noted. Finally, in grave no. 206 adult bones had been piled in the centre of the pit. The first three examples are most likely to be interpreted as some ritual body mutilation practices and comparable finds from Hierakonpolis HK43 and Adaïma confirm that such obscure customs had been in use. The latter example can be easily explained as a

secondary burial, the remaining ones may be incomplete well due to post-depositional intrusions.

A somehow reverse phenomenon, but still related to unexplained practices of body treatment, are graves where only fragments of skeletons (according to Wainwright's disputable identification) were registered. These are the cases of graves nos 40, 61, 71, 95 and 281. There, pieces of skulls and phalanges were discovered in pots that had been meant as funerary goods of the main grave occupant (Stevenson 2006: 23). In the context, a unique structure, labeled as grave no. 108 (Petrie et al. 1912: 8), is also worth mentioning. There, the only discovered human bones were a few phalanges, while the whole pit was full of ashes and charcoal. The structure could have possibly played the function of a hearth related to burial custom rituals, which are presently undefined and obscure, however, since we have no more data, the actual function and significance of the structure remain unknown.

Ritual related activity may also be reflected by observations made in graves nos 11 and 263. In the former, some linen had been wrapped around bones of a young individual, while in the latter an adult body was found with thick pads of fabric that covered his/her hands and pelvis. These two examples are sometimes quoted as the beginnings of mummification (Stevenson 2006: 19), tentatively comparable with discoveries made at Hierakonpolis (Jones 2002).

Thus, Gerzeh appears to be a site composed of structurally simple graves but, what is interesting, rather wealthily equipped with a relatively wide range of functional objects, including those of personal use, frequently made of precious materials.

## THE NAQADA CULTURE ENTERS THE NILE DELTA

In the period of NIIC the Delta cultural picture was no longer as homogenous as before. Apart from settlement remains of the mature Lower Egyptian culture, in the archaeological material registered in the area appeared the first Naqadan elements. However, the problem of the developed Naqada culture arrival in the Delta and the process of the local unit supplanting or evolving into another cultural quality, is still far from being explained. The cultural situation in the Late Predynastic period is difficult to be properly assessed, because in the Delta only three cemeteries were precisely dated: Kafr Hassan Dawood (Tassie, van Wetering 2003: 502; Tucker 2003: 532), Minshat Abu Omar I (Kroeper, Wildung 1985; 1994; 2000) and Kom el-Khilgan 2 (Midant-Reynes et al. 2003; 2004; Buchez, Midant-Reynes 2011) – two of them being clearly connected with the Lower Egyptian culture (see above). Besides them, a group of partially published sites was registered, some of which were also imprecisely dated – in the Delta: Minshat Ezzat (el-Baghdadi 1999; 2003), el-Huseiniya (Krzyżaniak 1989: 271; Mostafa 1988a; 1988b) and Beni Amir (el-Hagg Ragab 1992; el-

Moneim 1996); others merely general – located in the Delta Khelwet Abu Musallem (Leclant 1973a: 396), as well as outside the Delta: et-Tibbin (Leclant 1973b: 404), Gurob (Loat 1905: 2; Brunton, Engelbach 1927) and el-Bashkatib near Lahun (Petrie et al. 1923: 21-22); or even unreliable as Gezira Sangaha and Tell el-Ginn (Krzyżaniak 1989: 271). In addition, the material collected at the sites is mostly uncharacteristic – simple pit burials in a contracted side position, with bodies sometimes wrapped in leather and devoid of offerings – that is why it could probably date to some earlier periods. Nevertheless, the sites' presence itself proves that the new culture was already settled in the territory, however, it does not provide information about its relation to the previously popular local cultural unit.

In the situation the only cemetery site useful for further analyses of the quoted issue remains Kafr Hassan Dawood, where the deceased were buried in simple oval and small pits dug in a sandy ground. The average grave dimensions were: 1-1.5 x 0.8m. The grave walls were only rarely plastered with mud. The fact that all these graves were simple in their form and infants were continuously interred in pots without offerings or any differentiation do not point to a complicated social structure of the community.

Burials of Naqadan tradition in the Delta related to the early period (that is NIID2) were definitely simple and not very interestingly furnished. The offerings repertoire was rather limited and a set of typical grave goods was composed of a single pottery vessel and, much less frequently, of some other categories of items like cosmetic objects (among them simple stone palettes), personal ornaments or bone spoons.

No clearly preferable, commonly followed body orientation was noted: in Kafr Hassan Dawood it was the contracted left side position with heads southwards. As far as it can be said on the basis of very fragmentary publications, the same concerns Minshat Ezzat, while in Beni Amir heads were turned northwards. It is possible that the upset of the rules imported from the south illustrates the accommodation process of the incoming people to new conditions, however, it should be remembered that this is hardly sufficient material for such a discussion. There is also another subject to raise, which is the surprising simplicity of burials and offerings in comparison to the South. Of course, it can be explained by the scarcity of accessible data but it is also possible that the early Naqadan settlers, who certainly were not conquerors, did not represent the elites of their culture and at the time were not wealthy or influential but rather immigrants in unfavourable position, thus, simple burials were the most suitable solution.

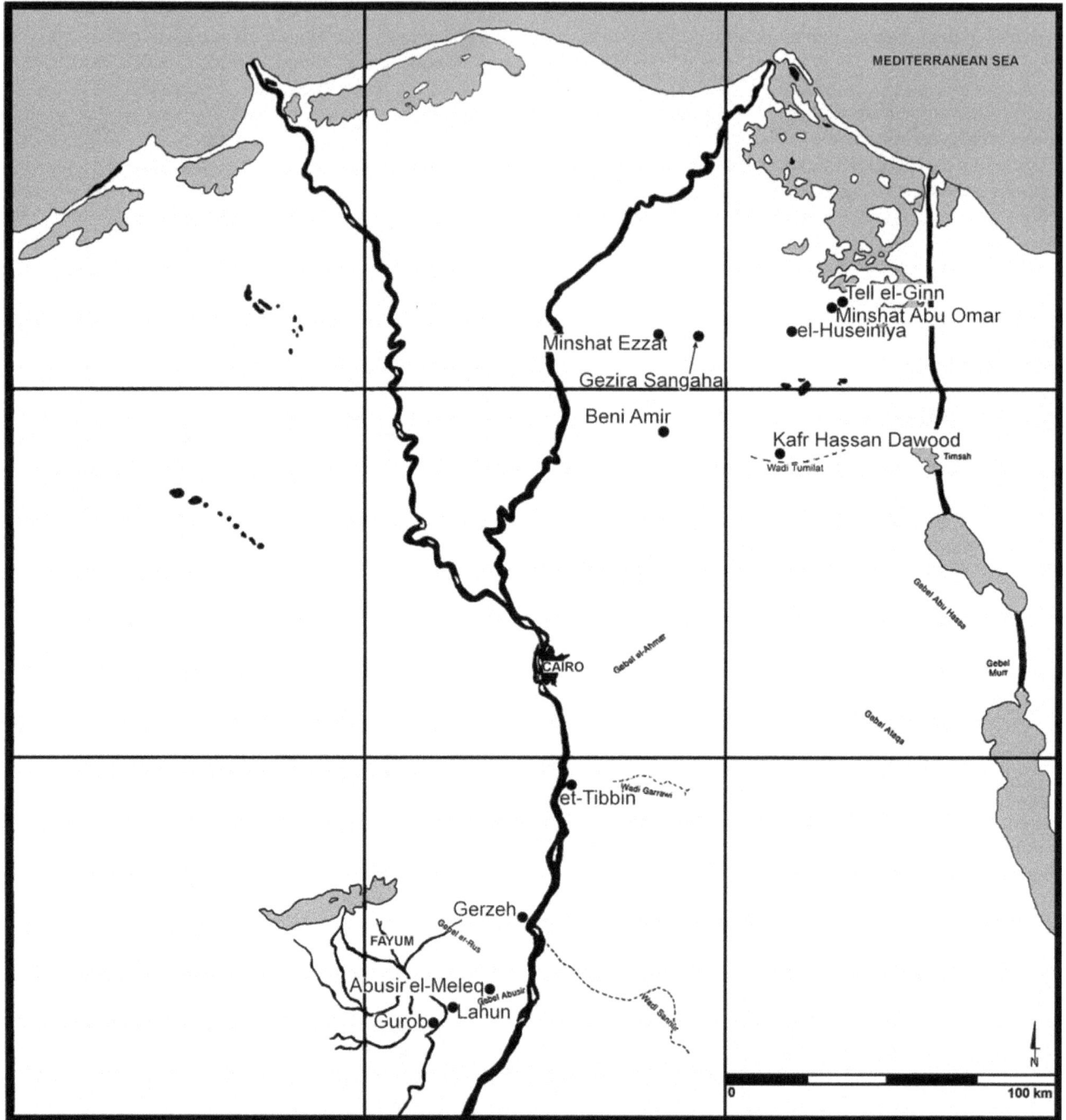

*Map no. 3. Burial related sites used in the period of the Lower Egyptian-Naqadan transition (NIID2)*

## THE ISSUE OF ABUSIR EL-MELEQ

In the period when the presence of the first Naqadan settlers was gradually becoming a normal element of the Delta cultural picture, that is NIID2, ca. 300km south, in the Fayum oasis area a cemetery in Abusir el-Meleq (Möller 1926; Scharff 1926) was founded. Except for Gerzeh (at the end of its occupation), small Gurob and a single, uncharacteristic and very widely dated burial from el-Bashkatib near Lahun (Petrie et al. 1923: 24), no other traces of burial practices were registered in the region. It is surprising that the burial customs from Abusir el-Meleq seem very homogenous. The total number of burials registered at the site reached at least 850, which forms quite reliable material for statistical analyses.

With only a few exceptions a consequent preference towards the contracted left-sided position (99%) with heads turned southwards (98.75%) and facing west (98.45%) was observed. The majority of identified bones belonged to infants and small children (40%), and the remaining 35% and 16% were males and females, respectively (Castillos 1982a: 155). Pottery coffins were found in four graves, three of which contained child burials. In addition, only a single wooden coffin was registered at the site (Seeher 1999: 92). Graves were simple pit burials, oval or round in their shape, sometimes partially or thoroughly plastered with mud; however, the more structurally sophisticated type of rectangular pits lined with mud brick predominated. Few

32

graves of the latter construction type were divided into two chambers – an actual burial one and the other of storage function (Scharff 1926: 108-165). The average depth of burials in Abusir el-Meleq was 0.8-1.2m and total dimensions of majority of them were 0.7-2.26m of length and 0.45-1.3m of width. The largest structures were 3.19m long and 1.7m wide. Remains of wood and mats were interpreted as internal wall lining and ceiling constructions. 15 graves clustered in the northern part of the site comprised a sort of mud brier where the dead with grave goods had been placed.

As far as it can be estimated in the situation when numerous burials were robbed in the antiquity, jars representing the wavy-handled type usually stood near the deceased heads while large storage vessels near the feet. Animal bones registered within graves were interpreted as food offerings. The most precious objects were usually found close to the deceased hands or over the body. Vessels and large flint knives were often broken before they were interred.

Grave goods were diversified and composed mainly of pottery and stone vessels. The remaining articles were: miniature vessels of ivory, shell, horn, faïence and copper; personal adornments, such as beads, pins, bracelets (one with relief decoration representing a serpent, others with crocodiles) and cosmetic objects like spoons, sticks, combs – frequently made of bone and decorated. Also the majority of cosmetic palettes were decorated examples. Among other objects copper tools, six pear-shaped mace heads and animal figurines should be mentioned. Grave no. 1035 revealed a cylindrical seal made of ivory and decorated with three rows of animals (Scharff 1926: 65-70; Seeher 1999: 92-93).

In general, the cemetery in Abusir el-Meleq is wealthier than the ones already mentioned, however, it should not be disregarded that the site was also a bit younger and the more affluent furnishing practice might result from the difference in dating and reflect the general development direction of burial customs registered in the Delta.

As the archaeological material suggests, the considerably far distance of Abusir el-Meleq from the Delta did not have any influence on the differences that arose between these two regions. And thus, a conclusion can be drawn that the cultural picture registered in the eastern Delta was not of local character and should be regarded as the actual view of the general situation of the period. The Abusir el-Meleq publication proposes that people buried in the cemetery represented two different types which should belong to more robust descendants of the local Lower Egyptian cultural unit and Naqadan newcomers. At present, the problem is that the anthropological examination was done at the beginning of the 20th century and therefore, the data is not fully reliable, now, on the other hand there is not enough comparative material for such a study. From the physical anthropological point of view the question remains unsolved, however, if the two distinct groups of people really existed it would perfectly suit the theory about mutual merging of the outgoing

Lower Egyptian culture and the north expanding Naqadan formation.

Interesting conclusions come to mind when the distribution pattern of sites with any registered burial remains in Northern Egypt and of the NIID2 period, is under examination (Map no. 3). A clear concentration of sites in the eastern Delta may be observed, as well as popularity of the Fayum oasis region and surprising – in comparison to the previous period – lack of activity remains in the present Cairo area. It is possible that the situation reflects the actual state of research and intense interest attested within the latest twenty-year period by the eastern Delta. It is also possible that the observed concentration of sites in the region and time corresponds to intentional activity related to e.g. the control of Palestinian trade routes which were used by the Lower Egyptian people (see Mączyńska 2004). The questions will only be answered when more data is accessible for future analyses.

### 3.4. NORTHERN EGYPT AT THE END OF THE PREDYNASTIC PERIOD

17 cemetery sites from the Northern Egypt area are dated to the end of the predynastic period (Map no. 4). There are among them sites which were in use in the previous period, for example: Kom el-Khilgan 3, Kafr Hassan Dawood, flourishing Abusir el-Meleq, clearly diverging Minshat Abu Omar III and Gurob, where the use of four early sites (the oldest of them was abandoned by the end of NIIIA1 and the remaining cemeteries O, C and C2 were founded in NIIIA2) coincides in period NIIIA. In the same period also other cemeteries were established (large sites of different features than before) in Abusir North (Radwan 1991;1995; 2000; 2003), Tarkhan (Petrie et al. 1913; Petrie 1914; Castillos 1982; Seidlmayer 1988; Ellis 1992; 1996; Wilkinson 1996) and Helwan (Saad 1942; 1943; 1947a; 1947b; 1951; 1965; Köhler 1998; 2000; 2000-2001; 2001; 2003; 2004a; 2004b; 2006; 2007; 2008). There, burials with distinctive features were registered, that is highly structurally complicated and wealthily equipped, interpreted as belonging to the emerging elites. Apart from the above mentioned sites, there are also some less precisely dated ones, whose use is estimated around NIIIA, too. This group includes: Beni Amir (el-Moneim 1996a; el-Hagg Ragab 1992), el-Huseiniya (Mostafa 1988a; 1988b; Krzyżaniak 1989: 271) and Minshat Ezzat (el-Baghdadi 1999; 2003), which surely existed in the period in question, but possibly also earlier; sites that offer little characteristic material, like: Khelwet Abu Musallem (Leclant 1973a: 396), et-Tibbin (Leclant 1973b: 404), probably founded around the time Tell el-Daba'a el-Qanan (el-Baghdadi 2005 – unfortunately, of an imprecise date, too) or questionable Gezira Sangaha and Tell el-Ginn. The whole accounts for definitely richer analysis material than that known from NIID2. There is also a clear increase in diversity and the abandonment of previously popular practices when the Lower Egyptian culture was at the forefront. On the one

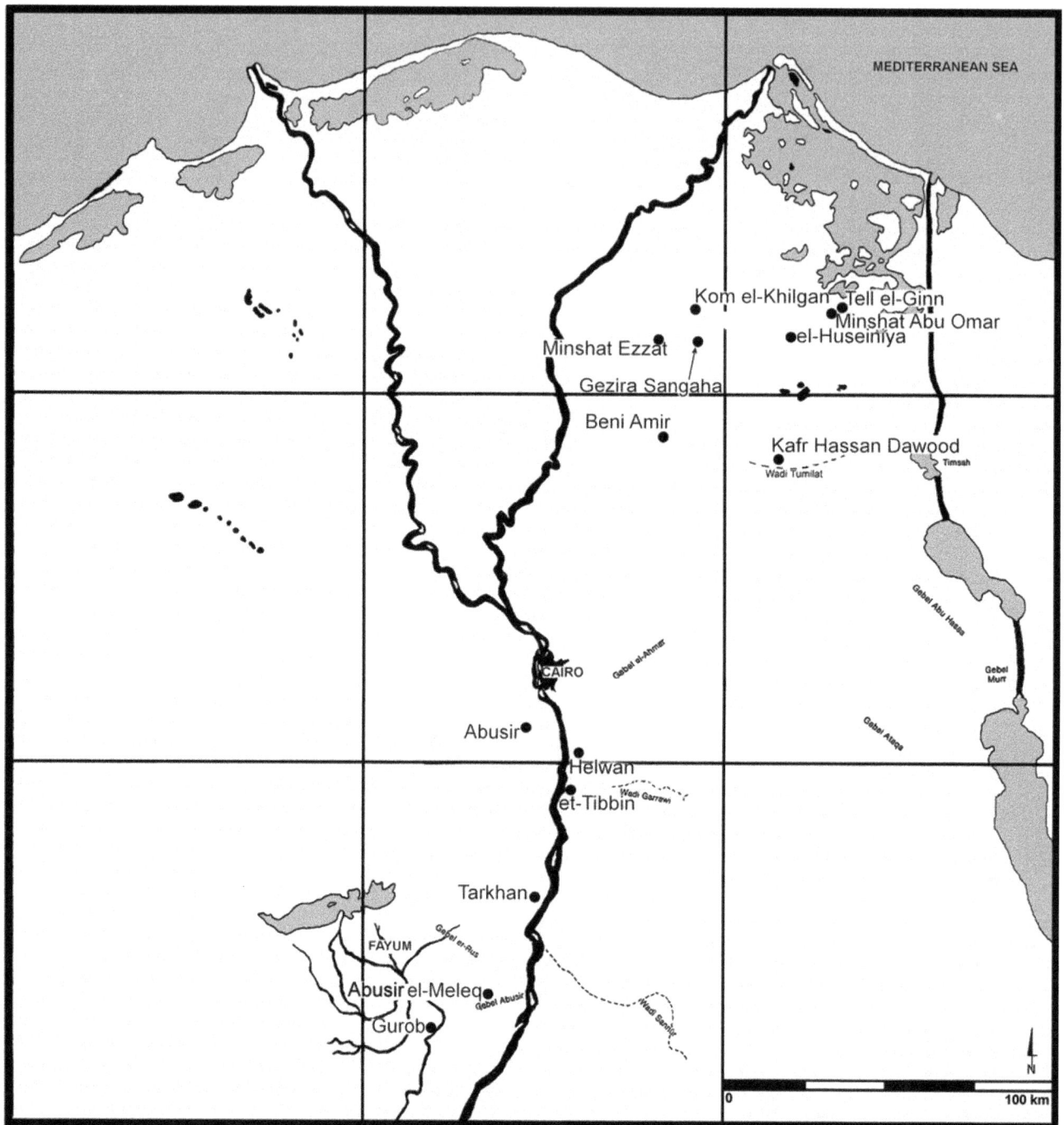

*Map no. 4. Cemeteries dated to NIIIA*

hand, we deal with continuation and development of the leading sites from the preceding period (situated in the Delta in particular) and, on the other hand, high intensification of activity near the Delta base in the present Cairo area is observed. It was there that cemeteries like Abusir and Helwan emerged, which deserve special attention as they forecast the Early Dynastic period.

In the case of the actual Delta the leading sites are Minshat Abu Omar III, Kafr Hassan Dawood and Kom el-Khilgan 3, and after them those less precisely dated ones: Beni Amir, el-Huseiniya, Minshat Ezzat and Tell el-Daba'a el-Qanan that play a supplementary role being only a background illustration for the information

provided by the former. The most significant change in the material is greater consistency in following burial custom rules. And thus, the deceased were interred in the contracted position mainly on their left side, the head turned northwards, with eventual slight declination eastwards. Still, simple pit burials known from the previous period predominated, but more and more popular became also those additionally plastered with mud (like in Kafr Hassan Dawood or Kom el-Khilgan) or lined with mud bricks ones (a case rather typical for Minshat Abu Omar). The most popular grave shape was still oval and oblong with rounded edges – the ones plastered with mud – although rectangular pit graves lined with mud bricks (especially Minshat Abu Omar), which were just being introduced, were growing in popularity. It is worth stressing that the appearance of rectangular grave shape coincides with the introduction of coffins made of mats, wood or mud. Graves of these types were often additionally inlayed and covered with mats. What is interesting, structures of mud brick were in general better equipped. An exception to the rule is the case of Kafr Hassan Dawood where even wealthy burials inevitably kept a structurally simple form.

The issues of offerings variety noted in graves of the period as well as the increasing structural complexity indicate that the society itself was also more and more stratified. A good example is formed by Minshat Abu Omar III, where in comparison to the preceding phases a far more significant number of graves furnished in over 10 objects is observed. Simultaneously, grave goods comprised a vaster repertoire of luxurious objects and therefore – against the epoch background – such offering sets were treated as rich. Also the increasing quantity of valuable items in terms of the material and precision with which they were made together with growing average grave dimensions lead to the conclusion that the Delta was just entering its prosperity epoch, which began at the turn of the Pre- and Protodynastic periods.

Outside the Delta, however, Gurob and flourishing Abusir el-Meleq set good examples of the older tradition continuation on these sites next to newly founded cemeteries, in the present Cairo area in particular (Helwan, Abusir North and a little more distant Tarkhan). The sites were relatively large and reflected a growing diversity of the society within that time as they also comprised burials of wealthier classes. The situation was noted in Tarkhan phase 1, that is from the very beginning of the site history when a separated "hill" cemetery was established, which obviously had been meant for the elites. It is also accepted that Helwan and Abusir North in NIIIA were already entering the era of their magnificence. The majority of graves that were registered there were pit burials, rather small, roughly rectangular and sometimes lined with mud bricks. In the light of this kind of archaeological data, it is acknowledged that the elites arrived there in a later period.

In the cemeteries, the deceased were buried in the contracted left-sided position, the head southwards on a daily basis. The exception was Gurob, where in contrast to the previous period, the preferable dead orientation changed in favour of the northern direction. However, on all these cemeteries the striking feature is deep similarity of traditions – the same known also from the Delta structural models (simple oval pits sometimes plastered with mud or rectangular pits lined with mud bricks), mats which inlayed grave bottoms and covered the whole burials, more and more popular coffins made of various and above mentioned materials, as well as a vast repertoire of grave goods of types known also from the Delta – together with the wide range of luxurious articles – although more frequently represented. In this context, graves from Tarkhan, where bodies had been placed on a sort of mud bed or brier – against the background of remaining discoveries connected with the period – may

be recognized as a local variant, which would find its continuation in the following epoch.

Despite a different attitude toward a few issues of the burial customs in general, that is opposite bodies' orientation and fewer objects accompanying the deceased, in the whole area in question of the NIIIA period, a gradual but consistent standardization of rules may be observed. It is exemplified by the spreading popularity of mud bricks in building material function, by the simultaneously introduced burials in coffins, mainly in rectangular shape, but also in oval as is the case in Karf Hassan Dawood (Tucker 2003: 532). Especially bricks, the new – roughly cuboid – building material could have played a significant role in popularization of the rectangular grave shape, which in the earlier period had been less common. Also, the general rules concerning grave goods stabilized and according to them, only few burials were left unfurnished. Unfortunately, it is impossible to express binding opinions since burials were frequently plundered shortly after funerals. However, it may be easily assumed that the increasing pillaging practices in a way reflect the typically growing number of offerings. Robbers deprived us of the possibility to assess properly the rules of assembling offering sets. In their search for valuable articles, they often looted whole burials and therefore our knowledge of the organization of internal grave space is limited. Nevertheless, the quite impressive number of graves that escaped robbery allows the assessment of the set of grave goods typical for the period.

The most abundant group of objects represented in graves are pottery vessels in a vast repertoire of types, as well as numerous categories of items interpreted as luxurious: imported, stone and sporadically copper vessels; stone, bone and copper tools; palettes and other cosmetic objects; numerous items of bone; beads of various materials and personal adornments like pendants and bracelets. It seems significant that regardless of some mere local differences in the burial customs, an offering set was invariably composed of objects from the above mentioned categories and in very similar types. At the same time a general tendency toward wealthier grave equipment in cemeteries located outside the Delta was noted. This vague inclination also reflects the presence of so-called elite burials, that is graves with plenty of objects (usually over 10 items of various categories of goods), which included luxurious articles of great value. The phenomenon of rich burials is known in the Delta in cemeteries of Minshat Abu Omar and Kafr Hassan Dawood, nevertheless, graves of this kind are rarely represented and describing them as belonging to the elite members seems to be an exaggeration. The case looks differently on the younger site of Tarkhan, located farther south, where the ratio of rich burials to those commonly furnished is more balanced. Moreover, rich graves were from the very beginning situated in smaller and separated "hill" cemeteries. The juxtaposition of the facts leads to the conclusion that in the southern area we deal with flourishing and well established tradition, while in the

Delta in the period of NIIIA we observe the process of establishing new customs that just drove local practices out.

## 3.5. TOWARDS THE UNITED KINGDOM – DYNASTIES 0 AND 1

### NORTHERN EGYPT IN THE TIMES OF DYNASTY 0

The first observation that comes to mind when comparing sites distribution in Northern Egypt by the end of the Predynastic period and on the threshold of the Early Dynastic one (Map no. 4) is the obvious intensification of activity expressed by a higher number of burial related sites from 17 in the NIIIA period to 24 during Dynasty 0. The second observation is the shift in increasing settlement interest to the northern part of the Nile Valley apart from the eastern Delta, which still remained popular. On the one hand, the higher site density in previously occupied regions is observed, while on the other hand, the regions themselves were constantly growing. In general, however, a short glimpse on the sites map only confirms the statement that during the Dynasty 0 time we deal with continuation of the development trend started in the NIIIA period.

The beginning of NIIIB coincides with the moment when the previously flourishing cemetery in Abusir el-Meleq (Scharff 1926) was abandoned. A few other sites had their direct continuation without any changes visible in the material. These were: Gurob, Kom el-Khilgan 3, Kafr Hassan Dawood, Tarkhan phase 1, Minshat Abu Omar III and Minshat Ezzat, where conditions stabilized in the NIIIA period and were being continued during Dynasty 0 as well. Cemeteries in el-Huseiniya and Beni Amir are of little precise date, therefore they do not provide significant information, except for the fact that material collected there perfectly fits the picture known from other Delta sites of the period. As for the cemeteries in Abusir North and Helwan, they were still awaiting their full significance, only beginning their long history. At the same time, the case of Tell el-Daba'a el-Qanan (el-Baghdadi 2005) seems to be really interesting. The cemetery there dated to the NIIIA period was abandoned to be reoccupied in the Early Dynastic age within the same archaeological site but, unfortunately, the exact moment of the reoccupation is impossible to establish.

Among sites that came out on the map for the first time especially a few should be mentioned. These are the precisely dated ones: Turah phase 1 (Junker 1912; Castillos 1982b; Wilkinson 1996), Abu Roash 300 (Klasens 1958a – the first from a long sequence of cemeteries founded in the site) and Tell el-Farkha (Dębowska-Ludwin 2009; 2011b; 2012). The sites of Tell el-Iswid (van den Brink 1989; Midant-Reynes, Denoix 2011), Tell el-Murra (Jucha 2012; Kazimierczak 2012; Kozłowska 2012), Tell es-Samara (Leclant, Minault-Gout 2001: 366; el-Baghdadi 2005) and Tell Basta (el-Sawi 1979) are also interesting, although incompletely published. Nevertheless, almost all of them were founded in the second half of Dynasty 0. The remaining sites are single burials of an imprecise date, like Merimde (Eiwanger 1979: 28) and Dimeh (Caton-Thompson, Gardiner 1934: 86), or of medium graves' number, like el-Qatta (Leclant 1950: 494; 1952: 247; 1954: 74), but of similarly imprecise chronology, as well as those only generally dated to Dynasty 0. The latter are rather small cemeteries, which probably belonged to a single family and were seriously plundered, like in Kafr Ghattati (Engles 1990). The burial ground in Tell el-Ginn, although mentioned in the subject literature, should rather be recognized as unconfirmed (Bietak 1975: 99, footnote 364a).

On the continuously occupied sites, except for a few cases, no visibly recognizable changes in burial customs were registered. However, the newly founded sites – or at least those with precise dates – appeared not earlier than the second part of Dynasty 0. The only exception to the rule is Tell el-Farkha where sepulchral activity is dated earlier than the second half of Dynasty 0 but still within the period of NIIIB. Quite numerous sites with imprecise dates generally described as "Early Dynastic" do not provide crucial data comprising only the epoch's background. The comparison of published data collected at cemetery sites from Northern Egypt and used in the Dynasty 0 times definitively points to the standardization of burial custom rules, which were practiced in the period in the whole area of interest. Also the main differences between the Nile Delta and the northern Nile Valley were little by little being blurred and particular divergences should be rather explained as local variants of specific sites (e.g. the lack of mud bricks typical for Kafr Hassan Dawood).

Generalizing, the deceased were buried in the contracted position on their side. In the period in question the left side prevailed, as well as body orientation to the north or north-east, although there are cemeteries where the southern direction was more popular (Tarkhan), and the other were also registered. The deceased were put on mats that inlayed the inner part of graves and often covered the whole burial together with a complete set of offerings (a good example is set by Tell el-Farkha where straw mats of this kind are frequently preserved as white fibres that still keep the weave arrangement of the original object – Fig. 6). Quite widespread became also coffins, mostly in rectangular shape, though, from Kafr Hassan Dawood are known some oval objects fitting the typical oval shape of graves at the site. The coffins were made of mud, badly fired pottery, wood and plaiting, and sometimes they were closed by covers of the same material (Turah, Kafr Hassan Dawood). They were deposited in burial chambers or directly in pits dug in the ground (Turah, el-Qatta, Kom el-Khilgan). The majority of burials was oriented along the north-south axis with possible small declinations regardless of the deceased head was turned to the north or south.

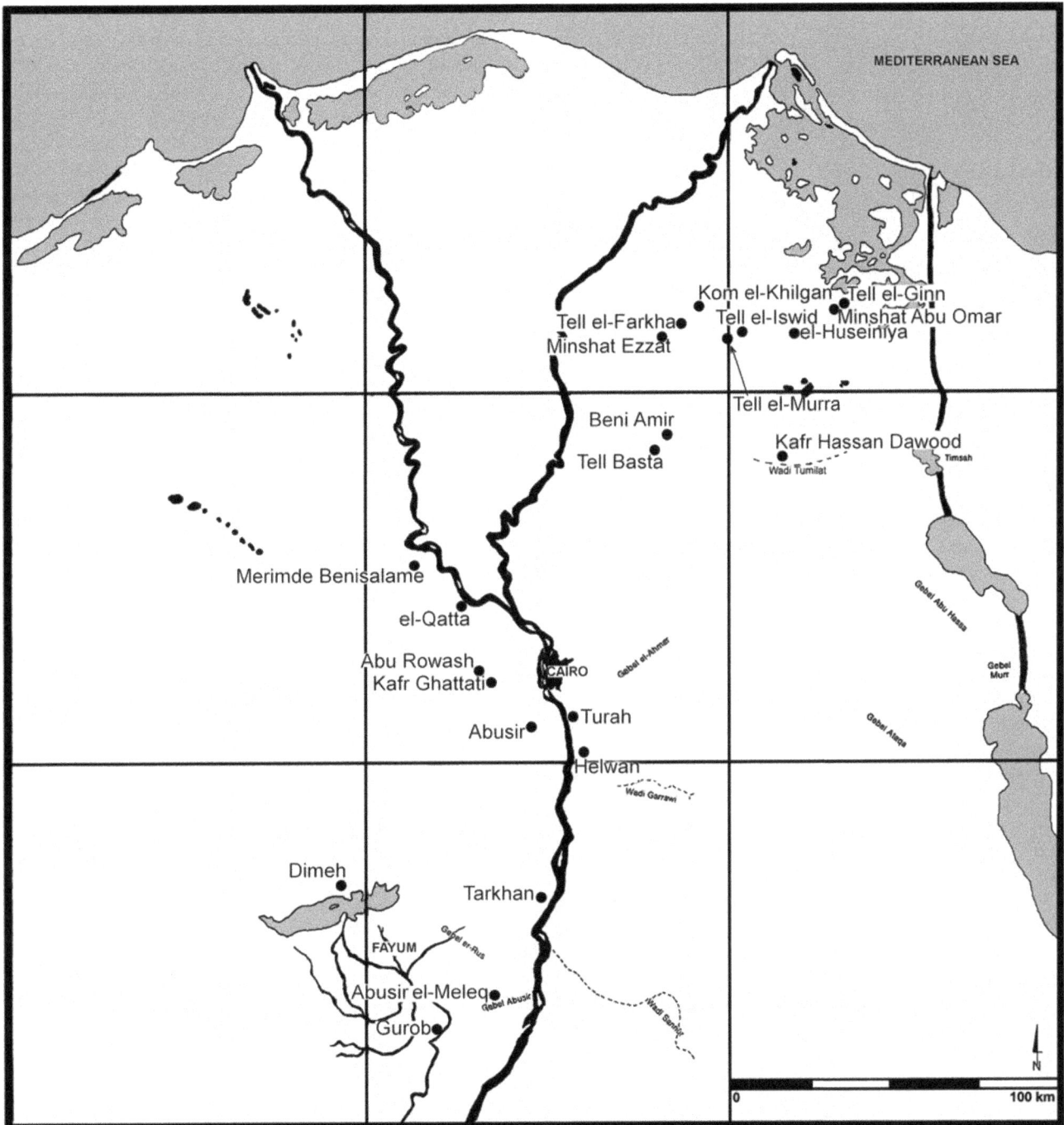

*Map no. 5. Cemetery sites dated to Dynasty 0*

Like in previous periods, the structurally simplest pit burials were still popular. Usually they were shallow and oval in shape (Kom el-Khilgan, Kafr Hassan Dawood, Tarkhan, Turah) but also nearly round or rectangular (Turah, Tarkhan, Abu Roash 300, el-Huseiniya, probably Tell Basta). With only few exceptions, like grave no. 1008 in Karf Hassan Dawood (Hassan 2000: 39), this burial category remained unfurnished, which in combination with little constructional effort allow to draw the conclusion that this type of burials was characteristic for people of lower material and/or social status. This opinion may also be supported by the fact that graves of the type were usually discovered next to other and more advanced structures like rectangular and oblong pit graves lined with a single row of mud bricks that are characteristic of the period in question and the later ones. The graves were most probably the next development stage of a burial form where a previously simple grave pit was first reinforced by mud paste applied on its inner walls or by wood (the latter in particular seems to be a solution soon given up and occasionally practiced since the material availability was always limited unlike the omnipresent Nile mud). The following stage was probably partial and, finally, thorough wall lining with sun-dried mud bricks of a standardized shape and size. A regular burial chamber that had been created by brick walls was roofed with mats (like e.g. in Tell el-Farkha), sometimes with wood or in single cases (Abu Roash 300) with stone slabs (Klasens 1958a: 34).

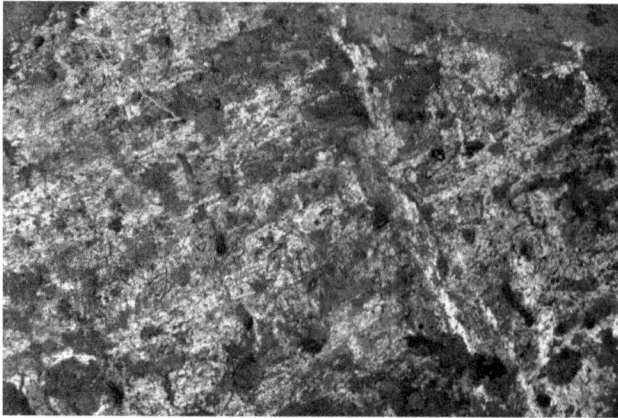

*Fig. 6. Mineralised remains of a mat that covered a burial*

The majority of pit graves lined with mud bricks was single-chambered. Their dimensions fluctuate between ca. 1m-2.5m of length and 0.8-1.5m of width. It was presumably thanks to the constantly growing number of offerings that the inner space in larger graves (ca. 5m long and 2m wide) was more and more often divided into the actual burial chamber, where the deceased together with the smallest and most precious objects of his/her equipment were placed, and side chambers. The latter were of storage function, usually tightly packed with pottery.

At least a few types of division into smaller chambers were registered:
- In the first of them, while the general north-south orientation was applied, a single storage chamber was placed at one of the shorter pit sides, at the north or south.
- There are also examples where additional chambers were placed on both shorter sides of a grave pit or with two little ones at one shorter side, moreover, the external edges of the chambers sometimes consisted of rough and unlined pit's walls.
- Also four-chamber-structures are known, they had a single burial chamber, two little side chambers at one shorter grave side and the third one bigger and adjacent to the smaller rooms.
- In isolated cases (e.g. in Abu Roash 300) five-chamber-tombs were attested – a burial chamber and two storage rooms at both shorter structure sides.

It seems, however, that the more and more complicated inner grave layout progressed in time and structures with larger number of chambers are those solutions that emerged a bit later, possibly even during Dynasty 1. Unfortunately, particular graves and cemeteries are far too imprecisely dated to decide the case. A slightly different answer to the question how the growing offerings amount should be arranged into a grave was found in Abu Roash 300. There, a unique category of burials was registered – pit graves with side chamber placed in front of the deceased face in the eastern grave part.

Differentiated publication state of particular sites means that naming the actual number of burials dated to the period of Dynasty 0 is impossible. However, in a very cautious way, the number may be assessed at around 2 104. In such a quantity numerous unconventional structural solutions are also present. One of these cases is grave no. 8 from Tell el-Farkha (Dębowska-Ludwin 2009: 462). It was a relatively uncomplicated construction that combined advantages of oval simple pit burials and those lined with mud bricks. In this case bricks were paving the whole bottom of an almost round pit (1.3m in diameter), where a tightly contracted body with no offerings was interred (Fig. 7). Another atypical structure that is worth a mention here is grave no. 137 from Tell Basta (el-Sawi 1979: 63) dated to the turn of Dynasties 0 and 1. It was elongated, built of mud bricks and oriented along the north-south axis. Its substructure comprised a vertical shaft ended with entrances to two burial chambers (!), each of them measuring 1.9 x 1.9 x 2m.

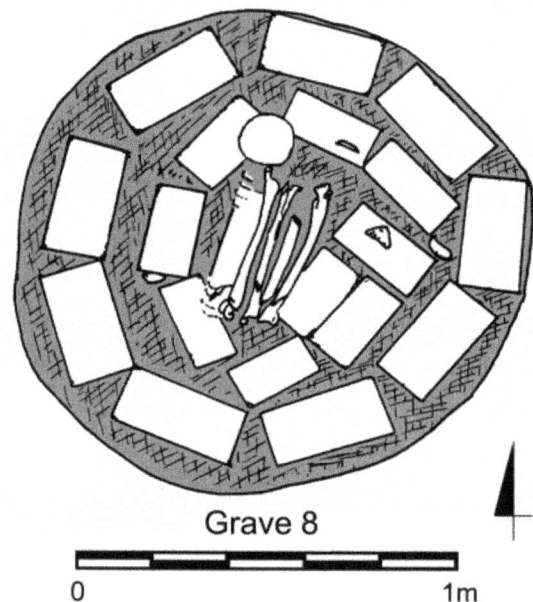

Grave 8

0                                                        1m

*Fig. 7. Example of an atypical oval grave structure – grave no. 8 from Tell el-Farkha*

Nevertheless, the most interesting structure among those atypical and dated to the period in question is a monumental construction found at the Eastern Kom at Tell el-Farkha (Fig. 8). The only appropriate interpretation of its purpose seems to be a burial related structure. There are numerous factors that point to this assumption. The most significant is its surprising – for the period – size (ca. 16 x 18m) and architectural solutions applied as massive brick walls surpassing 2m of their maximum thickness, four large exterior chambers and the main one with a deep shaft, the whole surrounded by thick walls composed of two and three adjacent walls. Fieldworks around the impressive construction have not been completed yet, however, it seems the eastern façade of the building forms also the oldest example of so-called niche decoration with additional white plaster (Fig. 9).

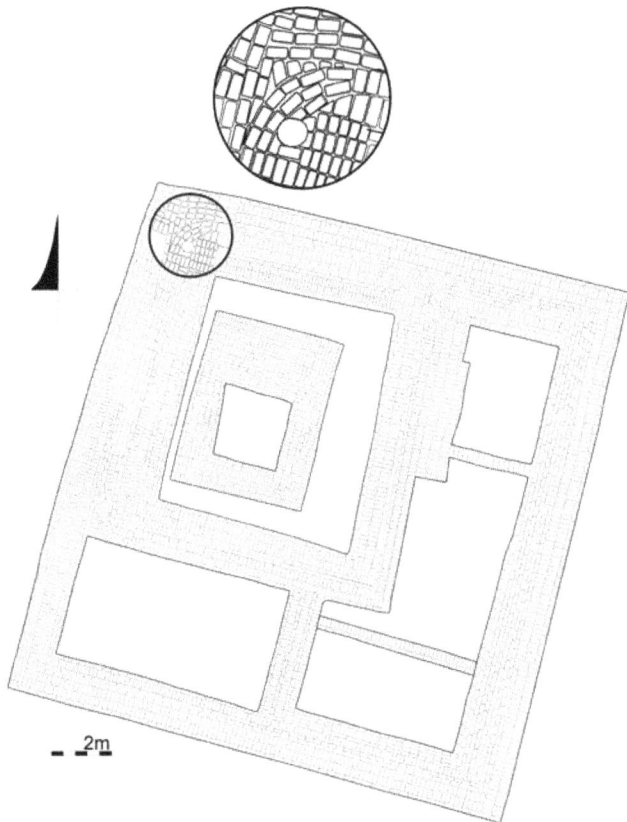

*Fig. 8. General layout of the great mastaba at Tell el-Farkha (niche decoration of the eastern façade remains unmarked due to preliminary state of fieldworks in the area)*

No entrances or communication openings of any kind were registered, although the structure was splendidly preserved to the impressive height of over 2m. The side chambers were compactly filled with brick rubble and, except for it, were devoid of any other movables in burial offerings function. At the bottom of the shaft, which was also secured with rubble, nothing but few little pottery vessels were discovered, which were badly eroded by groundwater. Since not even a skeleton was found, the actual function of the impressive structure remains uncertain. However, it is highly possible that remains of the structure's owner simply did not survive in the strongly adverse soil conditions and because of high and fluctuating groundwater level. Also symbolic character of the construction may be considered as a cenotaph kind. Independent of all those questions and propositions, the presence of such a complicated structure alone, interpreted as of burial importance, should be taken as a proof of social stratification actually existing at that time, as well as a signal of the beginning of burial monumentalism. And after all, the most intriguing issue is the surprisingly early date of the structure connected with the very beginning of the age in question, that is the turn of the NIIIA2 and NIIIB1 periods. The early date means that we deal here with the oldest structure of this type in Northern Egypt (Ciałowicz 2008a: 505–510).

Another interesting question concerns the way burials were marked on a cemetery surface. The most inconvenient case is – at present – the fact that Early Dynastic sites lie in layers deep beneath later strata or as they were resting in a site's surface layers they are severely damaged now. In these conditions it is difficult to state what the original surface of many Early Dynastic cemeteries was. Data concerning preserved remains of grave marking are, regrettably, not numerous. And so in Kafr Hassan Dawood in many cases mounds built on the cemetery surface of mud, sand and gravel were registered over some burials (Tucker 2003: 532). In Tarkhan (Petrie 1914: 2) little mounds of sand covered with natural gypsum were similarly attested, where they covered only smaller graves. In Tell el-Iswid South and Tell el-Farkha numerous burials were secured with a mud brick cover. In the former site the cover was described as a three-layer-mantle of irregularly thrown mud bricks (van den Brink 1989: 64-65), while in the latter the covers had regular rectangular shape and were built over burial chambers (Fig. 10). They were constructed over the top of a mound of earth that a burial chamber was filled with and so bricks were consequently laid over to create a regular shape, probably flat in its upper part. If the subterranean part had been a rather small pit lined with only a single row of bricks the superstructure would have been larger in its size, but if a burial part had had thick and massive walls, the upper part would have been constructed exactly over the underground walls, so their measurements would have been the same. The most elaborated brick tombs with superstructures deserve the name of a mastaba.

An illustration comes from Tell el-Farkha again. Grave no. 100 (Dębowska-Ludwin et al. 2010) was rather monumental with its large (6.2 x 4.1m) and massive construction composed of a single burial chamber surrounded by thick walls up to 2m wide. The outer surface of its walls was slightly sloping, plastered and from north, east and south decorated with niche façades (Fig. 11). The date of NIIIB makes the tomb the oldest example of this kind of structure known from Lower Egypt. The special character of the tomb was reinforced by four subsidiary child burials – a practice usually seen as restricted to the Dynasty 1 period.

Another interesting example is grave no. 63 still from Tell el-Farkha (Dębowska-Ludwin 2011a: 260-262). It

*Fig. 9. Partially exposed eastern façade of the great mastaba from Tell el-Farkha with possible niche-decoration*

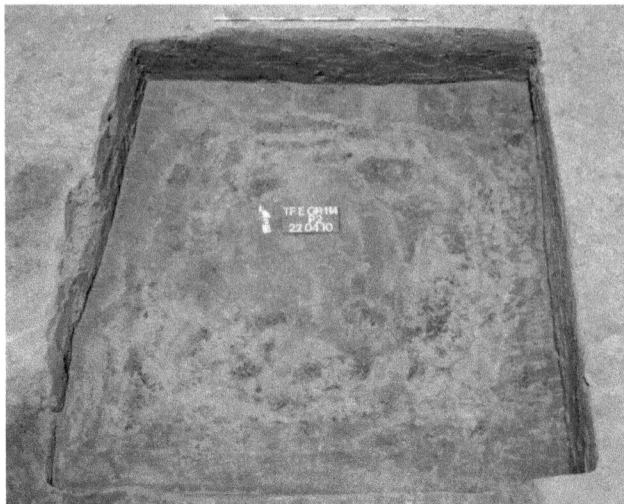

*Fig. 10. Example of a grave superstructure from the Dynasty 0 period – grave no. 114 from Tell el-Farkha*

was dated probably to the very end of the period in question and measured ca. 5 x 3m. Its most interesting architectural feature was a niche decoration of the outer eastern façade – four two-step-niches covered the whole wall of its superstructure (Fig. 12).

The characteristic regular shape of a superstructure – often additionally plastered with mud-and-sand mortar – as well as its usually larger dimensions than those of a substructure suggest that this part of a grave structure was meant to be visible over the ground level. The observation is also supported by a portion of preserved original cemetery surface discovered at Tell el-Farkha, which was covered with a relatively thick layer of plant material preserved as white mineral fibres mixed with many fragments of pottery and some bones. The whole tightly pressed stratum was leaning over neighbouring superstructures of graves nos 63 and 114.

The best preserved constructions in Tell el-Farkha measured over 1m of height (e.g. graves nos 1 or 94) and were found over burials that had been primarily located on the tell's slope overbuilt as a result of later human activity at the spot, which probably enabled them to survive. Rare examples known from Abu Roash 300 also imply that the method of burial securing with a brick cover was relatively common and also there traces of a muddy plaster were registered (Klasens 1958a: 35). The above mentioned grave securing solutions concern complicated constructions only, while simple pit burials were presumably left unmarked. A good example of the situation is Kom el-Khilgan, where considerably numerous burials intersected others even the closely dated ones (Tristan 2005: 51).

The review of archaeological materials enables the statement that pit graves lined with mud bricks were in principle always furnished and cases when empty burials of this form were registered concern plundered tombs, most probably as far as in the antiquity since any burglary

traces are difficult to find. The average offering set was composed mainly of:

- pottery vessels in great variety of forms typical for the period;
- stone vessels and their miniatures made of basalt, travertine, limestone, greywacke, marble, dolomite, breccia and porphyry, as well as composite ones;
- also bodily adornments were found in many burials: bracelets of greywacke, flint, limestone, shell, horn, bone and elephant or hippopotamus ivory; necklaces of greywacke, limestone, serpentine, amethyst, onyx, steatite, carnelian and bone or singular beads;
- toilet objects like cosmetic palettes in geometrical shapes and grinders used with them, tattoo needles, spoons, a copper mirror (discovered in Tell Basta), bone combs, cosmetic sticks, hairpins, boxes;
- fragments of other objects of ivory and copper with mostly undefined purpose because of their poor preservation state;
- tools like flint knives, scrapers and sickle blades, copper fish-hooks, chisels, axes, stone querns (attested in Tell el-Iswid South);
- finally, so-called symbolic pottery fragments that were discovered in the majority of burials in Kafr Hassan Dawood in deceased hands, in front of their faces or by their pelvises.

To summarize, during the Dynasty 0 times the general burial standard was gradually rising. Simple pit burials characteristic of earlier periods were still in use; however, pit burials lined with mud bricks enjoyed much wider popularity. The increasing number of more differentiated grave goods was also part of the scheme. Probably in response to the threat of robberies some of the most carefully composed burials from Tell el-Farkha were covered with a layer of greasy, very humid and probably liquid mud. It was poured into the burial chambers over the deceased bodies and all of their offerings. Unfortunately, this fantastic "safety device" was also

*Fig. 11. Elaborated superstructure with niche façade dated to Dynasty 0 – grave no. 100 from Tell el-Farkha*

*Fig. 12. Perfectly modelled niche façade in grave no. 63 from Tell el-Farkha*

responsible for higher humidity level within the protected chambers and thus, for highly advanced decomposition of all objects deposited inside (Pawlikowski, Dębowska-Ludwin 2011). The presence of mud was also attested in some pottery and stone jars that were offered to the deceased and were usually empty (with the exception of the mud). Altogether it shows that the protective function of mud was not the only one. Possibly more important was its cult significance, connected with the afterlife and rebirth conceptions. Similar role of a kind of magical protection was probably played by the presence of ochre, which was attested in some burials beneath the mud. A great example is grave no. 99 with its burial chamber thoroughly covered with a layer of red ochre (Fig. 13). All of these illustrate the growth of care of the burial form itself but also the increase in economic and life conditions in the area, probably thanks to political situation development. The political stability also reflects the process of burial customs standardization, the spread of uniform building techniques and rules of burial

*Fig. 13. Burial chamber in grave no. 99 from Tell el-Farkha covered with red ochre*

furnishing. The last bastion of local tradition seems to be the clearly unique cemetery – against the background of the remaining sites – in Kafr Hassan Dawood, where not a single brick was registered. Unfortunately, its actual political position remains unknown.

The eastern Delta in particular enjoyed its prosperity period during the reign of Dynasty 0 and the prosperity lasted until the middle of the following dynasty. Archaeological sites registered in the region are interesting, quite numerous and composed of wealthy middle class representatives burials. What is more, except for a few graves with especially rich offerings, the so-called elite graves phenomenon (at least at the scale of far south located areas) remains hardly attested. The exceptions come from Kafr Hassan Dawood, e.g. grave no. 1008, the biggest one at the site, oval in its shape (1.8 x 1.5m) equipped with the largest number of objects and their categories like the pot with the *serekh* of Ka; a group of burials from Minshat Abu Omar or the mastaba and graves of NIIIB from Tell el-Farkha, where latest fieldworks brought into light exceptional and impressive structures of a very early date. All these data point to a high average life standard in the whole region but also signals the emergence of elites. Political position of the three centres remains undefined, however, recent discoveries in Tell el-Farkha (the shrine, votive deposite and golden figurines – see Chłodnicki et al. 2012) indicate that the latter site could have been of far greater importance in structures of power of that time than it seemed just a few years earlier from now.

In this unclear picture people's movements in the Delta, which were registered in quite numerous newly founded sites, seem to be significant. Among them at least two are worth mentioning: Tell el-Daba'a el-Qanan and Tell el-Farkha ones again. On the former site the cemetery from the earlier period was abandoned and another one was established not far from it but, unfortunately, at an insufficiently specified moment. It may be regarded as highly possible that one group of people had departed from the site and another one settled there shortly after. Regrettably, our comparative material is not complete enough to prove the thesis. More interpretation possibility is offered by the site of Tell el-Farkha, where a similarly puzzling situation was discovered (Ciałowicz 2008a). The above mentioned monumental construction was abandoned shortly after it was erected and then, in the place that became a new mound, a cemetery was founded not much later. The burial ground was of character typical for its epoch and did not far diverge from the scheme, although it surely was not a continuation of recent events on the site.

**THE PROSPERITY PERIOD – NORTHERN EGYPT DURING DYNASTY 1**

During the times of Dynasty 1 the number of sites dated to the period grows rapidly to 43 (Map no. 6). Among cemeteries of use continued from the previous epoch the following should be mentioned: Tell Basta, dated to the

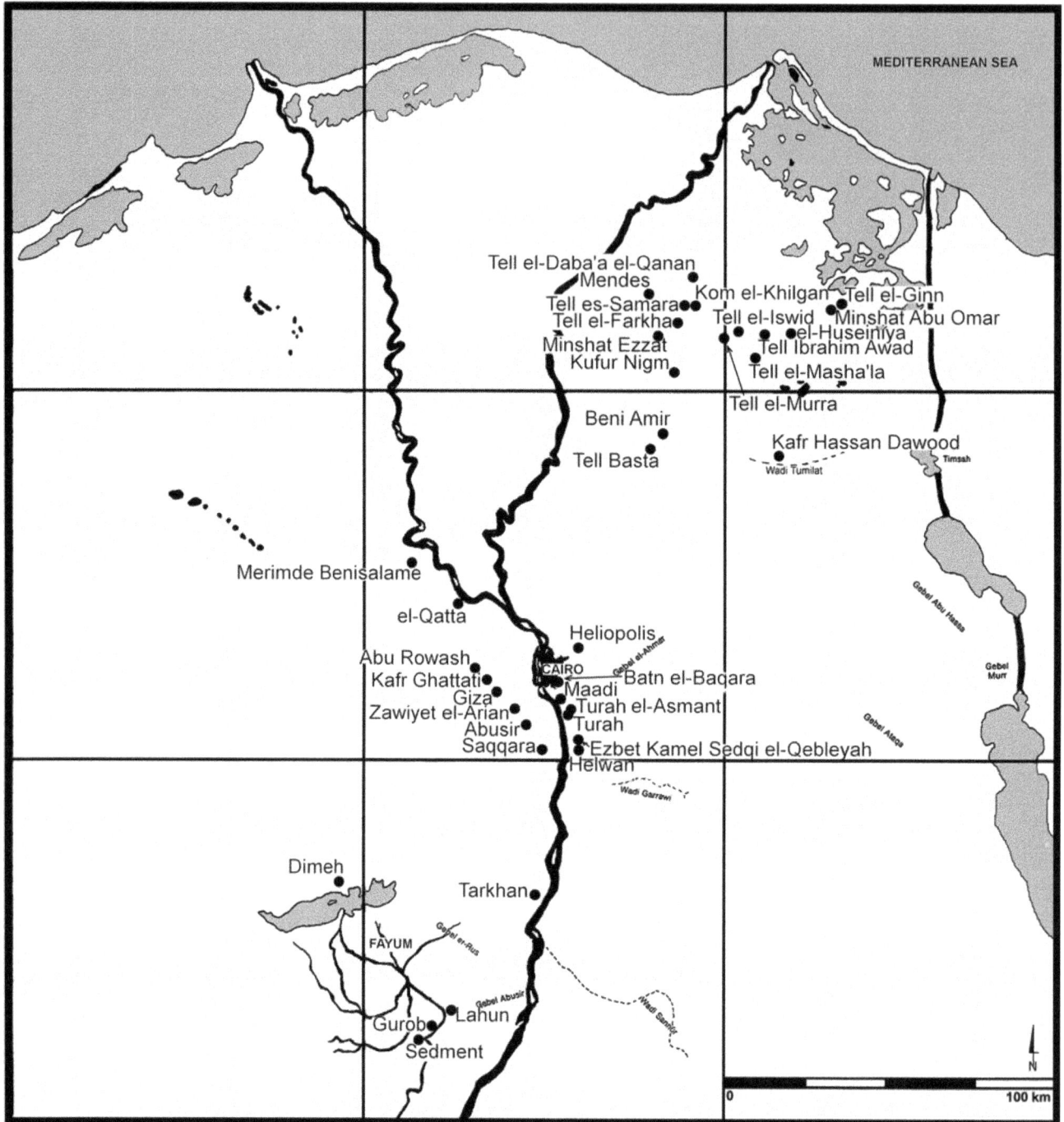

*Map no. 6. Cemetery sites dated to Dynasty 1*

turn of Dynasties 0 and 1; Kafr Hassan Dawood, with its climax during the reign of Narmer and sudden abandonment during Aha; Minshat Ezzat left by the time of Den, el-Huseiniya, occupied only a bit longer; Minshat Abu Omar IV, or Tell el-Iswid, Tell el-Daba'a el-Qanan, Tell es-Samara, Tell el-Murra, Beni Amir and Tell el-Farkha. All the sites revealed little changes in burial customs, for example a noticeable increase in the wealth of burials registered until the middle of the dynasty, then followed by a slump. Like before, cemeteries in Merimde, el-Qatta, Gurob, Dimeh, Kafr Ghattati and Tell el-Ginn also in this period provide material insignificant in number and of imprecise date, which is insufficient for observation of changes in burial customs. A visible difference is noted in the case of the largest necropolises

in Turah, Helwan, Abusir North and Tarkhan, which in the period of Dynasty 1 experienced their highest magnificence. They served as burial places for most influential people of the society including fully developed elites and extended bureaucratic machine.

The distribution of new sites from Dynasty 1 seems to be significant. In contradiction to previous periods, burials in new Delta locations appeared only in Kufur Nigm (Bakr 1988; 1994; 2003; Tassie, van Wetering 2003: 505, footnote 3), Tell Ibrahim Awad (van den Brink 1992; van Haarlem 1996; 1998a; 1998b; 2000; 2001), Mendes (Hansen 1965; 1967) and reoccupied Tell el-Masha'la (el-Hagg Ragab 1992). Three of them were composed of

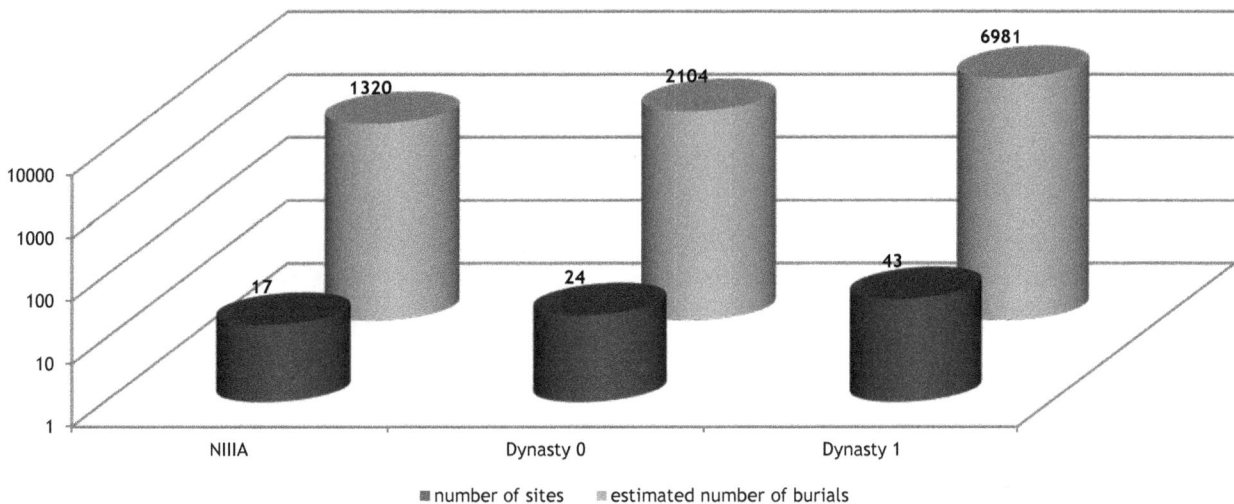

*Chart no. 2. Number of sites and estimated number of graves attributed to a particular period*

typical for their times wealthy equipped burials of brick structure, while in Mendes few registered graves used bricks only as burial covers. Human activity clearly shifted towards the new centres of power in the area of the northern Nile Valley. And thus, we deal with a series of more and more wealthy and diversified cemeteries in Abu Roash – from site 300 founded during Dynasty 0, through sites 1957 (Klasens 1957), 400 (Klasens 1959), North (Hawass 1980) and M (Montet 1938; Klasens 1960a; Baud 2005; Tristant 2008; Tristant, Smythe 2011) to site 800 (Klasens 1960) – which start a long row of necropolises on the left river bank. Abu Roash is then followed by grave no. 2 in Giza South (Daressy 1905; Petrie 1907), Zawiyet el-Aryan (Dunham 1978), Abusir (Bonnet 1928; Jeffereys, Tavares 1994), Saqqara North (Emery 1938; 1939; 1949; 1954; 1958; Firth 1931; Quibell 1923; Youssef 1996; Tavares 1999: 703-704) and Saqqara Serapeum (Macramallah 1940; Castillos 1976; Kaiser 1985). The opposite bank of the Nile was occupied by sites registered in Batn el-Baqara (Boghdady 1932), Maadi (Brunton 1939), Turah el-Asmant (el-Khouli 1968; Yacoub 1981; el-Sadeek, Murphy 1983) and Ezbet Kamel Sedqi el-Qebleyah (el-Banna 1990). Finally, the list of sites registered in the period for the first time is closed by necropolises located farther north in the area of the Fayum oasis, that is in Lahun (Petrie et al. 1923) and Sedment (Petrie, Brunton 1924a; 1924b). To sum up, we deal with a flourishing centre rich in impressive tombs of state officials of various rank that separated the peripherally situated Delta from the similarly peripheral Fayum area. The Delta, at least to the middle of Dynasty 1, followed the course chosen in the previous period, while the Fayum region was under direct influence of the capital.

Comparison of numbers from Dynasty 1 and older periods appears to be very interesting. Rapid increase in human activity is illustrated by Chart no. 2. Also the continuation of cultural standards from NIIIA period and Dynasty 0 is obvious, that is continuously gaining momentum rise of the number of both sites and burials, as well as proliferation of these two values in the times of Dynasty 1. On the one hand, almost double number of cemeteries and triple number of burials point to overall economic stabilization of the society, certainly connected with political balance ensured by reign of kings of the recently unified kingdom. On the other hand, those rapid changes of quantity also prove further progress in burial customs, which reflected the evolution of society structure. To illustrate the situation, the ratio of large cemeteries, that is over 100 burials, to the complete number of sites registered in the times of Dynasty 0 from ca. 21% increased to ca. 31% during the proceeding Dynasty 1. It is worth noticing that only three out of 13 large cemeteries (Minshat Abu Omar, Kufur Nigm and Kafr Hassan Dawood) were located in the Delta. The juxtaposition proves then that the centre of power moved to the present Cairo area and that in the situation of the overall prosperity more and more care was invested in the afterlife and practices connected with it.

Changes in burial customs registered during Dynasty 1 are, undoubtedly, significant, however, their importance is based mostly on rapid bloom, development of previously formed elements by adjusting them to the needs of an affluent but centrally governed society. It was the king and the highest officials who set the tone of the society's expectations. That is why in the situation we deal with the powerful centre and the peripheral Delta and Fayum regions, which demonstrated numerous similarities but also important differences of regional character. The discussed material shows that the Delta was at first well positioned and possibly even kept a leading role in the region, however, around the middle of Dynasty 1 it lost its advantage to be finally turned into a kind of province.

## THE DELTA

Conditions noted in the Delta seem to be very specific. There, a significant number of cemeteries of very similar features was registered, which in the period in question reached their climax and then rapidly lost their significance. The tradition of clear social stratification in the region can be traced back to the Lower Egyptian times (see the residence from the Central Kom at Tell el-Farkha – Chapter 2), thus the idea of tombs' differentiation was well rooted here and can be seen as a continuation of older, local tendencies. The phenomenon is illustrated by Deltaic cemeteries, in particular by Minshat Abu Omar IV, Tell el-Farkha, Minshat Ezzat, Tell es-Samara and new in the list Kufur Nigm. Their development went according to the trend of the end of Dynasty 0. And so, we observe there more and more carefully equipped tombs of brick construction and clearly growing average dimensions of graves which had been built for continuously growing rich middle class with slowly developing elites differed by their higher material status. The most representative burials of the category were registered in Minshat Abu Omar (Kroeper 1992). They were multichambered, large structures (even as large as 4.90 x 3.25m) with interesting architectural features (tomb 2275) and despite some partial plundering, they still revealed over 125 items of funerary goods (tomb 2897).

In the context grave no. 6 from Tell el-Farkha (Dębowska-Ludwin 2009: 461) deserves attention as it was a massive, well-secured and free-standing structure in a small mastaba type built for a 10-12-year-old child and its 20 pottery vessels, as well as a beautiful necklace (Fig. 14). Such an effort and capital investment in the construction suggest a significant position of the child's family and, indirectly, a prosperity period that was being experienced by the whole community. What is more, the conclusion may easily concern also people of the Delta in general, particularly when data from less characteristic sites are also considered. Sites as: el-Huseiniya, Beni Amir, Tell el-Daba'a el-Qanan, Tell el-Iswid, Tell Basta, Tell el-Masha'la, Tell el-Murra and Tell Ibrahim Awad revealed similar features comfortably matching the development trend, while Kafr Hassan Dawood forms an example of a site continuing older and local traditions in its climax, too.

At the latter cemetery mud bricks were consequently unaccepted, but the general enriching process observed in the Delta society of the time was differently though also visibly marked in burials. And thus, increasing number of objects in a single grave and its larger average dimensions are among the markers. There were also built structures, which (although realized with the application of different methods) with the effort invested in their preparation, were counterparts of multichambered elite tombs known from other sites. A good illustration of the category of ideas is provided by a large grave no. 970 (6 x 4m) dated to the reign of Narmer (Hassan 2000: 39). The structure was oriented along the north-south axis and

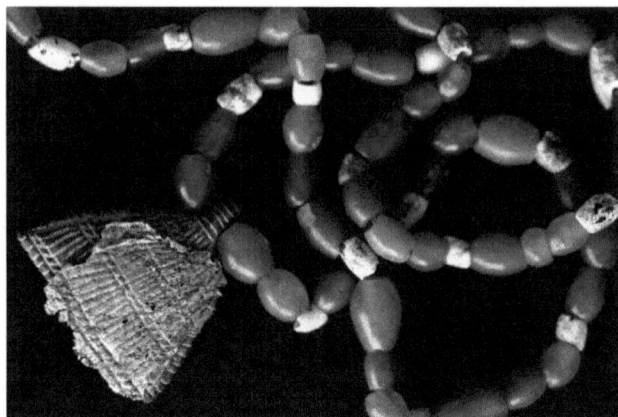

*Fig. 14. Necklace from grave no. 6 in Tell el-Farkha*

was surmounted by a kind of heap with a ramp that led towards it from the south. Due to its significant size and exceptional form, it may be interpreted as a burial enclosure. Another method used for favouring some of the burials was setting them in the oldest southern sector of the cemetery, evidently considered particularly representative (the richest burials nos 913 and 970 were registered there).

The prosperity period so vivid in Delta centres at the beginning of Dynasty 1 did not last long, since between the reigns of Aha and Den it was at least upset, if not collapsed. During the time some previously flourishing sites were abandoned (as e.g. Kafr Hassan Dawood left

*Fig. 15. Grave no. 9 from Tell el-Farkha*

*Fig. 16. Grave no. 50 from Tell el-Farkha*

during the reign of Aha or Minshat Ezzat – during the times of Den) and at the remaining ones the standard of a typical grave was gradually lowered. The situation is observed e.g. in Tell el-Farkha, where a typical middle class grave from late Dynasty 1 was smaller in size, less carefully equipped and rather carelessly secured. Changes in sepulchral data correlate in time with the foundation of a new centre of power in Memphis and reinforcement of its position as the capital of the united state. It was probably due to political factors, which temporarily destabilized the previously convenient overall situation in the Delta. The northern area regained its high position quite soon, however, it never reached its previous optimum again. It seems to be a situation somehow similar to that from the South, where some cemeteries like in Matmar (Brunton 1948), el-Ahaiwa (Reisner 1936), Naqada (Petrie, Quibell 1896; Kaiser 1961), Hierakonpolis HK6 (Hoffman 1982; Adams 1996, 1999b, 2000), Edfu (Leclant, Clerc 1994b), Nag el-Masaid (de Morgan 1984; Needler 1984) or Gebel el-Silsila (de Morgan 1897; Legrain 1903), experienced the same fate, probably also reflecting the centralization process.

As an illustration of the process two significant and undisturbed burials from Tell el-Farkha may be used (Dębowska-Ludwin 2011a: 259-260, 263-264). They are dated to the beginning and the end of the period in question and represent two distinct cemeteries used at the site in the period of Dynasty 1. The older one (no. 9 – Fig. 15), with its interesting form and diversified set of objects, represents well the first group of graves from the site. The overground part of the structure was massive and mud-bricked, preserved to the height of ca. 1m, with plastered outer surfaces and badly preserved niches on its eastern façade. The superstructure was oriented along the north-south axis with a declination to east and constructed over a heap of earth that had been built over the actual burial chamber. Perfectly preserved mats had inlayed the deep chamber of a visibly trapezoid section. Grave goods also represent an interesting set composed

of 27 pottery vessels (one with a Narmer *serekh*) in various shapes, also of Palestinian influence (Czarnowicz 2009), a miniature pot, two stone bowls, two cosmetic palettes of greywacke, a spoon of bone and beads (probably a bracelet) of carnelian and faience. The complete assemblage makes the impression of well-being and affluence having been experienced by the grave owner – a rather typical representative of people from the site. The younger above mentioned grave (no. 50 – Fig. 16) belongs to the second half of Dynasty 1 and reflects the ensuing situation of condition changes. This structure also appears to be interesting – it was two-chambered and overbuilt with a superstructure, however, its form was standardized, generally making less impression. The superstructure was preserved to the height of ca. 0.9m. It was a massive, very tight mud-bricked cover of a very regular rectangular shape and orientation almost perfectly along the north-south axis. The level of the superstructure foundation and the top of walls of the underground part (with orientation slightly deviated towards east) was divided by a distinct layer of earth. In the middle of the stratum, which was 0.4m thick, a deposit of five pottery objects was registered. They are interpreted as granary models (Kołodziejczyk 2009). Right beside the skeleton no objects were found and their majority had been gathered in the smaller, southern chamber of storage significance. Although, the deceased had been equipped in 37 vessels of pottery and 11 of stone, all the objects were in very similar forms. Therefore, in comparison to the older grave with no. 9 this tomb had been furnished with valuable objects but selected without panache typical for the older group of burials.

The standard type of grave in the period became pit burials inlayed with bricks that pushed simple pit graves on to the sidelines. The latter – except for Kafr Hassan Dawood – were used only for the smallest and poorest burials, in most cases devoid of any objects (the situation was registered in Beni Amir, el-Huseiniya, Kufur Nigm, Kom el-Khilgan, Minshat Abu Omar IV, Tell el-Iswid,

*Fig. 17. Traces of a simple roofing construction leaning against a wooden beam – grave no. 67 from Tell el-Farkha*

Tell el-Masha'la, Tell el-Farkha and Mendes). The straight majority of graves registered in the period is represented by rectangular pit structures lined with mud bricks. Some oval examples with bricks were also noted (Beni Amir), however, they were absolutely rare. Thus, during Dynasty 1 various sub-types of bricked graves were generally repeated from the previous period. The most popular were relatively simple single-chambered structures. Apart from them also more complicated, multichambered constructions were built, for example:

- two-chambered with a storeroom at one of the short sides (in case of Tell es-Samara the type predominated on the site);
- three-chambered – with a single storeroom at both short sides or two smaller at one side;
- four-chambered – with two storerooms at one side and a larger one at the opposite side;
- numerous other solutions were also attested, in which the number of inner rooms reached even 13 (Minshat Ezzat), quite atypical were examples with double burial chambers (Beni Amir, Tell Basta), too. All of them, however, belonged to exceptional structures that differ from the popularly repeated scheme.

Regardless of the number of rooms, the actual burial place was usually located in the central part of a structure, often being the largest chamber. Internally complicated or simple, graves in general were constructed in the same way. At first, a pit dug in the ground was lined with a

single row of bricks. Normally bricks were arranged parallel to the length of walls, but at the end of the period – usually in larger and multichambered structures – more and more often perpendicularly to the walls. The bottom and walls of such a chamber were inlayed with mats (great examples come from Tell el-Farkha, where plaiting works are preserved in a form of white inorganic substance), then the complete burial with offerings was covered with another mats or branches (Minshat Abu Omar, Tell el-Farkha – Fig. 17). The following step was to fill the pit in with earth and, finally, over the pit a massive, bricked superstructure was built. The last element was not registered in every case, therefore it is impossible to authoritatively judge if it was considered obligatory (as an example in Minshat Abu Omar, Tell es-Samara and Tell el-Daba'a el-Qanan they were totally unregistered). Solving the problem is again facilitated by the data from Tell el-Farkha, where – as it was mentioned in the previous chapter – superstructures were quite often preserved, at least in their lower parts, in the sector of the tell which was later overbuilt by younger strata. On that basis, it may be suggested that in a large part of cases, we presently deal with structures damaged in their uppermost, probably free-standing parts.

Judging by the growing average dimensions of a grave and its more complicated structural form in comparison to the previous period, the affluence of society was increasing in the first part of Dynasty 1. The conclusion is even stronger thanks to numerous atypical constructions of larger size and more internally complicated ones with the application of experimental building. These are

*Fig. 18. Atypical layout of grave no. 7 from Tell el-Farkha*

46

*Fig. 19. Burial enclosure from Tell el-Farkha – grave no. 55*

among the others: graves 125 and 127 from Kufur Nigm (Bakr 2003: 32-33) – exceptional because of the usage of fired bricks and pottery tiles for the reinforcement of a pit's walls or bottom; already quoted above grave no. 6 from Tell el-Farkha in a form of a small (3.45 x 2.56m), but very massive (mud-bricked superstructure preserved to the height of 0.5m and walls of the burial chamber with the same thickness) and undoubtedly, the free-standing mastaba; a large structure (8 x 4.5m, 2.6m high) from Tell Ibrahim Awad (van Haarlem 1996: 7) with perfectly preserved superstructure (up to 1.25m of height) also resembling a small mastaba that was composed of three little annexes located within walls surrounding the burial chamber; grave no. 7 from Tell el-Farkha (Dębowska-Ludwin 2009: 461-462) with a system of so-called side annexes adjacent to one of the longer sides of the actual burial chamber (Fig. 18); tomb 2275 from Minshat Abu Omar (Kroeper 1992: 134-136) with internal burial chamber walls decorated with niches, plastered, wood inlayed and painted white-and-red; a large (11 x 3.85m, the walls 1.4-0.8m thick), eight-chambered grave from Beni Amir (el-Moneim 1996a: 247-249), where arched vault made of bricks was registered; grave 137 from Tell Basta (el-Sawi 1979: 63) with a rarely occurring in the Delta scale shaft that lead to two underground burial chambers; a multichambered grave from Tell el-Masha'la (el-Hagg Ragab 1992: 212) with a court adjacent from the north and a niche in the grave's southern wall, and a large (6.5 x 3.6m) four-chambered construction from Tell Ibrahim Awad, dated to the end of Dynasty 1, with mud bricks used only additionally for supporting numerous layers of plaiting works stretched on wooden frames (van den Brink 1992: 51). And last but not least, the unique burial enclosure discovered at Tell el-Farkha labeled no. 55 (Dębowska-Ludwin 2011a: 264-266). It comprised a four-chambered tomb with a brick superstructure and was surrounded by a perimeter wall and one or two subsidiary burials (Fig. 19). This large complex measured ca. 9 x 7m, and its superstructure was preserved to the impressive height of over 1.5m. The eastern façade of the superstructure was decorated with two niches, one close to the northern corner, the second close to the southern one. An extremely large amount of rough pottery (mostly bread moulds) was concentrated by the niches, but within the perimeter wall, and suggests that the niches were of significance for ritual activity. The perimeter wall had clearly rounded corners and an entrance leading into the enclosure from the south. The subterranean portion of grave no. 55 is also interesting. It was composed of four chambers containing beautifully preserved mats and approximately one hundred items deposited as offerings, amongst them 33 stone vessels (Pryc 2009; 2012) and two copper harpoons. The main structure was accompanied by probably two much smaller burial constructions: graves nos 62 and 64. Pottery objects from the enclosure very tentatively suggest the date of late Dynasty 1, although early Dynasty 2 seems also plausible.

Aside from the chosen architectural solutions, features typical for burial customs of the region seem to include the commonly used coffins, made practically of all accessible materials, and consistent orientation of graves along the north-south axis with a characteristic small declination to east. The rule defining the preferable orientation of the deceased, which was set in the previous period, was still relevant in the times of Dynasty 1, and thus, bodies were interred in the contracted left side position, with heads northwards. Although some exceptions to this preference were registered they form only a small percentage of the total number of burials from the period.

When discussing the situation in the Delta during Dynasty 1 and its evolving – as far as it can be judged by sepulchral data – political conditions, one should bear in mind that many sites from the area were just in the process of their slow abandonment. The change started in the period between the reigns of Aha and Den (the reinforcement of central power) and was progressing till the end of Dynasty 1. Presumably by the reign of Andjeeb the site of el-Huseiniya was finally abandoned, the same happened to Kom el-Khilgan in the period of Semerkhet, while Minshat Abu Omar, Kufur Nigm, Tell Ibrahim Awad and Tell el-Masha'la were left around the time of Qa'a. Thus, from 17 cemeteries known from the period of Dynasty 1, only eight entered the following epoch.

### THE FAYUM OASIS AREA

In the period of Dynasty 1 the second – after the above discussed Delta – peripheral zone was the Fayum oasis area. There, burials related to the period in question were registered only on five sites: Gurob, Sedment, Lahun, Dimeh and Tarkhan. The latter, however, was deeply influenced by the central area and therefore, it will be discussed later. In comparison to the rather densely occupied Eastern Delta, such a scarcity of sites makes the region relatively insignificant. The largest structures known from other zones were never found there, but even without them burial customs were coherent and consistently practiced.

The most frequent (Dimeh, Gurob, Sedment, Mayana n. Sedment, Bashkatib n. Lahun) were relatively shallow graves and among them simple pit burials in oval or rectangular shapes. Pit burials lined with mud bricks were also popular, mostly single-chambered, but more internally complicated examples were registered, too. Numerous solutions known from the Delta were applied also in the Fayum region as tombs with one or two storerooms located at one of the shorter structure's sides. A type of local popularity in Bashkatib n. Lahun was represented by somewhat transitional graves with an almost square burial chamber and bricks used only for a

single central wall, which divided the part meant for the deceased from the other one reserved for grave goods, stored behind the owner's back (Petrie et al. 1923: 22). In the enumeration an exception is set by a single grave with two storerooms at one of the structure's short sides and the third one parallel to the tomb's length. Invariably, however, all constructions of the type were secured from the above with branches and filled in with earth, which was a solution widely implemented in the Delta, too.

The second category of burials were structures generally deeper (registered in Bashkatib n. Lahun, Sedment and Mayana n. Sedment). These were graves equipped with staircases and shafts. The first type was composed of a staircase (straight or bent at the right angle) of three to 15 steps, a short vestibule and the actual burial chamber of various shapes. The entrance to the chamber was usually secured with a stone slab or bricked wall. The main underground part, which was the chamber, could be small and simple or large with its ceiling supported by a pillar. It could also be enlarged by side niches in the number from one to four. In one case (Mayana n. Sedment, grave 684 – Petrie, Brunton 1924: 14) the surface over a tomb with a staircase had been levelled, which may point to a kind of superstructure built there. The excavators (Petrie, Brunton 1924: 14) suggest it could even be a mastaba. The second type of deep graves were a little less complicated shaft structures (Mayana n. Sedment, Bashkatib n. Lahun, Kom el-Iswid n. Lahun). These constructions were composed of a vertical shaft from 0.82 up to 5.25m deep, which led to the actual burial chamber in form of a small niche or a room, regular in shape, sometimes also enlarged by side niches. The entrance to the chamber was – again – secured by a wall of bricks or stones and only exceptionally preceded by a little vestibule. A single construction of the type usually comprised one burial chamber, although examples with two chambers at the same level placed side by side, facing each other or one over the other were also registered. In an isolated case, one shaft led to four chambers cut in each of its. Exceptional are also two graves from Bashkatib n. Lahun (Petrie et al. 1923: 22-23), where at the shaft's bottom human skeletal remains were found. W.M.F. Petrie considered them subsidiary burials, however, the relatively simple form and scarcity of offerings in both main structures would form rather atypical context for these extra burials.

Against the background of diversified grave forms, it is striking how homogenous burial customs were and to what extent the range of objects that had been offered to the deceased was standardized. And thus, people in the Fayum area were consistently buried in the contracted, left side position, with heads northwards, very often in rectangular wooden coffins. Other bodies orientations were also practiced, but – just like it was the case in the Delta – only as marginal examples. Also objects typical for funerary goods were similar:
- the most popularly registered were pottery vessels;
- stone vessels and their models of greywacke and travertine;
- flint tools;

- animal bones;
- beads of carnelian and limestone; bracelets; pendants;
- cosmetic palettes; combs of ivory;
- fragmentarily preserved items of ivory and copper;
- copper tools;
- shells;
- seals;
- headrests;
- pieces of cloth.

In Bashkatib n. Lahun (Petrie et al. 1923: 25) it was possible to establish the chronological sequence of particular grave types' popularity. According to it, the predominance of simple pit burials was clearly characteristic for the first half of the period in question, structures with staircases were built during the reigns of Djet and Den, while the ones with shafts were introduced as the latest – that is at the time of Den. In Mayana n. Sedment (Petrie, Brunton 1924: 14) an interesting cemetery layout was observed, where – in the excavators' opinion – graves that belonged to small families or inhabitants of little settlements were clustered together. This observation was supported by the fact that small groups of structures with staircases had been surrounded by shallow and simple pit burials or small shaft graves.

Juxtaposition of the above presented data points to the changes direction of a typical grave for the time of Dynasty 1 in the area. At the beginning, we deal with the predominance of pit burials – simple and lined with bricks, which in general, corresponds to the situation attested in the Delta. Conditions changed during the reigns of Djet and Den – and here again there is a chronological coincidence with the Delta, where in the same period a temporal break of prosperity was registered, which was probably caused by the shift of the power centre to the area of Memphis – when new construction types appeared: first graves with staircases, a bit later the ones with shafts. Therefore, in contradiction to the Delta, where the development came in accordance to the direction chosen during the Dynasty 0 times, in the Fayum area we clearly deal with a different version of the progress, evidently influenced by the centre. The situation might have arisen from various political conditions in the area, but also from different geological formations typical for the Nile Valley and the Delta. Since hewing deep shafts and staircases in soft Deltaic soils was far more technically difficult than it was in the Valley as it required the application of special lining and shoring practices. Possibly, both factors were important for the case.

## THE CENTRE

The area reveals a surprising cemetery concentration in the number of 22, which means that the majority of sites used in the period all around the northern part of Egypt was located in the very region. What is more, only eight of the places (situated in a peripheral area, little characteristic Merimde Benisalame; similarly

uncharacteristic el-Qatta and Kafr Ghattati; continuing Abu Roash 300 and flourishing Abusir North, Turah, Helwan and Tarkhan) had been constantly occupied since the previous period. The remaining 14 (the long sequence in Abu Roash 1957, 400, 800, M and North, Abusir, Giza South, Zawiyet el-Aryan, Saqqara Serapeum and the most significant among them Saqqara North, as well as located on the right Nile bank: Batn el-Baqara, Maadi or short-time extensions of much larger cemeteries like Turah el-Asmant and Ezbet Kamel Sedqi el-Qebleyah) represent newly founded necropolises of the age in accordance with the actual trends. In comparison to the already discussed peripheral areas, the cemeteries registered in the center reveal numerous common features, which attest the overly high life standard and degree of social inequality.

The sepulchral material offers a great variety of burial structures which were used according to the social rank of the deceased but also depending on the geomorphologic character of the ground where a site was located. Apart from those typical, a significant number of constructions is represented by only single examples. And thus, simple pit graves with the least representative poor inhumations of people probably from the bottom rung of the social ladder are still popular in this period. The presence of such burials was registered on the majority of cemeteries at that time, where they were most often shaped rectangular (Abu Roash 300, Tarkhan, Turah, Turah el-Asmant, Helwan, Ezbet Kamel, Abu Roash 1957, Abu Roash 400, Saqqara Serapeum, Abu Roash 800), rectangular with clearly rounded edges (Abu Roash 1957), square (Ezbet Kamel, Saqqara Serapeum), oval (Tarkhan, Turah, Turah el-Asmant, Ezbet Kamel, Abu Roash 1957, Saqqara Serapeum), round (Turah, Abu Roash 1957, Saqqara Serapeum) and irregular, e.g. triangular or kidney-shaped (Saqqara Serapeum). At sites covered with layers of loose gravel like in e.g. Abu Roash simple pit graves had walls additionally secured from falling down by partial lining with mud (Turah, Abu Roash North), mud bricks (Abu Roash 300, Turah, Abu Roash 1957, Abu Roash 400, Abu Roash 800), stones (Abu Roash 300, 1957, 400 and 800) or wood (Tarkhan, Turah) and plaiting works (Turah). Organic material was attested in few cases, mostly at those sites where soil conditions were especially favourable for its preservation. The usage of this kind of partial grave wall lining appears to have clearly practical meaning and the lining material was probably chosen according to its local availability. A specific variant of pit graves are relatively large and almost square pits with rough edges divided in their middle by a little brick wall into the actual burial chamber and a storage niche located in front of the deceased face (Abu Roash 1957, 400 and 800). Also, pit burials furnished with a few steps formed in the ground (Ezbet Kamel, Saqqara Serapeum, Abu Roash 800) or a short staircase (Kafr Ghattati) have been registered. Examples where the deceased were buried in coffins put right into small and very simple pits (el-Qatta, Turah) can also be regarded as types of pit burials. In a single case in burial no. 467 from Abu Roash 400 the pit's edges were reinforced with rough stones plastered with black mud (Klasens 1959: 42, Pl. XXIII.1).

Similarly as in the previously discussed areas, the most popular were burial structures based on mud bricks. And also there the most common and known from the largest group of cemeteries is the type of a single-chambered rectangular pit grave lined with a single row of mud bricks arranged parallel to the pit walls (Abu Roash 300, Kafr Ghattati, Merimde Benisalame, el-Qatta, Tarkhan, Turah, Turah el-Asmant, Helwan, Ezbet Kamel, Abu Roash 1957, Maadi, Zawiyet el-Arian, Abu Roash 400, North and 800, Abusir), sometimes with rounded edges (Abu Roash 300, Zawiyet el-Arian) or massive walls up to half a meter thick (Saqqara Serapeum). Also in Turah a special single-chambered, rectangular grave type was noted closed with bricked barrel vault usually restricted to child burials (Junker 1912: 20-21). A development of limited possibilities offered by a bricked single-chambered grave was another type registered in Turah (Junker 1912: 21) and Abu Roash 400 (Klasens 1959: 42), where at one of shorter walls of the classic bricked structure an adjacent simple and rather irregular pit was found that played the role of a hurriedly built storage chamber.

Numerous types of multi-chambered graves registered at the cemeteries of central localization location are already known from peripheral areas with no real differences in their shape or structural features. There were multi-chambered constructions in variants based on variable number of inner rooms, which were created by separation of some storage space from the actual burial chamber with suitably arranged bricked partition walls. And thus, researchers have identified:

- two-chamber structures with a small storage room by one of shorter grave walls (Abu Roash 300, Turah, Turah el-Asmant, Ezbet Kamel, Abu Roash 1957, Maadi, Abu Roash 400, M and 800);
- three-chamber ones composed of two stores by one of shorter grave walls (Abu Roash 300, Turah, Turah el-Asmant, Ezbet Kamel, Abu Roash 1957 and M);
- three-chamber structures with two magazines at one shorter grave wall with the gable end rough, devoid of bricks (Turah, Turah el-Asmant);
- three-chamber graves – with a single store at each of shorter structure walls (Turah, Ezbet Kamel, Abu Roash M and 800, Abusir), sometimes with their gable ends left rough (Saqqara Serapeum);
- four-chamber – with two smaller storage rooms and one larger at one of shorter grave walls (Turah) or with two magazines at one short grave end and one larger magazin at the other end (Ezbet Kamel);
- five-chamber – with two storage rooms at both short grave ends (Abu Roash 300 and 1957), sometimes with their gable ends left rough (Saqqara Serapeum);
- finally, seven-chamber – the actual burial chamber and six storage ones (Tarkhan).

Pit structures usually had no complicated roofing solutions. In their straight majority they were covered with mats or branches and then filled up, however, at some sites – mostly those where organic material is usually better preserved – also the presence of wooden roofing was registered. These examples come mostly from Abu Roash (300, 400, 800) but also from Tarkhan and Saqqara Serapeum. Another novelty is the introduction and more and more common use of stone in burial constructions (Abu Roash 300 and 800, Helwan).

Apart from the mentioned structures that are known from the previous periods in the time of Dynasty 1, some more structurally complicated solutions were also popularized. They were usually based on a level much below the present surface, their sub-ground part was composed of the actual burial chamber, some storage rooms and sometimes of a vestibule, possibly with additional stores at its both sides. Chambers' walls were lined with mud brick, but there are also some examples where stone was used for the purpose. In addition, the same material was applied as security solution for a burial chamber entrance. The most interesting element of this type of tombs is the entrance to the whole structure which was provided by a staircase – straight (Tarkhan, Turah el-Asmant, Helwan, Ezbet Kamel, Abusir) or bent at the right angle (Helwan, Ezbet Kamel). In few cases apart from a staircase a tomb was also furnished with an additional shaft (Tarkhan, Ezbet Kamel). Another structural solution that implied a little lesser effort, but also located a burial relatively deep below the surface were shaft graves (Turah, Turah el-Asmant, Ezbet Kamel, Abusir). The burial chamber function was played by a side niche, which at the beginning of the practice was dug at some height from the shaft bottom level. The niche entrance was often bricked in with mud bricks or blocked with a stone slab. A development of the variant which was much less popular and registered at generally richer cemeteries were tombs with more complicated layout of inner rooms, sometimes separately hewn in bedrock, lined with stone slabs and secured with a massive stone portcullis (Helwan, Batn el-Baqara). In an isolated case a tomb (no. 10B-2,3 from Abusir) with a single shaft that lead to two burial chambers was registered (Bonnet 1928: 4).

A specific structural solution characteristic for the lower part of the Nile Valley and the period of Dynasty 1 are also subsidiary burials that belonged to the largest mastabas built in the period mostly in Saqqara North and were arranged in long rows. Against the background of other graves they appear to be interesting, carefully made and relatively well furnished, but due to their special character they will be discussed with other subsidiary graves in a separate chapter.

When counting out burial structures discovered in the discussed area and dated to the period of Dynasty 1, apart from those that were typical, also those exceptional ones represented by singular examples should be mentioned here. One of these structures is tomb 27.w.1 discovered in Tura (Junker 1912: 25-26). It comprised a core made of a square bricked shaft, which from the south was closed by a wall, much longer than the dimensions of the shaft. Behind it another smaller shaft was placed that from its south was left devoid of bricks. In the half of length of the northern wall which created the main shaft a hole was made. It enabled entering the structure through a straight, six-step staircase leading from the north. The whole construction was encircled by a bricked wall that measured 16 x 9.5m and 7m of height and was oriented along the north-south axis. What deserves special attention, for reasons presently unknown, the tomb was never used. Another atypical structure was grave no. 186 from Turah el-Asmant (el-Khouli 1968: 73) – a rectangular pit measuring 5 x 3m and 3m of depth, which was accessible through six steps arranged along the pit's northern wall. At the bottom of the pit and by its eastern wall a bricked chamber was built that was probably meant for the burial. The chamber measured 2.2 x 2.5m. It is also worth drawing some attention to an interesting construction labeled as tomb no. 137/76 also from Turah el-Asmant (el-Sadeek, Murphy 1983: 159). Regardless of its severe damage it was possible to establish the size of the structure at not less than 10.5 x 5m and 3m of height. It was composed of at least two large and almost square chambers with niches in its northern and eastern walls, connected by inner passages.

There are also other examples of atypical sepulchral structures from the central area. Tomb Z124, known from Zawijet el-Arian (Dunham 1978: 18-19), was composed of a two-step pit that measured 1.97 x 1.34 in its upper part and 1.76 x 1.06m below the step, where a roofing structure of three thick beams was placed alternatively with two layers of wooden planks additionally covered with a reed mat. The deceased was placed in a coffin 1.34 x 0.73m in size, and over it a brier was put made of four wooden beams with two longer ones ended with decorative knobs. In the beams little holes were made, through which straps of plaiting were driven that were formerly creating the inner part of the brier. The wooden coffin and roof of the structure were found in a perfect state of preservation. Another atypical tomb from the same site was grave Z401 (Dunham 1978: 25-26) of quite impressive dimensions (9 x 3m) atypical for pit structures lined with mud bricks. It was oriented along the north-south axis and the pit was divided into three almost identical rooms (dimensions 2.37 x 2.05-1.96m) arranged in a row and plastered, created by partition walls 0.7m of thickness. Both the bricks and plaster were burnt during the fire of the grave, probably set by robbers. In Saqqara Serapeum (Macramallah 1940: 8) the most interesting structures include type I (rectangular with a superstructure), known from only a single example. Its sub-ground part was composed of a deep and large rectangular chamber, hewn into bedrock, while its over-ground part was created by a circle of local limestone arranged around the chamber.

A great variety of the hitherto discussed possibilities indicates that aside from the progressing complication of inner layout of graves' substructures, Dynasty 1 also witnesses a growing interest in grave superstructures. They evolved from simple brick covers, attested in the previous period, to large-sized and multi-chambered mastabas that were one of the numerous elements of burial enclosures built for representatives of the highest layers of the society. We deal here with the simplest preserved solutions (similarly as it was in the Delta, the original surface of many sites was destroyed and thus, we possess only limited luckily saved material), like masses of bricks arranged in layers and securing a burial from the above (Abu Roash 300 and 1957) or low and rectangular superstructures built of mud bricks over a burial chamber of slightly larger size than the sub-ground part, sometimes plastered or even painted in colours (Abu Roash 300). There were also registered constructions commonly known as little mastabas – relatively small and simple that constituted a reminiscence of the greatest sepulchral structures but on a much reduced scale. Such examples come from Helwan, Abu Roash 800 and Tarkhan, where they were a kind of mounds reinforced with brick walls that gave them their rectangular form, sometimes decorated with niches or on the pattern of the largest structures extended with additional side elements as a sort of small vestibule and courtyard (Tarkhan).

## GREAT MASTABAS

The largest tombs of the mastaba type were much evolving during the years of their popularity. They were the most abundant at the necropolis of the highest rank state officials in Saqqara North (that is why the development sequence of this type of burials is much based on the history of this particular site), but also in Tarkhan, Abusir North, Abu Roash M, Giza South and very badly preserved in Helwan, where they were registered in the richest sectors of the cemetery, however, surrounded by numerous graves of average society members. It is highly significant that the largest group of these exclusive structures was built during the reign of Den, which corresponds to the convenient development conditions attested in the period in sepulchral material connected with the lower society groups also in the peripheral areas.

The structure type characteristic for the early Dynasty 1 is well represented by tomb 3357 (Emery 1939: 10-17) that starts the long sequence of dignitaries' burials in Saqqara North. The structure measured 41.5 x 15.5m and dates to the reign of Aha. The tomb was composed of a rectangular pit cut into bedrock and gravel and divided into five smaller rooms by bricked walls. The largest and central room played the role of the actual burial chamber. A rectangular, large mastaba was planted on the surface level and its inside space was divided into storerooms, while its outer façade was decorated with niches. There were no visible traces of any entrance, which means that the structure was completed after the burial. Additionally, the construction was encircled by a double perimeter wall that measured 48 x 22m, and to the north from the tomb also a series of low buildings was registered, described as "a model estate" (Emery 1954: 171). Two of them had arched vaults, another three were rounded and may represent granaries, while further north a barge was discovered.

Other examples of tombs of the type are structures located also in Saqqara North. One of them is the large (42.6 x 16m) tomb 3503 (Emery 1954: 128-170), dated to the times of queen Merytneith, which was furnished with a perimeter wall, a barge and 20 human subsidiary burials. The tomb attributed to Sekhemka[7], no. 3504 (Emery 1954: 5-127), had a traditional layout, it measured 49.5 x 20m and constitutes the earliest example of a superstructure surrounded by a low bench with heads of 300 bulls modelled in clay. Tombs 3507 (Emery 1958: 73-97) and 3505 (Emery 1958: 5-36) from Saqqara North, dated to the reigns of Den and Qa'a, were also furnished with such a bench with bull heads, similarly as the largest mastaba from Abusir North labelled with number XVII (Radwan 2000: 510-511).

Three large mastabas from Tarkhan are dated to the period of Djet – they are the largest preserved structures from the site, although probably not the only ones that were ever built there: 1060 (Petrie et al. 1913: 13-20), 2038 and 2050 (Petrie 1914: 4-9). They were all of similar size (31.6-34.8m long, 12.7-15.4m wide) and construction. Their main part was a bricked body with a niche decorated façade (nine to 10 niches at the longer walls, four to five at the shorter ones), some of the niches preserved remains of red paint and wooden panels, while the rest of the façade was covered with white plaster. The inner space of their superstructures was filled up with sand and gravel, thus it had no rooms. In mastaba 1060 there were two additional storage rooms cut into bedrock by the sub-ground burial chamber, which could have been covered with a limestone roofing. All underground chambers in mastaba 1060 were white plastered, while mastaba 2038 was characteristic because of a steep passage that led to a completely empty burial chamber. However, little can be said about the construction details of the pit, since it was preserved as nothing more but a depression in gravel and bedrock, heavily weathered and irregular, ca. 6m deep. Basing on the lack of any partition walls in the inside or brick lining, W.M.F. Petrie (1914: 4-5) decided it once comprised a wooden burial chamber, however, he did not mention any wood remains discovered there. The underground part of mastaba 2050 did not preserve its original features, either. Each of the Tarkhan mastabas was surrounded by a narrow passage between the superstructure façade and the perimeter wall. In addition, mastaba 2038 was accessible through an outside vestibule located by the eastern, longer side of the construction. In the corridor around mastabas 2038 and 2050 subsidiary burials were discovered.

From the same period comes also tomb 2 from Giza South. It was a mastaba built of mud bricks, oriented almost ideally along the north-south axis, which measured ca. 10 x 37m. It was composed of five rooms. The main, sub-ground chamber was 3.5m deep and 15.7 x 7.5m in size. It was located centrally and had eight pilasters – two at each longer side, one at shorter side and in every corner. The pilasters were 2.3m high and supported the roof of the chamber made of perishable materials and covered with 1m deep layer of earth. The centre of the chamber was divided by a narrow (0.2m)

and irregular wall without a door. Clear traces of fire were registered there, however, its intensity was different in various parts of the building (Daressy 1905: 99-101). Four storage rooms were located, two at each shorter side of the main chamber. Rooms A and B were constructed in the southern part of the structure. They measured 2.6 x 2.71m and were parted by a wall 1.18m thick, partially damaged at the west, similarly as the north-eastern corner of room A. Storage rooms D and E located in the northern part were slightly smaller (2.45 x 2.35m in size) and were divided by a wall 1m thick. This sector of the building bore no traces of fire and thus, remains of wooden roof beams were discovered here. All additional chambers were located on a less deeper level than the actual burial place, that is 1.65m below the surface (Daressy 1905: 101). During the second phase of research W.M.F. Petrie (1939: 3) discovered in the burial and southern chambers the presence of wooden panelling, preserved as charcoals and remains of beams and posts that once held the construction. The outer walls of the superstructure were decorated with white painted niches, where in two cases pottery vessels were discovered, left there before the whole wall was secured with a very closely built wall 0.55-0.62m thick (Petrie 1907: 3). Not far from the main body of the mastaba and along each of its sides a row of subsidiary burials was found (Petrie 1907: 3-5).

The middle of Dynasty 1 was a period of numerous innovations, with a significant number of tombs built during the reign of Den and simultaneously growing care for the structures' form which led to the introduction of staircases. In Abu Roash M as many as 14 large mastabas were built (Montet 1938: 63-69). Their common features were: niche and painted decoration of outer walls of massive superstructures; wooden drums found fitted crosswise into the upper parts of niches; storerooms located in superstructures in number from one to four; the largest room from a superstructure had its floor level lowered below the surface and beneath there was the entrance to the actual burial space; a kind of a wooden chest in the actual burial chamber (similarly as in Abydos in royal tombs from the reign of Djer [e.g. Petrie 1900: 14; Engel 1996]); a substructure composed of a shaft and one to four rooms; a singular burial chamber closed with a stone portcullis; side magazines without their own closing; lack of goods in the shaft; a perimeter wall around the whole structure; a corridor between the main mastaba body and the wall; subsidiary burials arranged in rows along longer mastaba walls closed by the perimeter wall and lack of entrance to burial structures. The largest tomb in Abu Roash M is mastaba VII (Montet 1938: 38-46) with maximum dimensions of the main building 9 x 21m and walls up to 2.2m thick, while the whole enclosure measured ca. 30 x 20m (Tristant, Smythe 2011: 318). The eastern façade was preserved to the height of 1m and decorated with niches (in three of them horizontal beams were registered) and colour plaster – white, black and red. In the corridor that ran around the main mastaba body and in its slightly broader eastern part eight subsidiary burials were found, arranged exactly below the paved passage in a single row. Within the mastaba's main

---

[7] For the discussion on the identification of the large mastabas' owners and some doubts concerning the commonly accepted attributions see Morris 2007.

body an upper chamber with a floor lowered below the surface was discovered in the south-western corner of the building. The chamber was accompanied by a single storeroom localized located at the same level. A shaft ca. 4m deep led to a single underground chamber closed with a large stone portcullis crushed by robbers but partially found *in situ*. The most architecturally complicated structure from Abu Roash M is tomb M 25 (Klasens 1960a: 110-111). Its underground part was composed of four storerooms arranged into two at both shorter sides of the burial chamber. In this case the chamber floor was paved with wood and the whole underground part was closed with double wooden roofing. The tomb was additionally furnished with two barges modelled in clay.

Staircases introduced in tombs in Saqqara North from the period of Den were placed at the eastern side of those structures and had their beginnings outside of them in the place leading right to the actual burial chamber. The underground layout remained unchanged, that is a rectangular pit cut into bedrock and divided by partition walls into the actual burial chamber and storerooms. The only change was the larger depth of such rooms (the earlier ones did not exceeded 4m). Tomb 3038 (Emery 1949: 82-94) measured 37 x 13.85m, it was situated at the northern edge of the plateau and is dated to the reign of Andjeeb. Originally, it had a mound of earth with a bricked staircase over the burial chamber. Later the mound was changed into a stepped form. Similar mounds were registered in tombs 3507 (Emery 1958: 76), 3111 (Emery 1949: 95-98) and 3471 (Emery 1949: 13-17). They were considered prototypes of the pyramid of Netcherikhet (Djoser), although they were probably constructions that tried to incorporate elements of early Upper Egyptian tomb into the mastaba type of Saqqara (Tavares 1999: 701). Also in Helwan few preserved remains of superstructures in the form of large mastabas with niche façades were registered (Köhler 2004: 297), which topped tombs with their underground parts furnished with staircases.

During late Dynasty 1 the previously typical niche façade was abandoned in favour of full façades with false doors at the northern and southern edge of their eastern wall. A superstructure had then a solid core made of rubble or mud bricks, a staircase was L-shaped and started at the east to enter the burial chamber from the north. Additional rooms were grouped at both staircase's sides, not around the burial chamber as it was previously. A good example is set by mastaba V from Abusir North (Radwan 1991) and known from Saqqara North tomb 3383 (Emery 1949: 125-129) with measurements 30.5 x 14m and tomb 3500 (Emery 1958: 98-109) that measured 31.9 x 15.9m. The latter kept the east-west axis of the burial chamber, while the north-south axis was already predominant in the period. The structure was entered from the east, moreover, it was furnished with the youngest subsidiary burials that differed in their shape and structure from other early examples.

With the end of Dynasty 1 the system of open construction of burial chambers was abandoned. Tombs 3120 (Emery 1949: 121-124) and 3121 (Emery 1949: 116-120) dated to the reign of Qa'a were furnished in a chamber hewn in bedrock, while their superstructures were unchanged – filled with rubble, solid and usually devoid of niche decoration. Also from the period comes the largest (measurements 35.2 x 24.3) Early Dynastic mastaba from Saqqara North – it was tomb 3505 (Emery 1958: 5-36). the entrance to the burial chamber lead from the east through a north-south ramp that turned at the right angle. The solid superstructure had a niched façade, a double perimeter wall and a mortuary shrine at the north.

*BURIAL CUSTOMS*

The burial customs which were practiced in the area seem homogenous. A general rule was to orient burial structures along the north-south axis with only small declination to the east, regardless of the body position placed inside. The deceased themselves were in their straight majority buried in the contracted, left-side position with their heads northwards[8]. Then, there was no different practice observed than in the remaining part of Northern Egypt. Similarly popular were coffins – rectangular, made of wood, pottery or stone, so also in this case there were no new, surprising solutions attested, just as it was with grave goods.

Offerings were numerous, composed of interesting sets with higher number of luxurious objects also in terms of their craftsmanship, which can be justified by a generally higher standard of living, the affluence of local people, but also by the closeness of the best workshops which specialized in products satisfying the needs of the highest state elites. The repertoire of objects is, nevertheless, already known:

- pottery vessels often offered in hundreds, produced locally but also imported, mostly from the Levant;
- numerous stone vessels made of colorful and valuable materials (alabaster/travertine, limestone, greywacke, dolomite, black basalt, steatite, serpentine, porphyry, tuff, rock crystal, breccia, amphibolite, quarz);
- copper vessels;
- ivory vessels;
- tools, weapons and their models – wooden sickles with flint blades, wooden sticks, arrows with quivers of leather, bone or wood, bunches of arrows, arrow heads, harpoons, flint knives and scrapers, whetstones, wooden spears with ivory heads, copper tools as knives, saws, hatchets, hoes, chisels, tools for making incisions, punctuators, spikes, needles, knife and hatchet handles made of sandstone and wood, hatchets, axes, javelins, mace-heads;
- copper plates of unknown use;
- discs made of limestone, copper, ivory, horn and wood;

---

[8] Still, it should be kept in mind that numerous grave robberies deprived us of much information on the original order in a burial, especially when the most impressive structures were mostly completely looted.

- wooden and bone plaques inscribed and uninscribed;
- sets of game pieces, sometimes still in leather pouches, marbles (or tokens), gaming sticks and boards;
- zoo- and anthropomorphic figures;
- flint nodules;
- seals and their impressions;
- furniture and their elements: bull-shaped legs of ivory, copper bed knobs, copper nails for wooden elements, wooden chairs and beds, a large stone table with movable legs;
- rhinoceros horns models made of pottery;
- cosmetic palettes of greywacke;
- cosmetic and decorative spoons, needles or awls, combs, hair-needles and sticks of ivory;
- personal adornments like: decorated copper bracelets, bracelets made of shells, ivory or leather, pendants, amulets and beads of various materials;
- decorative boxes;
- fragments of walking sticks;
- golden foil cut into long pieces;
- animal bones – some with intentionally cut grooves;
- leather bags and baskets;
- fragments of mats from floors, fabrics, papyrus roles, pieces of string;
- shoe fragments;
- inscriptions on ivory plaques, wooden objects, stone vessels, pottery and impressed in clay;
- inscribed stelea;
- food offerings;
- and finally, a long series of undefined objects, such as: a wooden item in form of a disc with one of its sides convex, the other one flat; an incrusted wooden box where the disc was closed; a piece of limestone with black painted figures of a bull and donkey; numerous objects of ivory; so-called castanets that is a boomerang-shaped object ended with a carved animal head, etc.

## DYNASTY 1 SUMMARY

The closest vicinity of the new capital center visibly influenced burial customs practiced in the whole Northern Egypt. The central area was densely strewn with cemeteries meant for each layer of the society. Graves that were built there represent in fact all known variants of structures often accompanied by side elements, such as: granary models, barges, subsidiary burials. Numerous structures were furnished with objects of the highest quality, also in artistic terms. The center of these changes seems to be the most distinguished necropolis located in Saqqara North, where for a long time only the largest mastabas were constructed. The cemetery was founded during the reign of Aha and was continuously used till Dynasty 3. The distribution pattern of structures dated to particular years reflects the history of the beginnings of the pharaonic state. And thus, the turning point seems to be the first prosperity period that occurred during the reign of Den, when the largest group of structures was constructed. This conclusion on the common prosperity experienced by the people of the area is certified by discoveries from other sites, like: Abu Roash M, Helwan,

Batn el-Baqara, Turah, Tarkhan, where the increased building activity was also registered. Additionally, more precise research done on the two latter sites (Wilkinson 1996) confirmed the presence of this phase in the state's history when after the end of state formative process during the reign of Narmer central power went through a period of temporal destabilization that ended with the reign of Djet (the large mastabas in Tarkhan) and finally stabilized by Den. It is then possible that the foundation of such a representative necropolis of the highest state elites in Saqqara North was a propaganda campaign aimed at emphasizing the state presence in the landscape of Northern Egypt.

To sum up, the whole sepulchral material which is accessible from Northern Egypt from the period of Dynasty 1 is quite rich and shows that burial customs practiced at the time were very homogenous. Regardless of the exact location and burial construction, the general rule at the period was burying the deceased in the contracted left side position with their heads northwards, often in coffins made of wood, pottery or plaiting – probably in consideration of local availability of particular material. The repertoire of objects that was composed of typical offerings was also homogenous, though interesting and wider than it was in previous periods, and more abundant in so-called luxurious items. The commonly predominant building material was sun-dried mud brick of standardized measurements, at least within a single structure. Brick was used for constructing the most sophisticated buildings meant for the highest and wealthiest society layers, but also for pit structures lined with bricks, which were typical in this period and registered in the whole discussed area. Local differences lay in a lesser or wider variety of burials at particular sites, more or less abundant presence of complicated multi-chambered structures. Similarly, burial pits in the whole discussed area were registered in the same simple forms, invariably serving as burials for the lowest layers of society.

Among all those similarities of key significance also local variability cannot be forgotten. And thus, the Delta seems to continue its own development line started at the beginning of Dynasty 0, which around the middle of Dynasty 1 was politically dominated by the new centre of power and as a result, was gradually losing its panache, which probably reflects the slow decline of the area's importance. The second peripheral region was the Fayum Oasis area, which for the whole discussed period was evolving under a clear influence of the centre, displaying numerous common features and – at the same time – much poorer sepulchral material. In the centre, however, the sudden emergence of numerous new sites with simultaneously flourishing older cemeteries is absolutely striking. It was there that the largest number of necropolises was registered, the largest structural differentiation of tombs funded in the area, the richest offering sets and the largest sepulchral construction built for the ruling elites. It is worth mentioning here that graves with shafts and staircases that belong to the youngest structures (they were introduced around the reigns of Djet and Den) represent examples which are more elaborated in their form and consumed high building effort. Moreover, they are generally unknown (with the exception of Tell Basta and a few very deep examples from Tell el-Farkha) in the Delta. However, the latter situation should be presumably justified – as it was already suggested – by local differences in geomorphology of the areas.

The site distribution pattern with settlement concentration in the northern part of the Nile Valley, the more intensively occupied agricultural Fayum areas and gradually more and more abandoned eastern Delta (previously densely populated) also seem to be important factors that are the evidence for significant changes of the Egyptian state and society at the very beginning of their history.

## 3.6. THE TIMES OF DYNASTY 2

The first conclusion concerning the times of Dynasty 2 is a sudden decrease in the number of registered sites to 25, although their distribution pattern remained more or less the same (Map no. 7). Simultaneously, the general amount of burials attributed to the period also decreased and only Helwan stood out with its far over 100 graves, while the remaining ones did not exceed the limit of 50, on average. However, it is surprising that the straight majority of these sites were cemeteries continuously used from the previous period, since in new location only five burial grounds appeared, while in the Delta exclusively old cemeteries were declining. The new localities are: Saqqara – the Royal Cemetery (Hassan 1938; Munro 1983; 1993a; Dodson 1996; van Wetering 2004; Dreyer 2007; Lacher 2011), Saqqara South (Raven et al. 2003a, 2003b; van Walsem 2003; 2004; Regulski 2011; Regulski et al. 2010), Wardan (Larsen 1956), Ma'asara (Hughes 1941) and after a long break the reoccupied site in Gerzeh (Petrie et al. 1912: 2). Unfortunately, in many cases graves were attributed to the period only in general (el-Qatta, Mendes, Dimeh, and Gurob in particular), which creates severe difficulties in defining characteristic features of burial customs. In the case of middle class representatives' burials no significant changes were observed and elite graves were much less popular. Among not numerous structural novelties were doubtlessly the first royal burials funded in Saqqara. On the other hand, additional outside elements of graves that were introduced during Dynasty 1 disappeared, like: subsidiary burials, boat burials, model buildings or granaries, neither chapels nor burial temples were registered and their function was taken over by so-called false doors. The exception was made by royal galleries which comprised some of the elements in a rethought conception. Generally, in comparison to the boom attested in the previous epoch a sort of building slowdown is observed, which probably reflects another central authority's stability upset.

As it was already mentioned, particularly significant changes in sepulchral material were not attested. Graves attributed to the period repeated types known from older times and thus, in general they may be divided into the simplest pit burials and a bit more elaborated pit graves lined with mud bricks, as well as deeper structures equipped in a staircase or shaft. Moreover, the last two categories were sometimes covered with a superstructure in a small mastaba type, although, examples of them were definitively fewer and found only in the central region (e.g. Helwan). In the whole juxtaposition the Delta looks surprisingly bland, especially when its previous diversity is taken into consideration. Only eight cemeteries from the period are known here (Beni Amir, Mendes, Tell es-Samara, Tell el-Iswid South, Tell el-Farkha, Tell el-Murra, Tell el-Daba'a el-Qanan, Tell el-Ginn). They had only few graves, in majority of cases severely impoverished when compared to their own history, slowly entering their decline. All these graves surely belonged to a much more stratified and usually poorer society. Still, mud bricked structures were being built, however, publications are so imprecise that it is difficult to say anything closer on their subtypes. It seems that rectangular or roughly rectangular single and double chamber graves were being constructed (e.g. Tell es-Samara), since we lack data on those more complicated ones. At the same time, equally popular were the simplest grave types only inlayed with mats and eventually covered with a mud brick mantle (Mendes).

A good example is provided by the site of Tell el-Farkha, where a rather small group of Early Dynastic graves belongs to early Dynasty 2. The majority of them are poor pit burials, mostly devoid of any object, often cut into older and much more elaborated sepulchral structures (Fig. 20).

The situation illustrates a significant decline if not of the whole region, at least of the particular site. Unfortunately, data from the region are too imprecisely dated and do not allow to continue this line of reasoning. It is interesting that two sites (Tell el-Farkha and Tell el-Iswid South) were characterized by the surprising alternation of typical settlement strata rich in fragile remains of outbuildings with layers full of burials. This observation, together with the fact that we deal only with small cemeteries may lead to the conclusion that in the period of Dynasty 2 in the eastern Delta shifts of small groups of poor people were quite common and that the people did not take much care of burial customs.

In the context the Fayum oasis region comes definitively better out. There were five sites used there (Gerzeh, Lahun, Sedment, Gurob and Dimeh – the two latter offered uncharacteristic and imprecisely dated material), however, similarly small. Except for the smaller number of graves and lesser diversity of their types (in case of burial pit lined with mud bricks, in particular, simple and rectangular structures like in the Delta predominated) no clear changes were registered. What draws attention is the greater popularity of structures dug deeper in hard ground, that is graves with a long staircase (Sedment,

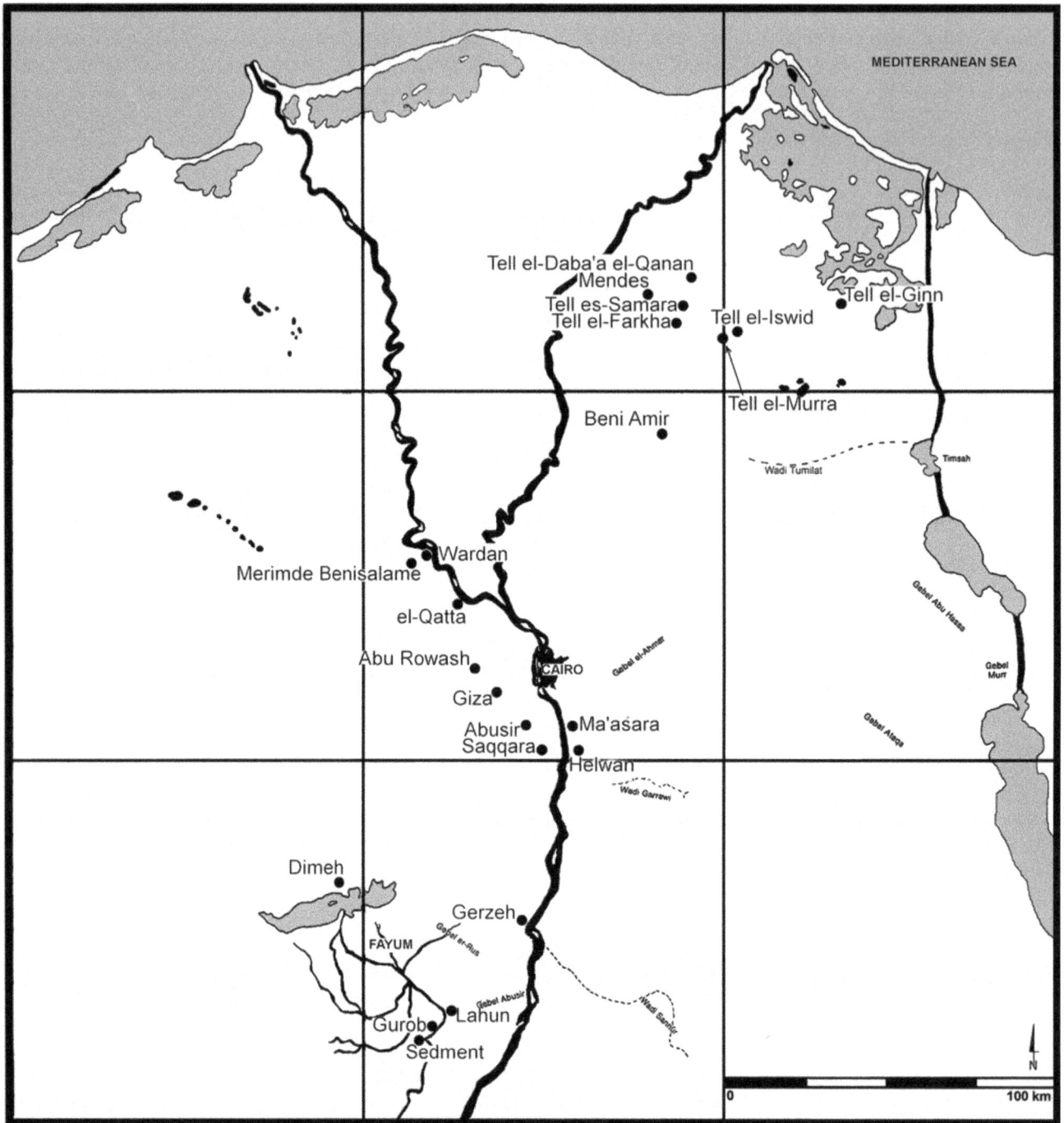

*Map no. 7. Cemeteries used during Dynasty 2*

Dyke cemetery in Lahun) and with shafts (Dyke cemetery in Lahun, Bashkatib near Lahun), which were of an unchanged inside chambers layout (single niches or separately hewn rooms with emphasis to on the latter solution) whose entrances were more and more often secured with stone portcullises. Only two of the graves from Dyke cemetery in Lahun (Petrie et al. 1923: 25) deserve special attention thanks to their structural features – an oblique corridor in one of them, or stone lintel and brick staircase walls in the second one.

Despite a clear development slowdown also in the times of Dynasty 2 the region of the very northern Nile Valley remained the most interesting and most intensively used. There were 12 sites registered there, the majority of

which was continuously occupied from previous periods (Abu Roash 800, Abusir, Abusir North, Giza South, Saqqara North, Helwan as well as localized a bit peripherally by the Delta base and also discussed here Merimde Benisalame and el-Qatta), while only four cemeteries were newly founded (Wardan, Ma'asara, Saqqara South and Saqqara – the Royal Cemetery). Similarly as in the preceding period, burials of middle class representatives and of the highest state elite, as well as for the first time royal graves were registered there. The former were discovered on every, but the royal cemetery. They were inevitably simple in their pit form – oval, rectangular or almost square with a niche for equipment (Abu Roash 800) or lined with mud bricks – mostly rectangular, oblong and single chambered, although, the presence of two- or three-chambered ones of the types attested in previous times was also discovered. Private graves that had staircases and shafts were found in Abu Roash 800, Abusir and Helwan, in the shape already described in the preceding chapter. They displayed only one difference, which is a wider application of stone for wall lining, ceilings and burial chambers' entrances protection interchangeably with still popular mud bricks.

Also in this period, the largest structures seem to be reserved for the elites, exclusively. They were usually located in regular cemeteries in the company of burials that belonged to less influential people (Abu Roash 800, Helwan), however, a tendency toward a more compact burial arrangement within borders of sites delimited in the period of Dynasty 1 was obviously observed. And thus, the primarily regular organization of structures in Saqqara North was changed by numerous younger constructions erected in between the older ones, even at the expense of the latter. The typical mastaba shape at the beginning of Dynasty 2 was not significantly different, since a grave layout of the previous period was kept. An alternation was the fact that substructure was hewn in bedrock, that is an L-shaped staircase, a burial chamber and storage rooms. Bricks were still used for dividing large, hewn chambers and a burial chamber was placed in south, as a rule. Inside the superstructures of a few graves large amount of so-called table pottery was registered, which indicates that the custom of feeding the dead was in practice then. In the middle of Dynasty 2 a typical grave layout resembled a house with numerous rooms separately hewn in bedrock and the previously popular bricked partition walls vanished then. An example is provided by tomb 2302 from Saqqara (Quibell 1923: 29-30) dated to the reign of Ninetjer. Tombs 2307 (Quibell 1923: 31) and 2337 (Quibell 1923: 35-36) had even rooms tentatively identified as bathrooms and latrines. Their superstructure comprised a mantle of mud bricks over a core of rubble or mud and the façades remained even with two false doors. By the end of Dynasty 2 in Saqqara North first examples of shaft graves with model staircases were introduced (Tavares 1999: 702).

Also the so-called Covington tomb from Giza South is dated to the end of the period in question – its rectangular mud bricked and plastered superstructure, with clearly archaizing niche façade was closed by a perimeter wall. Over the wall basis and in the north-western corner of the structure 25 wooden pegs were found stacked into the wall (Covington 1905: 205), moreover, they were arranged in an atypical, irregular and broken line, in some parts even zigzag like. The burial chamber had one niche and was placed along the east-west axis of the structure, slightly moved west from the north-south axis. The chamber was dug into hard and brownish mud to the natural bedrock level that was the chamber's bottom (Covington 1905: 215). The main chamber was situated on the second subterranean level of the mastaba and was secured with a regularly cut portcullis of white limestone. The other underground rooms were small chambers and a gallery of 16 rooms arranged in a complicated layout.

The substructure was accessible through a steep, 17-meter-long corridor with stairs. The corridor began with four narrow steps that were running from west and turned at the right angle, finally, it ended with a five-meter-deep shaft (Covington 1905: 209). The passage between the shaft and the underground chambers was blocked with another, this time oval, portcullis of white limestone.

It is worth a mention that some structures, which were atypical for the whole northern Egypt, were found in the north-eastern part of the necropolis in Helwan. These were two giant grave pits with entrances from north that D. Jeffreys (1999: 368) interprets as built to resemble the oblong tomb of king Khasekhemwy in Abydos but rendered on a smaller scale affordable for local elites.

The sepulchral material reveals that a common practice was to hew substructures deeper and deeper in bedrock with simultaneous more and more complicated layout, and that the process was crowned by the new tomb type restricted for kings only. There were two royal galleries registered in Saqqara in a separated sector and labeled A and B. They are attributed to Hetepsekhemwy/Raneb and Ninetjer, that is the first/second and third ruler of Dynasty 2. The most characteristic feature of these galleries are their underground rooms – chambers, niches, storage rooms and corridors – in a highly complicated layout, which were arranged in long labyrinths covering the vast area of even a few hectares. The entrance into tombs A and B leads through an oblique corridor from the north, tomb B was additionally furnished with shafts that could be of communication importance. The galleries represent many significant design details. Both comprised sectors of rooms interpreted as a model palace with banquet/living-rooms, sleeping-rooms, bathrooms/latrines and offices, model cult places, where the actual burial chamber was surrounded with courtyards and model houses, model residence and magazines (Lacher 2011). However, the Ninetjer gallery was visibly smaller than the one of his predecessor and it had a new compound – a model city, which evidently raised its quality.

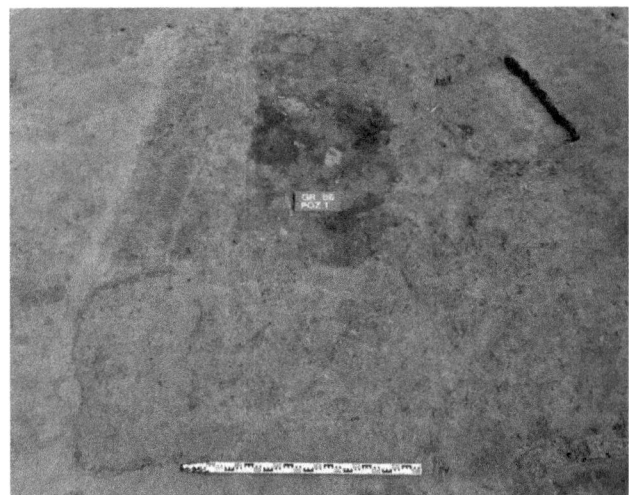

*Fig. 20. Simple and poor Dynasty 2 burials cut into older sepulchral structures at Tell el-Farkha*

*Fig. 21. Typical early Dynasty 2 burial structure – grave no. 111 from Tell el-Farkha*

was found below the nearby tomb of Maya also of New Kingdom. It was suggested (Regulski 2011: 304) that we deal here with a separated cemetery at Saqqara South which represented a different social stratum – neither royal nor the highest state officials known from the northern part of the vast locality. This assumption would correlate with another observation (Köhler 2008a: 398) that Early Dynastic society at Memphis was highly structured and complex, divided into numerous discrete strata.

Graves dated to Dynasty 2 were mostly equipped with rich and interesting offerings. In general, the scope of possible objects that comprised typical grave goods was the same as it was before, although luxurious articles were found more often and in a bit wider range. And thus:

- invariably pottery predominated;
- it was followed by stone vessels made of limestone, travertine, granite, breccia, diorite, greywacke, porphyry, tuff, marble, basalt, dolomite, amphibolite, anortozite, quartz and rock crystal;
- offerings could consist of imported objects and tools of copper (among them also their miniature models) and flint;
- numerous were stone balls of still discussed function – possibly elements of a presently unknown game or tokens used for some goods counting – made of carnelian, agate, colour limestone and quartz;
- various beads and pendants of carnelian, faïence, limestone, travertine, amethyst, ivory, steatite and rock crystal;
- small articles of ivory and copper (e.g. miniature vessels, so-called castanets with curved animal head, pins, plaques, spoons, harpoons);
- cosmetic palettes, cosmetic caskets of greywacke and ivory;
- whetstones;
- cylindrical seals;
- shells;
- furniture pieces;
- stone tables;
- stelea and many, many other;
- it is also worth stressing that there were plenty of inscribed objects among those above quoted.

Regrettably, many structural features are presently impossible to be reconstructed due to later bustling building activity at the site. Also for the same reason the original surface over the subterranean structures was destroyed and therefore, scarce remains of superstructure were traced over tomb B, exclusively. The preserved elements were: an oblong and levelled strip of ground paved with mud and ended with a step with a kind of ramp, where – probably – the actual superstructure was erected. Some scholars (van Wetering 2004: 1066) accept the possibility the superstructure could have the shape of a small mastaba or a chapel. The royal galleries are, undoubtedly, the most interesting structures of the period of Dynasty 2. Moreover, there is a quite common view (Jeffreys, Tavares 1994: 150) that similar galleries from the site could also be sepulchral structures of Dynasty 2, later included into the mortuary complex of Netjerikhet (Djoser).

Gallery C (Raven et al. 2003a: 98-100) of similar layout composition with corridors, niches and an entrance shaft, though of much smaller dimensions, was previously reported as the third royal tomb of Dynasty 2 in Saqqara. However, it was recently reinterpreted as belonging to a high status official, possibly a royal family member, but not a king. The tomb was discovered below a New Kingdom burial structure that was built for Meryneith and after another similar construction of the same date

Burial customs were unchanged and still homogenous, that is the dead were placed in the contracted left side position, heads oriented northwards with obvious exceptions that only proved the general rule. Bodies were commonly interred in coffins made of materials and in shape types already known from the time of Dynasty 1. Unfortunately, a significant number of graves was plundered and their original internal arrangement was disturbed, which severely affects data accessible for analyses. Most probably, it was the greater probability of finding precious metals that could be one of reasons for increased robberies frequency in comparison to previous epochs.

Burial customs in the period of Dynasty 2 in the light of archaeological data seem to be a straight continuation of preceding epochs achievements. The way bodies were treated did not change nor did the model according to which the dead were equipped with a wide range of functional objects with slightly more popular luxurious articles. Invariably, different types of graves reflected social and material diversity of deceased, and so the simplest pit burials were still common among the poorest society classes, while the quite wealthy middle class was buried in graves lined with mud bricks (Fig. 21). However, introduction of particular structure types belongs to Dynasty 1 achievements, whereas, during Dynasty 2 stone material was far more frequently and boldly used for building, walls' lining, floors' paving, roofing and – the most important – for almost omnipresent portcullises placed in specially curved furrows. All these indicate a greater care for burial security, in the period more exposed to robberies. Therefore, it is possible that the care resulted in gradual decrease in the external burial form, since the largest tombs lost their previously obligatory additional elements, such as subsidiary burials, boats, model buildings, chapels or superstructure niche-decorated façades. The lack was compensated by further extension and complication of graves' substructures hewn deeper and deeper into bedrock that found its culmination in the form of royal galleries discovered in Saqqara. And that is the fact of kings burials appearance in the Memphite necropolis at the same time when the previously highly independently developing Delta region declined, which proves the process of the new state reinforcement with its power centre located in Memphis.

# 4. OTHER DECEASED RELATED PRACTICES

## 4.1. CHILD BURIALS

From the moment when we register the first remains of burial customs in Northern Egypt child burials were specially treated. Older children were usually treated according to the rules typical for the remaining adult part of population, while the youngest, newborns and fetuses had the right for extraordinary burial conditions. The moment when a child was crossing the barrier and gained the right to a burial with adult representatives of their society is difficult to be established. Judging by the registered material, their age could have been not the only factor and some basic abilities like sitting, walking or speaking – something that remains invisible in the specific skeletal material – could have played a role in the differentiation. It is also possible that small size and sensitivity of these littlest bodies forced disparate but practically inspired practices.

The cultures of Merimde and Omari, although the character of their burial customs remains uncertain – intra- or extramural – brought a lot of material for research as in Merimde only child burials constitute over 55% (Castillos 1982c: 171-172) of the whole grave number. It remains unclear, however, whether it results from the high mortality of newborns (obviously an important factor) or the fact that the presently excavated part of the site was a special zone, where such burials were concentrated. Less problematic in the case is Omari (Debono, Mortensen 1990: 75), where some concentration of older child burials was attested in particular sectors of the cemetery. Nevertheless, the issue of newborn burials seems to be much worse since only a single grave of this type, placed in a leather bag, was registered and thus, it constitutes no comparable material.

In the Lower Egyptian culture the commonly practiced custom was burying fetuses, newborns and the youngest children in a settlement area, which stands in contradiction to extramural burial practices, typical for the unit. Older children, after they crossed the undefined age/ability barrier, were buried within regular cemeteries, but in restricted zones (Maadi). The practice, however, is not fully clarified since the settlement in Maadi with its 54 children graves (Rizkana, Seeher 1989: 65) is not the single one excavated and other settlement sites connected with the cultural unit brought very little or no burial remains. Possibly, the situation may be explained by the very early date of the settlement in Maadi and the fact that its large part was successfully excavated. Despite the doubt, it can be said that the Lower Egyptian culture was the first to introduce the long practiced custom according to which newborns were interred in pottery jars of typically functional forms, while older children in simple pits. Burials of the youngest representatives of these early cultural units were usually left unfurnished, which may hint – although not necessarily – that the societies were socio-economically unstratified.

Rules referring to child burials in the Naqada culture were clear as early as at the oldest Northern Egyptian site of the unit in Gerzeh. Child burials there constitute (similarly as in the previous cultures) a high percent of the whole registered grave number. It seems typical that children were buried in pottery jars put in separate pits. In Minshat Abu Omar four pottery jar types were distinguished which were used for child burial purposes (Kroeper 1994: 19). These were examples of typical settlement pottery in popular storage shapes that were produced for practical use and surely not burial purposes, which does not correspond to examples known from adult burials and makes their proper dating hardly effective. In sporadic cases (e.g. Gerzeh, Kufur Nigm) jars with a burial were additionally covered from the above with a large pottery fragment. Also a sporadic discovery were offerings in these burials, since nothing but small and few objects were registered (e.g. Kom el-Khilgan). However, it is surprising that in contrast with the beginning of the Gerzean period at its end the number of child burials clearly diminished. It is then possible that some part of them – as was the case in the Lower Egyptian culture – was placed within settlements and was destroyed while the latter were growing and/or the practice of jar burials of newborns was nothing but one of numerous possibilities, regrettably, the only one that was preserved to our times. The remaining practices like burials in perishable woven, plaited or leather bags, as well as put right into grave pits were faster disintegrated and thus, unregistered. Nevertheless, the concentration of child burials in jars observed in particular sectors of a cemetery (e.g. Minshat Abu Omar – Kroeper 1994: 28) deserves extra stressing.

As long as newborn and youngest children burials were organized according to the mentioned and special rules, older children were buried like adult representatives of their population and thus, they belong to the second category. An interesting phenomenon is observed when wealthily-equipped child burials are first introduced. The graves belonged to wealthy young individuals, whose high rank was probably derived from the actual position of their affluent or influential family. Examples of such practices are: early grave 67 from Gerzeh (Petrie et al. 1912: 5) – the richest at the site or Early Dynastic grave no. 6 from Tell el-Farkha (Dębowska-Ludwin 2009: 461) – furnished with a gold ornament. The tendency towards wealthy child burials is another hint for the processes of growing social inequality that was taking place at the end of the Predynastic and the beginning of Early Dynastic periods.

Structurally atypical is a unique category of graves registered in Turah (Junker 1912: 20-21), where a group of relatively small brick tombs was found – single-chambered and with bricked barrel vaults, which were covered with a mound of earth and in their majority they were meant for children.

The vast majority of discussed child burials was represented by single inhumations of popular types, however burials of children accompanied by adults account for a small percentage of the whole number. As a general rule, newborns were put into an average grave pit next to an adult person, sometimes – like in a single example from Gerzeh – in the adult pelvis area (mother and child died before delivery?) or in a jar. In some other cases even older children were buried with adults (e.g. Tell el-Farkha). Interpretation of these instances remains open (see Dębowska-Ludwin 2010). Usually, they were recognized as burials of women deceased around giving birth to their offspring that died together with mothers. To resolve the doubt DNA analyses could be of major importance, however, such results have not been published yet and – on the other hand – the skeletal material in its present state of preservation is mostly useless for such research.

As far as it can be defined, newborns and small children buried in jars were placed in the contracted left-side position with their heads northwards, that is similarly as in the case of adults. However, the rule seems to be less strictly followed and numerous exceptions were registered. It is also worth stressing that the special case of child burials was not the subject of essential regional differentiation, in terms of preferable bodies' position, typical offering sets or grave construction details.
The end of the Early Dynastic period brought a very small number of child burials. It is difficult to explain the situation. Possibly, it may have resulted from generally limited sepulchral material at that time, but it should be also considered that a new and archaeologically unregistered custom was introduced.

## 4.2. SUBSIDIARY BURIALS

They are a characteristic element of burial customs typical of the Dynasty 1 period and are always related to elite graves. They were registered only at six sites (Abu Roash M, Giza South, Abusir North, Saqqara North, Tarkhan and Tell el-Farkha) invariably close to the largest structures in the mastaba type in number from one up to 62. Their complete number is difficult to be specified, mostly because of partial publication of Abusir North, however, it can be estimated at minimum 200. In their straight majority subsidiary burials are represented by human graves, nevertheless, there are among them also a few animal inhumations (see chapter 5.2).

Except for Tell el-Farkha that brought examples of very early and very late dates and thus of much atypical features, the remaining burials of this category are rather similar in their form. In general these graves were simple (usually single-chambered and lined with mud bricks), rectangular in their shape, of insignificant size (from 1.25 up to 2.55m of length and from 0.63 to 1.3m width – the largest found in Giza), commonly covered with wooden roofs and bricked superstructures in form of a little mound with rounded top surface often plastered and painted in colour. Also similar was their position along

sides of a mastaba main body, if numerous they were arranged in long rows composed of individual grave pits or long furrows cut into the ground and divided into particular burial chambers with small and bricked partition walls. In the case of tomb 2 from Giza both solutions were used as in the western row small rooms were allotted within a long furrow, while in the remaining rows separate pits were dug for each burial (Petrie 1907: 3-5).

There were three possibilities when choosing the typical distance of subsidiary burials from the main tomb. And thus, additional burials were located outside a mastaba perimeter wall (e.g. tomb 2 at Giza, graves nos 62 and 64 at Tell el-Farkha – Fig. 22), in the passage between the main mastaba body and the wall surrounding it (e.g. tomb VII in Abu Roash M) or in between layers of bricks a tomb was built of (a very early example from Tell el-Farkha – grave no. 100).

Also, the issue of the deceased orientation in particular grave pits appears to be coherent. It seems that the strongly preferable position was the one characteristic of the whole period, that is the contracted, left side, with heads northwards, and when such orientation was impossible – mostly in rows following the east-west axis – we can see attempts which meant to bring the situation

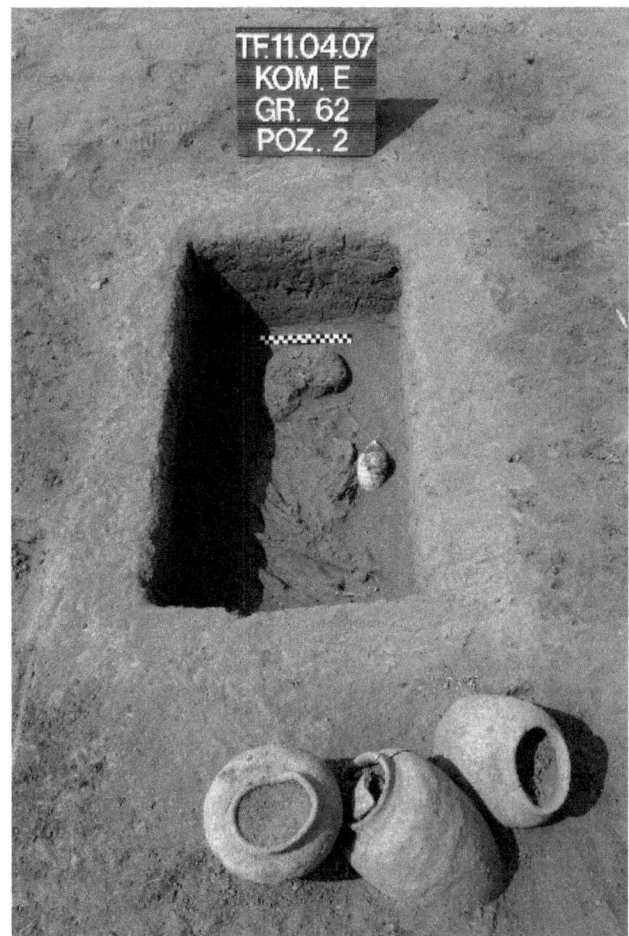

*Fig. 22. Subsidiary burial of late Dynasty 1/early Dynasty 2 from Tell el-Farkha – grave no. 62*

closer to the ideal one and bodies were arranged with their faces northwards.

In the context of all the quoted similarities, it is also worth mentioning that there were some exceptional cases. One of them is represented by a relatively large burial subsidiary to mastaba 3505 from Saqqara North (Emery 1954: 10), lined with stone, located within the passage around the tomb's main body and topped with a stele which could have belonged to the grave owner. As a matter of fact, stelae – although they were never popular in burials of this type – are also known from graves subsidiary to mastaba VII in Abu Roash M (Montet 1938: 64). An atypical solution were also two structures from Bashkatib n. Lahun, where at the bottom of their shafts human remains were registered and W.M.F. Petrie recognized them as subsidiary inhumations (Petrie et al. 1923: 23). Also grave no. 100 from Tell el-Farkha revealed four child burials put in between layers of bricks the southern mastaba wall was constructed of (Dębowska-Ludwin et al. 2010 – Fig. 23).

As far as the situation may be presently assessed, it seems that all subsidiary burials (except for the early examples from grave no. 100 in Tell el-Farkha) were furnished with grave goods, what is more, usually arranged in interesting and diversified sets. Despite numerous pillages, objects

which were discovered in such burials are:
- pottery and stone vessels;
- flint knives;
- objects made of ivory – spoons, vessels, sticks, hair pins, boxes, combs, so-called castanets etc.
- objects made of copper – tools and vessels;
- cosmetic palettes;
- golden needles;
- bracelets, beads;
- gaming sets – some items usually counted among them are probably tokens;
- other valauble items.

Along with the popular practice of placing the deceased in wooden coffins, such offerings indicate a relatively high status – at least the economic one – of their owners. That is why, it seems justified to recognize those deceased as members of the elite mastaba owner's retinue or his/her closest servants. In addition, it should be stressed that the homogenous character of offerings categories and coherence in terms of applied structural solutions which give the impression of sets with almost identical features, suggest these were burials contemporary of main mastabas. Regrettably, we do not possess any data which would enable us to reconstruct funeral circumstances and end the discussion on human sacrifices sent to the beyond with the elites.

Subsidiary burials were, of course, registered also in Upper Egypt, where they formed a significant element of royal burials. Thus, it was there that they were registered in highest numbers reaching as many as 318 in the tomb of Djer (Petrie 1901: 8-9; Dreyer 1990: 71-72). Except for the oldest inhumations subsidiary to the tomb of Aha (Dreyer 1990: 62-65) the remaining ones were arranged in rows around the main structure without its southern corner. From the reign of Semerkhet (Petrie 1900: 13; Vandier 1952: 628) the number of subsidiary burials has been diminishing and their rows were adjusted to the main tomb body. They represent examples of typical, single-chambered and bricked structures, also – as was the case in the North – interestingly equipped.

### 4.3. LOOSE HUMAN BONES REGISTERED WITHIN SETTLEMENTS AND DISORDERED BURIALS

It is a rather typical discovery known from the period of the Lower Egyptian culture (Maadi) and of Naqadan domination (e.g. Tell el-Farkha, Sa el-Hagar – Wilson, Gilbert 2003: 72). In general, these are single human bones registered in an accidental settlement context which could not constitute an actual burial, at least in the form in which they were found. In the majority of cases (Rizkana, Seeher 1989: 66) they are regarded as a result of older graves destruction or random translocations of single bones dragged around by wild animals or half-domestic dogs. The theory works well in case of limb bones, unfortunately, it hardly fits situations like separately registered mandibles (as it was in a settlement context at the Central Kom at Tell el-Farkha), human

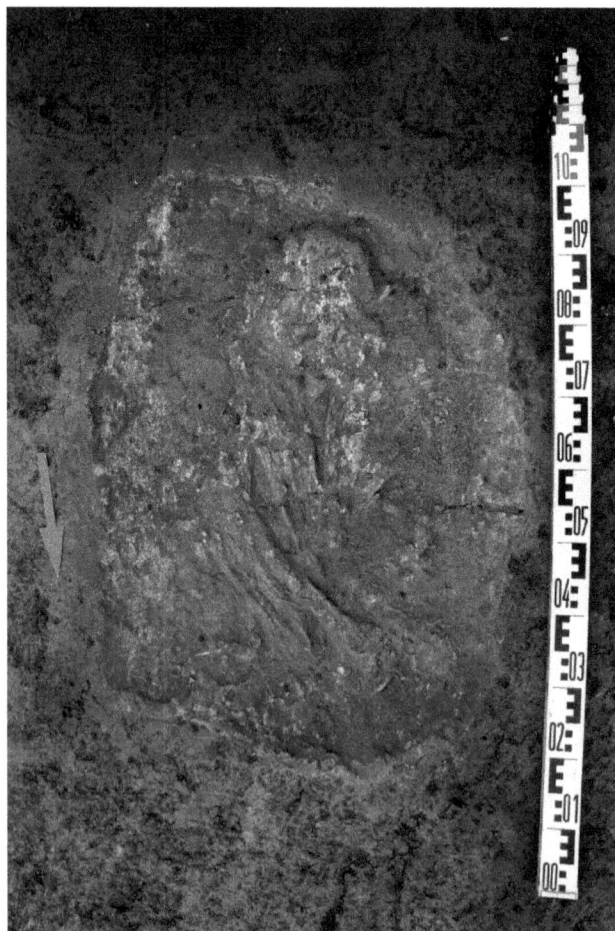

*Fig. 23. Subsidiary burial (100D) to grave no. 100 from Tell el-Farkha*

skull found at the top of an abandoned hearth (Maadi) or a few human phalanges unearthed in a structure filled with ash and charcoal labelled tomb 108 in Gerzeh.

Also the issue of incomplete and anatomically disordered burials is worth attention. The latter case may be interpreted as secondary burials, that is inhumations which belonged to people who had died outside a settlement and were later transported to the final cemetery destination. It is however much more difficult to assess the real significance of incomplete burials. Examples come from e.g. Gerzeh (Petrie et al. 1912: 8-10), where such graves were treated as remains of body mutilation practices – after the death or shortly before. Unfortunately, far younger Egyptian burial rituals descriptions quoted in the publication do not seem to be a sufficiently strong argument for the theory (Petrie et al. 1912: 11-15). Nevertheless, the case of Gerzeh is not alone, since incomplete burials are known from many other sites. Among them there should be mentioned Kafr Hassan Dawood (Tucker 2003: 523) or Tell el-Farkha (Dębowska-Ludwin 2010), where burials with skulls alone were also noted (grave no. 19), as well as phalanges thrown around the deceased body in grave no. 4 (Fig. 24). Similar practices were registered in Southern Egypt e.g. at the site of el-Adaima (Midant-Reynes et al. 1996; 2002a: 84), in Hierakonpolis (Friedman et al. 2002: 63-66) or Naqada. The famous and problematic tomb T5 (Petrie, Quibell 1896) comes from cemetery T in Naqada. It was there that the remains of numerous deceased arranged coincidentally, not in their proper anatomic position, were found. Although it is difficult to find here traces of ritual cannibalism – as the explorers wanted – we undoubtedly deal here with special practices applied to specific individuals. Special because they were significantly different from the standard. It remains an open question, whether tomb T5 is an example of a secondary burial or heralds the practice of subsidiary burials that were popular in the period of Dynasty 1, which probably covered remains of the main tomb elite owner's retinue.

*Fig. 24. Example of a partially disordered burial – grave no. 4 from Tell el-Farkha*

Unfortunately, discoveries of this kind fall outside full interpretation, mainly because of limited amount of data accessible for analyses. Probably, they testified to some forgotten burial related practices, however, we should stay aware that the actual causes of the presently registered state may be of various meanings.

# 5. SIDE BURIAL ELEMENTS

## 5.1. POTTERY PITS

They are connected solely to the activity of the Lower Egyptian culture. They were probably a supplementary element which was meant to compensate for relatively poor grave offerings, although their actual significance and rank remains unknown. Pottery pits, also called pottery groups, were found at cemeteries dated to the early (Wadi Digla, Heliopolis) and middle phase of the unit, too, in Sedment J and K, and es-Saff. They were invariably simple pits, structurally identical with those of burial use, different only in terms of their contents – typically functional complete and broken pottery vessels. In Wadi Digla they were concentrated in the central part of the cemetery, in four cases close to animal burials, however, the remaining sites do not demonstrate such a coincidence. It cannot be decided whether the pits full of pottery constituted a kind of supplementary equipment for one or a group of graves or an offering place connected with some burial practices in general. They may be possibly in relation to a few hearths registered at cemeteries of the Lower Egyptian culture of the period, their significance, however, also remains undefined.

## 5.2. ANIMAL BURIALS

They constitute one of the most interesting and imagination stimulating elements of Egyptian burial customs. They first came into light with the activity of the Lower Egyptian culture, where they formed a typical component of its customs and also most probably its original invention. Together with the decline of the unit, animal burials disappeared for a longer period of time to come out again in the prosperity time of the Early Dynastic age and to became a permanent element of the sepulchral sphere of ancient Egypt.

The oldest registered example, which heralds future popularity of the custom is a single dog burial dated to the beginning of the early phase of the culture and found within a small cemetery in Maadi. In later times, but still during the early phase, graves of lambs, dogs and goats should be regarded as an almost characteristic element of burial customs of the Lower Egyptian culture. Each animal was buried according to the rules typical of human individuals, in terms of simple pit construction, their orientation with heads southwards, localization within a typical extramural cemetery intended for a whole population and typical grave goods. The special significance of those burials is attested thanks to their richer offerings (at least in case of goats and lambs), which in the Lower Egyptian conditions and particularly during the early phase of the culture make them wealthy burials. Another special factor is the concentration of animal graves in special zones distinguished within regular cemeteries. The fact of such grouping and lack of

any possibility to connect particular animal burials with specific human graves does not induce to regard them as subsidiary burials and with the lack of other data makes their interpretation impossible.

Then, after a long brake the custom of burying animals in accordance with the rules normally applied to human individuals revived during the time of Dynasty 1. At the period, however, we undoubtedly deal with burials subsidiary to human ones. Not numerous examples are known from a few sites, where they were mostly registered next to tombs indicating wealth. Among the most interesting ones, triple burials of adult donkeys registered in Abusir North and Tarkhan should be mentioned. In the former case, the animals were buried in the standing position at the southern side of mastaba IV, put in a row and oriented along the east-west axis (Boessneck et al. 1992: 1-3), while in the latter similarly in the southern corridor around mastaba 2050 the donkey remains were discovered in an atypical grave of very elongated proportions divided into three chambers and partially dug under the perimeter wall of the main structure (Petrie 1914: 6). Single burials of donkeys and dogs from the period come also from Helwan and Abusir North still in the subsidiary context to human tombs. What is more, in Tarkhan in the mentioned mastaba 2050 there was additionally registered a unique subsidiary grave of a typical structural form and size which was hiding a duck skeleton (Petrie 1914: 6). Apart from this example two birds were registered in Turah el-Asmant in an atypical grave 191 (el-Khouli 1968: 74) in a small coffin of rough clay accompanied by miniature vessels and three unfired clay figurines representing tied and kneeling captives. Finally, the enumeration of those rather few preserved examples of animal burials dated to Dynasty 1 should be closed with grave no. 7 from Tell el-Farkha, where in the filling material of this interestingly furnished burial of an adult female and an infant besides many categories of goods, also a skeleton of a cobra *Naja Haje* (Abłamowicz 2004: 74) was registered, probably intentionally deposited there.

It is then clear that the approach to the issue of animal burials represented by the people of the Lower Egyptian culture and citizens of the united Egyptian kingdom of Dynasty 1 differed significantly. Originally, animals were treated with a special – even – respect, with their burials made up to wealthy human standards, later animals were appointed another clearly ancillary position within regular cemeteries used by more and more stratified populations. Regardless of the period we discuss, satisfying interpretation of the phenomenon still falls outside our cognition.

The phenomenon of animal burials was not strange either for the Upper Egyptian tradition. An excellent illustration of the subject are graves found in the south-western part of necropolis 6 in Hierakonpolis. In the vicinity of tomb 2 there were discovered remains of cattle, baboons, dogs, hippopotami, crocodiles and elephants (Hoffman 1982: 55), each buried in a separated pit or found in layers surrounding tombs and dated to the period from NIC to

NIII. Also interesting is tomb T13 from Hierakonpolis, dated to NIC-NIIA, where remains of a domesticated dogs were found over a human burial (Adams 2002: 20). Worth a mention are also remains of an elephant skeleton of *Loxodonta africana* from tomb T14, the NIC period. Another example is provided by at least seven young lions found in Abydos in tomb B16/12b-c (Boessneck, von den Driesch 1990: 86-89), most probably meant to keep company with king Aha in his eternal journey. Discoveries of relatively numerous independent animal burials and their remains in human graves, together with many objects of little plastic registered e.g. in Hierakonpolis (Adams 2002: 20-23) point to an important role played by animals in funerary beliefs also in Upper Egypt.

## 5.3. BOAT GRAVES

An interesting element of burial customs in ancient Egypt are boat/barge graves (O'Connor 1991) of only partially clear significance, however, they surely indicated a high social status of the tomb owner (Wilkinson 1996: 352-353). In Northern Egypt boat graves were registered at five sites (Abu Roash M, Abusir North, Saqqara North, Helwan and Ezbet Kamel Sedqi el-Qebleyah), each of them was located in the Memphis area, that is in the surroundings which focused the highest rank state elites. The number of boat graves is estimated at minimum 12. Since all known barge graves from the area are dated to the period between the reigns of Aha and Den, with the highest number from the end of the period, they seem to be characteristic of burial customs of Dynasty 1, with their temporary disappearance during Dynasty 2 and return at the Old Kingdom age.

In general, boats registered in Northern Egypt represented forms slightly different from examples known from the South. In the discussed area boats were shaped in two variants with the difference in stern and prow. In the first case both stern and prow were straight, in the second one – a stern was pointed and a prow rounded. The former type is similar to so-called Mesopotamian boats, used for sea sailing, the latter is a typical Egyptian papyrus boat used for the Nile navigation. The discovered boats were made of wood joined with ropes and before the funeral some elements of a cabin constructed on the main deck were partially dismantled (Emery 1958: 49) or were a kind of full size models made of bricks and mud. Two such examples are known from Abu Roash M tomb M25, where inside a panelled room in one case there was registered a human skeleton (Klasens 1960a: 110-111). Boat dimensions fluctuate significantly from the largest registered in Saqqara North and reaching up to 22.15m of length and 4.25m of width in their broadest part to the smallest known from Ezbet Kamel (3.8 x 1.4m).
Boat graves were planted on the surface, they were lined with mud bricks, plastered and filled up with sand (Saqqara North, tombs 3503 and 3506) or put into shallow pits with their shape following a boat outline with a low superstructure jutting over the surface level. Apart from those differences, it is unquestionable that

brick parts were built after a boat was placed in its final position. Such graves were subsidiary to large mastabas in Saqqara North and Abu Roash M or smaller structures in Helwan and Ezbet Kamel, which stood out at the background of the whole cemetery, most probably intended for an official of a high or middle rank. Boats themselves were usually oriented along the east-west axis and a shorter side of the main structure in a varying distance – from as far as 25m north from the model estate of tomb 3357 in Saqqara North to the closed space within the perimeter wall of tomb 3506 also in Saqqara North. Doubtlessly, boat graves built as side elements of impressive tombs were of symbolic significance, related to a deceased journey to the beyond, however, their closer interpretation, in the light of presently accessible data, remains impossible.

## 5.4. MODEL BUILDINGS

In the Early Dynastic period, the classic burial custom was enriched with other new elements, such as model buildings, which accompanied the most impressive tombs, both in terms of the state – e.g. Saqqara North – as well as particular sites, where they had been founded. Doubtlessly, the most interesting example is the so-called model estate (Emery 1954: 171). It is a structure (a complex of terraces and model buildings), which was discovered during surface cleaning in between tomb 3357 and its boat burial in 1937. At first the age of the structure was assessed as younger, but the idea was reconsidered thanks to pottery analyses, which proved it was actually a part of the burial complex devoted to the owner of tomb 3357, and thus dated to the reign of Aha. The structure's function remains undefined. W. Emery suggested it was a model of a palace or it took part in rituals connected with the owner's cult (he pointed to analogies with the complex of Netjerikhet), on the other hand, however, the model buildings bring into mind a series of granaries known from relief decoration of the Old Kingdom date, especially those three characteristically rounded. Regardless of its practical significance, the structure was unusual because of one feature – barrel vault which ran over the whole length of a passage located between the buildings. Unfortunately, it cannot be stated what the original size of the white plastered estate was. The material used for constructing the structure is worth a mention – it was rubble tightly covered with mud plaster which enabled to engrave details of the façade decoration.

Presence of other interesting structures interpreted as granaries or their models supports such an explanation of the function of the above described mysterious estate which accompanied tomb 3357 from Saqqara North. An especially interesting example is the northern chamber of the superstructure from tomb 3038 (Emery 1949: 85). It was furnished with a long bench 0.8m wide and 1.3m high, which ran along the chamber's eastern, northern and western walls. The bench supported nine granaries in the form of a cylindrical pottery container with a hole in their upper part. The hole was closed with a pottery stopper, while the second one located close to the

*Fig. 25. Granary models from grave no. 50 at Tell el-Farkha*

container bottom was corked and sealed. Worth a mention are also: the so-called model granary from tomb 2105 in Saqqara (Quibell 1923: 2) equipped with an atypical tunnel which lead to the burial located beneath; a pit interpreted as an imitation of four silos (Jeffreys 1999: 368) registered in Helwan, or representing the same idea but on a highly reduced scale miniature granary models of pottery registered in the context of grave no. 50 from Tell el-Farkha (see Kołodziejczyk 2009 – Fig. 25). Irrespective of the actual size of model granaries, their presence is observed in burial context, which supports their significance for burial customs. Possibly, then, we deal here with a kind of belief in rebirth represented by growing crops and known from pharaonic periods, e.g. from the cult of Osiris.

When discussing model buildings, also model staircases, latrines and bathrooms should be mentioned. They were registered e.g. in tombs 2302 and 2337 in Saqqara (Quibell 1923: 35-36). Their significance, similarly as in the case of granaries, was certainly symbolic, since it is bound up in time with the expansion of substructures equipped with numerous rooms which followed a typical layout of housing constructions inhabited by the tomb's owner before his or her death. And finally, a model palace and a whole model town recognised within gallery tombs of kings of Dynasty 2 from Saqqara should also be mentioned here as a relatively late continuation of the general idea.

## 5.5. MORTUARY CHAPELS

The oldest building in the history of ancient Egyptian architecture interpreted as a mortuary chapel accompanied tomb 3505 from Saqqara North and is dated to the reign of Qa'a. It was built by the northern and shorter side of the main tomb within the perimeter wall (Emery 1958: 10). The chapel was composed of a labyrinth of rooms and corridors, among which chamber labelled no. 7 was paved with a stone floor, while the others were floored with bricks and plastered. Walls of particular rooms were covered with mats and also plastered, in addition rooms nos 7 and 8 were painted

yellow and black. The chapel was accessible from outside and through it led the actual passage to the main tomb body.

A small statue annex accompanied tomb 2407 from Saqqara North. Its localization  resembles the above described chapel from tomb 3505, and therefore interpretation of its function is also connected with mortuary cult practices. Another structure, which remains unlabelled and which was discovered north to tomb 3030, represents a similar situation. The construction had a very complicated layout and was oriented along the north-south axis. It was unearthed in 1935 in Saqqara North and since then it has been only briefly mentioned in a few publications (Jeffreys, Tavares 1994: 148). It was a brick and rectangular building (12.85 x 11m in size, preserved to the height of 1.65m) with its inner walls plastered and painted white. Unfortunately, the structure was severely damaged during the construction of neighbouring tomb 3030. Probably the same happened to the tomb the building was originally connected to.

## 5.6. NICHES

Niches seem to be an element of North Egyptian origin. Most commonly they were two-stepped and decorated outer façades of early mastabas' superstructures and during a long period of time they were one of mastabas' characteristic features. However, niches were also registered inside a burial chamber of a visibly less impressive burial from Minshat Abu Omar labelled with no. 2275 (Kroeper 1992: 134-136).

The oldest examples of niches in sepulchral architecture come from Tell el-Farkha. The first of them, although still incompletely excavated is the large mastaba from the period NIIA2/NIIIB with its eastern (and possibly also southern) decorated with these elements (Fig. 8). More illustrations come from slightly younger graves dated to NIIIB (nos 63, 94 and 100) which preserved from one to four niches in their northern, southern and/or eastern façade. Further examples from the same site are dated to the period of Dynasty 1 (nos 55 and possibly 9). The

*Fig. 26. Example of a niche from grave no. 63 at Tell el-Farkha*

most impressive among them was grave no. 63 with accented corners of its northern wall and four beautifully modelled two-stepped niches, which were shaped in the eastern façade of the structure (Fig. 26). The enclosure of grave no. 55 comprised only two small niches, however, it belongs to the end of Dynasty 1. Although, these structures are interesting and rather significant, it should be kept in mind that they represent burials of local Deltaic elites and not state officials. The best constructions with niche decoration were registered at elite cemeteries in the Memphite area with the longest series from Saqqara North. During the reign of Qa'a in the period of numerous changes introduced into sepulchral architecture niched façades were gradually vanishing in keeping with a general trend which turned the constructors' interest from superstructures towards much deeper and more complicated underground rooms. A forecast of the tendency is tomb 3505 from Saqqara North, where the western wall was decorated with niches, however, they were much simplified and shallower. Another tomb dated to the reign of the same king from the same cemetery and labelled with no. 3500 was equipped only with two niches of a probable symbolic significance, while the remaining walls were left plain and undecorated. The niches were modelled in the eastern façade by its southern end and additionally furnished with rolls made of mud. W. Emery (1958: 100) explained them as a model for false door popular in later times. Niches interpreted as space for statues were found also in the case of graves nos 3120 and 3121.

Also another unique and relatively small structure registered in the Delta at Tell el-Mashala'a is dated to the reign of Dynasty 1. It was oriented along the north-south axis, the entrance led through a little courtyard and in its southern wall there was discovered a small niche (el-Hagg Ragab 1992: 212). Similarly, tomb 137/76 from Turah el-Asmant, although severely damaged, still

appears to be quite impressive (at least 10.5 x 5m) and preserved two large almost square rooms connected by inner passages with niches located in its northern and eastern walls (el-Sadeek, Murphy 1983: 159). At the same time so-called false door came to burial tradition typical of Dynasty 2, they were present e.g. in Saqqara North in tombs 2307 (Quibell 1923: 31) and 2337 (Quibell 1923: 35-36).

## 5.7. TUMULULI

They constitute a burial element rarely present at Northern Egyptian cemeteries. The few examples date back to the period of Dynasty 0, e.g. from Kafr Hassan Dawood (Tucker 2003: 532), where over many burials small heaps were registered. They were of simple construction, built on the surface of mud, sand and gravel. Similarly in Tarkhan, there were unearthed (Petrie 1914: 2) little heaps made of sand and covered with natural gypsum, which secured smaller graves. However, the most interesting tumulus which represent one of rebuilt phases of tomb 3507 in Saqqara North (Emery 1958: 77) then covered with a superstructure in a mastaba type decorated with niched façade is dated to the reign of Den. It was constructed of sand and rubble and covered with a single layer of bricks, which gave it a regular shape – convex in its section and rectangular in its layout with clearly marked sharp edges and dimensions 10.5 x 9.2 x 1.1m of height. A similar, though much worse preserved tumulus was discovered also in the superstructure of tomb 3471 (Emery 1958: 75), as well as in tombs 3038 and 3111 at the same site. According to A. Tavares (1999: 703) these mounds represent southern tradition and were among the elements meant to integrate southern and northern burial customs into a single construction.

# 6. EARLY NORTHERN EGYPTIAN BURIAL CUSTOMS IN CONCLUSION

In the early sepulchral material from Northern Egypt, a series of general rules can be distinguished which created the picture of burial customs. With emerging and vanishing cultures as well as economic and political changes, these rules were evolving, in some period being more strictly followed, in others treated rather freely. When discussing these changes, it should be kept in mind, however, they were nothing more than unwritten guidelines, not strict rules, which was reflected by numerous exceptional cases, original, unique, unsuccessful or forgotten solutions. The whole appears to be an interesting and diversified picture, in some moments predominated by particular tendencies with a noticeable development line. The number of graves and cemeteries used in certain periods illustrates a general growth tendency with its climax during the reign of Dynasty 1 (Chart no. 3).

The earliest registered remains of burial activity are connected with the cultures of Merimde and Omari. Unfortunately, they have brought material which forms no basis for explicit statement whether the dead were buried then within actually inhabited settlements or the fact they were discovered there reflects later shifts on the occupied area. Doubtlessly, extramural burial custom was developed by the Lower Egyptian culture and since its time it became a universally accepted pattern, though with an early exception which concerned fetuses and infants intentionally kept within settlements. With the passing time even this custom was less and less

A general rule seems to be burying the deceased in single graves. Taking into consideration the overall number of burials, cases with two individuals buried in a single tomb are in the minority and they usually comprised remains of young females and infants. There were, of course, registered graves with several adult individuals placed in a single chamber or tombs with two burial chambers, however, regardless of the period it was an absolutely marginal phenomenon. With the assumption that the largest sets of subsidiary burials connected with mastabas of Dynasty 1 were founded at the moment when the main burial was being closed, also these examples can be interpreted as a special form of mass burial. But they were very infrequently registered and were also marginally practiced customs. The most strictly observed rules were those of body position, material used for building burial structures and offering sets.

## 6.1. THE DECEASED POSITION

During the whole Pre- and Early Dynastic period in Northern Egypt there was a single popularly accepted rule. It was burying the deceased in a more or less contracted side position. Differences typical of particular epochs were based on greater popularity of right or left side and orientation of the heads towards a chosen direction. At the beginning, one can mention only general tendencies when one of numerous possible positions slightly predominated, however, the situation gradually standardized to became, finally, generally (although never strictly) followed rule over the whole territory influenced by the Naqadan culture. And thus, in the case of the Merimde culture the slightly preferable position of

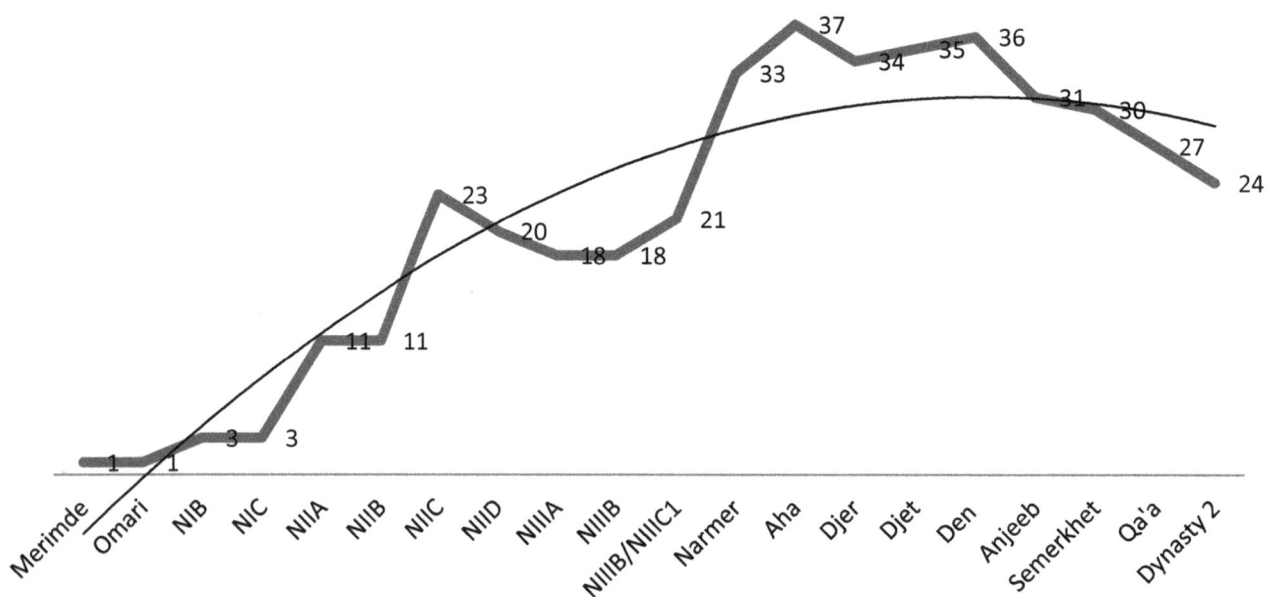

*Chart no. 3. Number of sites used in particular periods with the trend line of the development*

*Fig. 27. Basalt bowl "consumed" during disintegration of food offerings – grave no. 99 from Tell el-Farkha*

the dead was the right side one with the head southwards. The Omari culture burials were visibly predominated by those in the left side position, the head to south. The people of the Lower Egyptian culture in general preferred the right side position with heads turned southwards, although almost all other combinations were also rather frequently used. The next change (but the last one in the period in question) was connected with the expansion of the Naqada culture, when the previously popular customs were supplanted by a pattern imported from the South, that is the preference of the left side and head orientation to north. However, the important change was not introduced with a single move, but rather slowly and gradually, while a greater consistency in following strict burial rules dates not earlier than to the NIIIA period.

Interestingly, orientation of graves along the north-south axis and usually with a small declination to east became the most commonly followed rule. Moreover, a burial placed within such a structure could be oriented to north or south regardless of the chosen side. When a burial construction was oriented along any other axis it was usually caused by clearly practical factors as landform features or the need for adaptation to already existing structures. In the Early Dynastic period the rules concerning bodies orientation seem to be established and generally accepted, however, much information is presently inaccessible due to spreading burials' plundering and then numerous disturbances within burials.

From the times of the Merimde culture ancient communities tried to protect their deceased from direct contact with the earth which filled in a burial. The oldest solution was to wrap bodies in a mat or leather and its crowning was the introduction of coffins at the beginning of the Early Dynastic period, which were made of practically every accessible material – from mud, through plaiting and wood to pottery and sporadically even stone, sometimes covered with a lid of the same material shaped as flat or convex. By the end of the period in question coffins became a common element of burial customs registered at almost every site, both in wealthy graves of more elaborated architectural form and those poorer

placed in small and simple pits dug into the ground. The most valuable objects of an eventual offering set like metal items, jewellery, small personal objects, miniature vessels (especially of stone) etc. were actually closed inside coffins, just beside their owner.

Special rules concerned child burials. The youngest members of ancient Egyptian societies were from the very beginning buried in storage jars which played the role of later introduced coffins. In these burials fetus and infant bodies were posed similarly as it was in the case of adults, that is in the contracted position, usually left-sided, with the head to north, however, the general rule was less frequently followed in comparison to graves of the remaining parts of the society. The youngest child burials were located within settlement areas which were in use at the time, or within regular cemeteries in graves shared with young women customarily recognized as mothers who died in confinement. Unfortunately, lack of genetic material from these graves makes it impossible to achieve one hundred percent accuracy of such a statement. Burials of fetuses and infants were usually left devoid of offerings. From an undefined age on young members of those early communities were regarded sufficiently mature to be buried within regular cemeteries, then in accordance with the commonly followed rules.

## 6.2. GRAVE OFFERINGS

The idea of furnishing the deceased was known from the earliest manifestations of burial customs registered in Northern Egypt. Among numerous objects which comprised an offering set the most important – from the point of view of its frequency – was pottery, originally typically functional and together with the Naqadan expansion also produced exclusively for burial use. There were also many registered remains of food offerings, although it seems possible they were the most popular goods, due to their perishable nature they were rather rarely preserved (Fig. 27). Another category of items put into graves are personal adornments, objects of daily use, tools, stone vessels and their models, imported objects, pieces of games, tokens and a long series of undefined

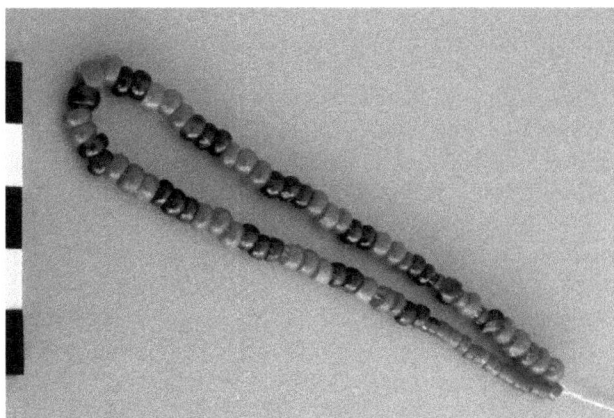

*Fig. 28. Necklace composed of carnelian beads – grave no. 98 from Tell el-Farkha*

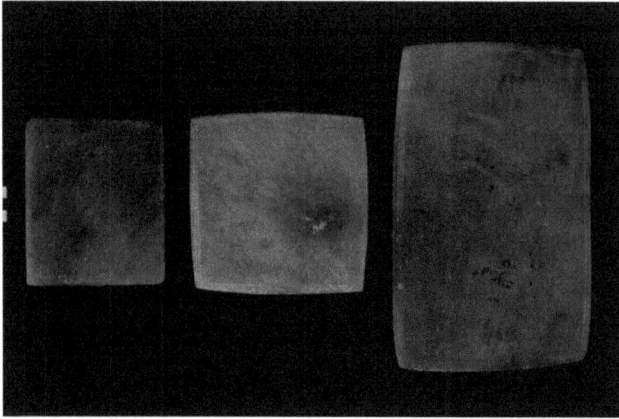

*Fig. 29. Geometric cosmetic palettes of greywacke –
grave no. 99 from Tell el-Farkha*

items. The number and quality of these objects was
changing in time, still indicating social status of their
owner and picturing evolution of the structure of the early
Egyptian society. Also, it seems that the idea of richly
equipped graves does not belong to native Lower
Egyptian tradition.

Originally, in the Merimde culture offerings for the dead
were rarely attested and if they were present they would
be mostly modest food offerings and few pottery vessels.
Graves of the Omari culture were definitely more often
equipped, moreover, with a vaster array of possible
objects like: pottery vessels, food offerings, wooden
items, shells, beads – still poorly and in single pieces.
Some differentiation in this respect is registered from the
times of the Lower Egyptian culture, which used to equip
around a half of its deceased with more numerous
categories of objects and during its evolution it tended
towards more and more affluent sets. A typical equipment
was composed of a single pottery jar chosen among
popular functional pottery types, very often badly worn
out. Sporadically registered objects of different categories
(flint tools, stone vessels, Nilotic mollusc shells, dyes,
personal objects made of bone, elements of personal
adornments, first discoveries of eroded copper objects)
were a kind of curiosity, hardly ever representing any
significant worth. A rule seems to be native origin of
particular artifacts accompanying burials.

The repertoire of offerings registered in cemeteries of
Naqadan tradition in the NII period was rather limited,
though in comparison to native Lower Egyptian customs
it was definitely richer. Typical burials were equipped
with: pottery jars, stone vessels of colour stones and their
models; beads and pendants from necklaces; zoomorphic,
shield-shaped and round cosmetic palettes; few flint
knives and copper tools; spoons and pins of ivory;
sporadically registered imported objects and other unique
items. It must be mentioned that there is a visible
tendency towards gradually richer grave equipment,
which is represented by the example of the cemetery in
Abusir el-Meleq. By the end of the Predynastic period
apart from the previously known categories of objects a
typical offering set was enlarged with numerous
luxurious objects like: imported vessels, stone, bone or

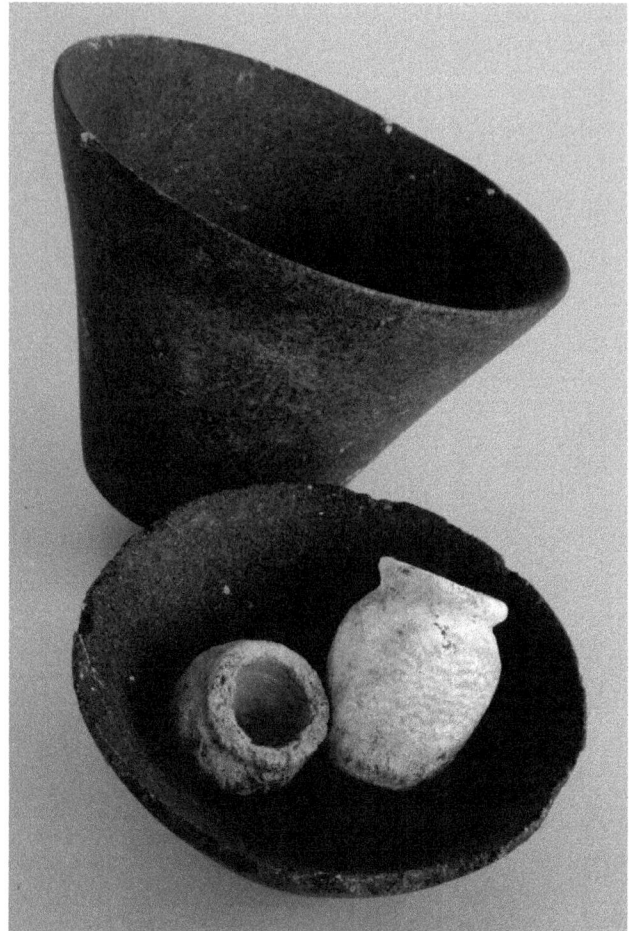

*Fig. 30. Stone vessels from grave no. 114 at Tell el-
Farkha*

rarely copper vessels. It seems significant that regardless
of some small local differences in burial customs typical
offering sets were invariably composed of objects of the
above quoted categories, what is more, representing very
similar types.

The time of Dynasty 0 brought mainly increasing number
of offerings, since in terms of goods categories those
registered in the previous period were the same. A
novelty is the use of a wider and wider range of colour
stones, that is basalt, travertine, limestone, greywacke,
marble, dolomite, breccia, serpentine, amethyst, onyx,
steatite, carnelian and porphyry (Fig. 28). Another
innovation is a wider set of cosmetics objects: in
particular cosmetic palettes in geometric forms (Fig. 29),
numerous boxes and fragments of ivory and copper
objects of often undefined function, copper tools and seal
impressions.

Similarly, offerings from the period of Dynasty 1 only
insignificantly changed and became richer and more
abundant in luxurious objects, many times produced in
the finest workshops. The repertoire of goods itself
basically remained the same:
• pottery vessels, often registered in hundreds of items,
produced locally but also imported, in particular
from the Levant;

Fig. 31. Deposit of travertine vessels from the cemetery at
Tell el-Farkha

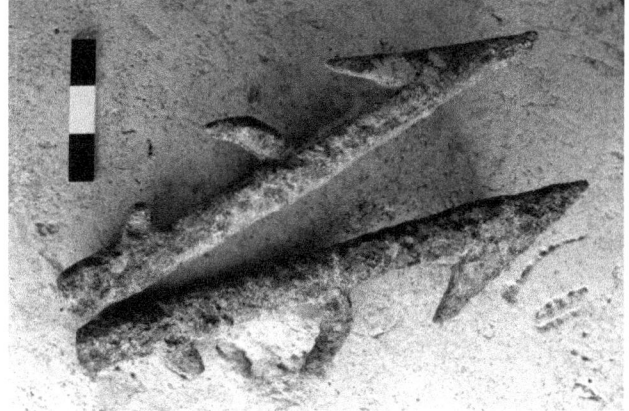

Fig. 32. Copper harpoons from grave no. 55 at Tell el-
Farkha

- numerous stone vessels made of colourful and valuable materials (alabaster/travertine, limestone, greywacke, dolomite, black basalt, steatite, serpentine, porphyry, tuff, rock crystal, breccia, amfibolite, quartz – Figs 30 and 31);
- copper vessels;
- tools and weapons, as well as their models – wooden sickles with flint blades, wooden sticks, leather, bone and wooden quivers with arrows, bunches of arrows, arrow heads, harpoons, flint knives and scrapers, wet stones, wooden spears with ivory heads, copper tools as: knives, saws, hatchets, hoes, chisels, harpoons (Fig. 32), tools for engravings, borers, needles, awls (Fig. 33), knife and hatchet hilts as well as complete axes, hatchet spears, mace heads;
- copper plaques of unknown significance;
- discs made of limestone, copper, ivory, horn or wood;
- wooden and bone plaques – uninscribed and with inscriptions;
- sets of game pieces, sometimes still resting in leather pouches as well as so-called marbles/tokens (Figs 34 and 35), game sticks and game boards;
- zoo- and antropomorphic figurines;
- flint nodules;

- seals and their impressions;
- furniture and their fragments: legs shaped as bull's limbs made of ivory which were parts of cases or game boards, copper knobs from beds, copper nails which bound wooden elements, wooden chairs and beds, headrests, a large stone table with movable legs;
- rhinoceros horns made of pottery;
- personal adornments, such as: copper bracelets with decoration, bracelets of shells, ivory or leather, pendants, amulets and beads of various materials;
- ivory vessels (Fig. 36);
- golden foil cut into straps;
- animals bones – some with intentionally incised furrows;
- decorative box; spoons (Fig. 37), bodkins and needles;
- leather bags, baskets, shells; fragments of mats from floors, pieces of cloths, flattened papyrus rolls, fragments of ropes; shoe elements;
- cosmetic palettes of greywacke, cosmetics sticks of ivory, combs, hair pins;
- fragments of walking sticks;
- inscriptions on ivory, wood, stone vessels, pottery and impressed in mud;
- inscribed stelae,
- food offerings
- and a long series of unusual objects of an undefined function like: a wooden object in the form of a disc

Fig. 33. Bone awl from grave no. 24 at Tell el-Farkha

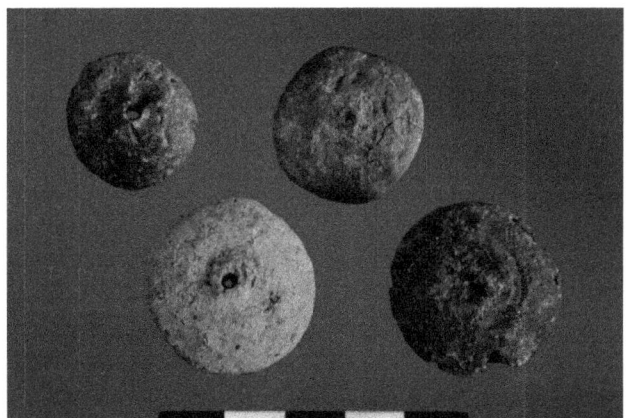

Fig. 34. Various types of tokens

*Fig. 35. Various types of tokens*

with an incrusted wooden box for it; a limestone fragment with black painted silhouettes of a bull and donkey; numerous objects of ivory; so-called castanets, etc.

In general, during Dynasty 2 the range of possible objects comprising an offering set is the same as in the previous period, though items of luxurious character seem to be more popular and present in a vaster array. Certainly, the most predominant are pottery vessels, then followed by vessels made of stone: limestone, travertine, granite, breccia, diorite, greywacke, porphyry, tuff, marble, basalt, amphibolite, anorthozite, quartz and rock crystal;

*Fig. 36. Miniature cylinder ivory vessel from grave no. 24 at Tell el-Farkha*

*Fig. 37. Bone spoon from grave no. 9 at Tell el-Farkha*

imported objects; there were also registered numerous tools of copper (among them their miniatures) and flint; numerous so-called marbles which seem to be tokens or elements of an unknown game made of carnelian, agate, colour limestone and quartz; various beads and pendants of carnelian, faience, limestone, travertine, amethyst, ivory, steatite and rock crystal; small objects of ivory and copper (e.g. miniature vessels, so-called castanets with a curved animal head, hairpins and needles, tablets, spoons, harpoons); cosmetic palettes; wet stones; cosmetic boxes of greywacke and ivory; cylindrical seals; shells; pieces of furniture; stone tables; stelae and many other objects often inscribed.

With the assumption that all these small items which constituted offering sets were objects of daily use and were meant to serve their owners in the afterlife, also additional architectural elements built with the most impressive tombs of Dynasty 1 like boats or subsidiary burials should be treated as a special category of grave goods. They were then offerings in the sense of objects of various scale, so their function was to serve the deceased and since state dignitaries of the highest level were probably used to luxury, they took with them also whole palaces, boats or hosts of servants.

## 6.3. CONSTRUCTION OF BURIAL CHAMBERS

The registered archaeological material displays a great diversity of burial structures' types. Appendices 3-5 gather them with the enumeration of sites, where particular constructions were discovered. The sites were arranged in alphabetical order with the exception of those where publications do not precise the form of graves registered there.

### SIMPLE PIT GRAVES

The simplest and the most popular grave construction during the whole period in question were simple pits, usually oval and round, less frequently elongated and rectangular, or close to rectangular with rounded edges, almost square and triangular, or the ones dug shallowly in the ground which were meant for the poorest. Average dimensions of such a pit did not exceed 1m in its widest point and enabled to bury only a tightly fitted human body.

However, with more and more abundant appearance of grave goods dimensions of typical pits were gradually growing to include a complete offering set. Up to the Naqadan expansion pit graves were the only used solution (it concerns also Gerzeh – the earliest Naqadan site in Northern Egypt), with a small and unsatisfactorily explained example of previously functional pits of habitation and economic significance adapted for burials and known from Omari. Already at the earliest development stage of the simple grave form the pits' bottom and walls were inlayed with mats and sporadically with branches to separate bodies from direct contact with plain earth. It is possible that not numerous stones registered in graves connected with the Omari and Lower Egyptian cultures had also a similar practical meaning as preventing collapse of grave pits' walls. During the Early Dynastic period the practice of reinforcing simple pits with every accessible material (stones but also bricks, wood, partial and total plastering with mud) is well evidenced although only at sites with surface covered with loose and unstable layers. It is worth stressing here that in the case of the Merimde, Omari and Lower Egyptian cultures simple pits were typical grave structures for all burials regardless of the number and quality of goods but after mud bricks were introduced pit graves started to be regarded mediocre and became representative for the poorest, usually unfurnished burials.

A slightly different solution to include the growing offering set in a grave was a category which emerged during Dynasty 1, namely a side niche placed to the east of the deceased.

## PIT GRAVES LINED WITH MUD BRICKS

From NIIC, that is the period of much intensified contacts between the classical Lower Egyptian culture and small Naqadan groups, which were slowly entering the Delta, mud bricks were also introduced to grave structures as a useful material which offered new and much wider possibilities of enlarging constructions, marking off rooms and complicating their layout. From the moment of its appearance in this function the new building material became inseparably connected with the most elaborated burial constructions in Egypt. It is worth mentioning that structures built of mud bricks were also more interestingly equipped. The new material cuboid in its shape could have played an important role in the popularization of rectangular grave shape, which in earlier times was a minority. And therefore, previously common simple pit graves were lined with bricks of standard shape and size, first partially and finally completely. Judging by recent discoveries e.g. at Tell el-Farkha (just to name the empty monumental mastaba or large mud brick structures like grave no. 100 with visibly smaller amount of offerings than storing capacity of the burial chamber), it is even possible that soon after their introduction as a practical means, bricks also gained some

additional importance which was accenting the social status of a grave owner. Apart from the tentative suggestion, thanks to the effort of brick lining, an actual burial chamber came into existence. Such a chamber was then covered with a kind of roof made of plaiting, mats or wood, in later periods sometimes even of stone slabs. The majority of these pit tombs lined with bricks was single-chambered and of average dimensions from 1m to ca. 2.5m of length and 0.8 to ca. 1.5m of width. Probably with the growing number of offering objects it became necessary to internally divide larger chambers of this type (ca. 5m long and 2m wide) into the actual burial chamber meant for the deceased and the smallest and most valuable objects of his/her equipment and side storage chambers often tightly packed mostly with pottery.

There were registered at least a few variants of internal chamber division:

- in the first of them in keeping with the general structure orientation along the north-south axis, storage chambers were located at one shorter end of a grave pit, that is to north or south;
- there are some three-chamber examples with side rooms at both shorter ends;
- there were also registered four-chamber structures with two smaller rooms at one shorter end and another larger room at the opposite end of a grave pit or adjoining the smaller rooms. In some cases outer walls of storage rooms were left rough and unlined;
- also some rather unique five-chamber tombs were discovered (the actual burial chamber and two storage rooms at both shorter ends).

It seems, however, that the internal layout of tombs was increasingly complicated with time and those structures with more rooms emerged a little later. The period of Dynasty 1 did not contribut largely to innovative solutions, being focused on continuation of previously chosen trends, complication of internal layout of tombs reaching even 13 chambers or sporadically occurring double burial chambers and more frequent presence of multi-chamber structures. One of rare novelties are barrel vaults which were registered only at some chosen sites in the central area and locally popular in Turah simple pits adjacent to typical bricked graves meant to fit offerings. A small number of graves undoubtedly dated to the period of Dynasty 2 makes it difficult to properly state what was the exact popularity of particular constructions lined with bricks. It seems that the most common were rectangular one-, two- or three-chamber graves of the types known from the previous period. Simultaneously, it was quite often registered that many structures, mostly at peripheral cemeteries, were built rather carelessly.

## GRAVES WITH STAIRCASES

This is a type which emerged around the times of Dynasty 1. Its presence is registered at sites located in the Nile Valley in areas whose geological structure facilitated digging deep trenches. They stand out because of a straight and then turning at the right angle staircases which led to the actual burial chamber, usually preceded with a vestibule. The burial chamber itself could be hewn into bedrock or had its walls lined with mud bricks, sometimes in later times even with stone. The chamber shape was usually square or rectangular, in some cases there was a bricked wall built centrally to separate the deceased from offerings placed behind his/her back. Dimensions of such a chamber were also diverse – from little to rather large with its ceiling supported by a pillar or enlarged with side niches in the number from one to four. A development of this type of grave are examples with additional storage chambers located at both sides of a vestibule, or with more and more numerous chambers separately hewn in the bedrock, typical at the end of the discussed. Also worth a mention here is the introduction and growing popularity of burial security by means of closing entrances with massive portcullises or by bricking them up. In addition these security solutions were repeatedly placed in various locations in staircases and vestibules. It is noteworthy that the increased popularity of these structures was noted during Dynasty 2.

## SHAFT GRAVES

The second type of deep and slightly less complicated graves were shaft constructions. They were composed of a vertical shaft 0.82-5.25m deep, which led to the actual burial chamber in a form of a small niche or a room of a regular shape sometimes enlarged with side niches. The chamber entrance was usually secured with a wall of bricks or little stones and only exceptionally preceded with a small vestibule. A single tomb of this construction was composed of a single chamber, however, there are registered examples with two burial chambers placed at the same level side by side, opposite each other or one over the another. By the end of Dynasty 1 and during Dynasty 2 tombs with a more expanded substructure composed of numerous rooms independently hewn into bedrock became popular. Their walls were lined with stone and entrances secured similarly as it was in the case of tombs with staircases. The only change observed by the end of the period in question was a rather bold use of stone both for wall lining, ceilings and entrances security next to the still popular mud bricks.

A composition of both hitherto described categories are tombs deeper in general and furnished with staircases and shafts, which however were not commonly represented.

## MASTABAS

They were the most impressive sepulchral structures built in the period in question. The oldest of them is the magnificent construction from Tell el-Farkha dated to the turn of NIIIA2/NIIIB1, which – taking into consideration its elaborated architectural form – probably was not a unique edifice of this type, however, it is the only one that has been discovered. Only a little younger structures from the site, like graves nos 100 and 63 were

outstanding against the background of the cemetery but hardly monumental. Therefore, the actual North Egyptian successors of the mastaba from Tell el-Farkha were great mastabas dated to Dynasty 1 with their largest concentration in Saqqara North – the site regarded as a major necropolis of the highest state officials at the time. All these structures were constructed of mud bricks, although through centuries of their popularity they visibly evolved and people started using stone for some of the elements. What is highly interesting is the fact that the building materials were used with full professional knowledge of the possibilities they offered, their strength and limitations (see La Loggia 2011). The oldest mastabas were composed of an expanded superstructure and relatively shallow substructure which included only the actual burial chamber and a few small storage rooms, while it was the superstructure that consumed the majority of efforts due to numerous rooms tightly fitted with most of the offerings. These early examples had no entrances or other communication facilities inside, that is why it is commonly accepted that burial chambers were closed just after the funeral and above them magnificent superstructures were built. More or less from the reign of Den in these tombs occurred first staircases which led from the outside to the deeper and deeper burial chamber. At first, staircases were straight, then they became elongated and by late Dynasty 1 they turned at the right angle and were often secured with brick walls or massive slabs of stone which blocked the entrance. Newly registered elements from about the middle of Dynasty 1 were also shafts which led to a deep substructure and ramps dated from the reign of Qa'a. Moving the major part of a mastaba below the surface level, which took place around the end of Dynasty 1, was accompanied by a change in the form of superstructure. It became an embankment of rubble and sand built around with bricks, which gave it its regular, simple and undecorated form.

A burial chamber was originally placed rather shallowly below the surface level. It was then a simple pit dug in the ground, sometimes divided into smaller rooms with brick and thin walls. Gradually a larger interest in its form was visible and thus, there were registered chambers lined with bricks, wood or finally with stone. Increasingly deeper dug substructures typical of the period from the middle of Dynasty 1 resulted in its complete hewing into bedrock and then dividing it into smaller rooms with brick walls and finally, from the middle of Dynasty 2, independently hewn rooms which comprised a substructure. Some of these rooms are interpreted as underground counterparts of typically housing elements, such as bathrooms and latrines. This complicated the layout of inner tomb rooms where a burial chamber corresponds to a bedroom, adjoining rooms to private apartments and a series of storage and side rooms to an economic part of a luxurious villa, leads to the conclusion that the early North Egyptian mastaba was meant to be home for the deceased, built following the example of a typical residence of the period.

Outer walls of a brick mastaba body were decorated with so-called niche façade (from the reign of Qa'a this solution was gradually vanishing in favour of plain façades and single niches, later converted into so-called false doors), sometimes painted white, black, red and yellow as well as surrounded with a bench with bull heads plastically modelled in mud. Elements connected with an earlier phase of the mastaba type development were also wooden beams placed horizontally in upper parts of niches and poles discovered at some distance from the mastaba body, also in front of the niches. The actual tomb composed of the above discussed elements was usually closed within a perimeter wall to create a kind of mortuary complex with a narrow corridor around the tomb body and often, although not always, with additional side elements as subsidiary burials, boats or a shrine. A probably significant part of such tombs were granaries and their models located inside the constructions but also outside the perimeter wall.

At many sites there were, of course, registered structures commonly called small mastabas. They obviously rendered the idea of the greatest tombs on a smaller scale, suitable for their owners' status – locally significant but not in the state hierarchy.

## GALLERIES

This type of tombs constitutes the crowning achievement in the process of substructures' expansion, being characteristic of royal burials in the Dynasty 2 period. Galleries were constructed on a complicated layout of numerous corridors, vestibules and chambers which covered the area even over a few hectares. Entrances to these deeply cut structures led through a shaft or staircase, however, the issue of whether the entrances were accessible when passing through possible superstructures is unsatisfactorily explained since scarce remains of an overground structure were preserved over only one gallery. There are two such galleries known, both located in Saqqara and dated to the beginning of Dynasty 2, but it is possible they were not unique and other structures of this type had been built. It is also highly possible they were later incorporated into e.g. the burial complex of king Netjerikhet/Djoser, thus they could constitute the direct link between the Early Dynastic period and the Old Kingdom and an important contribution to the Old Kingdom architecture.

## 6.4. SUPERSTRUCTURES

The issue of marking the actual place where a burial was located on the surface of cemeteries remains unclear. At many sites spatial distribution of graves points to their intentional arrangement to avoid mutual cutting of tombs, however, there are also such cemeteries (like e.g. Kom el-Khilgan) where burials often intersected the other ones. Although the original surface of the majority of early sites was badly damaged, it seems to be a rule that the poorest graves were not marked on cemeteries surfaces and various solutions applied within the long time in

question of constructing superstructures were reserved for tombs treated in a special manner, most probably due to social or economic status of their owners.

First remains of superstructures were registered already in Omari, where some kinds of canopies made of perishable materials were constructed over several burials, or stones were arranged in circles around burial pits. A visible development is noted not earlier than in Protodynastic, when small heaps of mud, sand and gravel emerged, sometimes covered with mud plaster. A more popular – especially during Dynasty 1 – type of superstructure of mostly pit graves lined with bricks was covering them with a bricked mantle or a more massive, regularly shaped cover. Such a cover in its outline repeated the shape of the substructure and was composed of regular layers of bricks or overbuilt on a heap of earth which a burial chamber was filled with. In some cases there was even a clear break between the sub- and superstructure and even a shift of their orientation, although they unquestionably belonged to a single construction. Most probably superstructures of this kind were meant to be visible on the surface and played the role of a tombstone, clearly marking the position of a burial.

In general, a growing interest in superstructures and consequently, their gradual complication is typical of the period of Dynasty 1. Superstructures evolved then rather quickly to large-sized and multi-chambered mastabas, which were only an element of sepulchral enclosures built over burials of representatives of the highest social elites. Smaller bricked structures usually erected over graves outstanding against the background of a particular site and meant to mark a higher local status of their owners can be regarded as a somehow transitional stage in the process. These structures are called small mastabas – a reminiscence of those magnificent sepulchral constructions but on a smaller scale. They were heaps reinforced with bricked walls, which gave them a regular shape, sometimes their outer walls were decorated with niches or enriched following the greatest examples with a kind of a vestibule or courtyard. It is probable that some boats discovered in the area of Helwan were connected to such smaller structures. During Dynasty 2 one can notice a gradual abandonment of such a complicated model of monumental superstructure and a shift of interest to the actual, underground parts of tombs.

## 6.5. SOCIAL STRATIFICATION

Social stratification is well evidenced in sepulchral material and it is exemplified by gradually more frequent burials of special construction and equipment against the background of remaining structures of a particular site. This kind of stratification which is archaeologically attestable dates from the period of intensified exchange of goods and ideas between the Lower Egyptian and Naqada cultures, since in older periods burials were equipped modestly and in principle, identically. The beginning of the process of emerging social differentiation within early societies in Northern Egypt is attested in Gerzeh, where there were registered burials which exceeded others in terms of the amount and quality of their equipment. Discoveries from Tell el-Farkha made at the settlement at the Central Kom prove that similar processes of social differentiation also took place within the late Lower Egyptian community (Chłodnicki 2011), unfortunately, no burials relevant to the settlement have been registered at the site yet. This phenomenon finally flourished in the form of elite burials of elaborated construction and much wealthier offering goods, especially abundant in luxurious objects, which are registered from the period of NIIIA. They became especially popular not earlier than Dynasty 0 and they found their climax in the form of great mastabas of state dignitaries, and finally in royal galleries located in Northern Egypt during Dynasty 2. There is an interesting situation noted in the Delta at the turn of Dynasties 0 and 1 when we deal with data which point to the overall prosperity period of local communities based on the wealthy middle class. Their elites built for themselves tombs which were nothing more than a kind of development of typical and common brick structures. There were some larger constructions registered like e.g. grave no 100 in Tell el-Farkha but except for a single and unique mastaba with no. 10 from the same site, no monumental constructions are known.

A phenomenon supplementing the emergence of elites in the early Egyptian society were richly furnished child burials, which appeared at the turn of Dynasties 0 and 1. It is accepted (Krzyżaniak 1992: 217) as a proof that those children were members of well-to-do families of high social status, at least in terms of their material situation, which influenced the social position of the youngest community representatives, devoid of personal merits.

## 6.6. BURIAL RITUALS

The following chapter is nothing more than an attempt to summarize some rarely registered remains which can be interpreted as of ritual character. The situation is even more difficult because only a small part of these rare finds is published, that is why, the generalization presented below is largely based on the cemetery from Tell el-Farkha, where the author is directly involved in fieldworks. In addition, tombs from the site were often well preserved and only ca. 5% of them were affected by robbers' activity, which helps observe and analyse some less frequently registered traces of ritually motivated activity. The importance of burial related beliefs so typical of the pharaonic civilization is well attested in later periods mainly thanks to art and written sources, but early stages of these extended practices may be observed in graves of regular Egyptians who lived and died in the Pre- and Early Dynastic periods.

Some graves from Tell el-Farkha preserved three elements which are best explained as related to ritual activity, since practical explanations seem to almost completely fail. These elements are ochre, pure sand and liquid mud – all of them deposited inside burial chambers, very close to a deceased, all found in tombs dated to the turn of Dynasties 0 and 1. Ochre, mostly red but sometimes also yellow, was usually registered just next to a buried body in the spine, pelvis or feet area (as it was in graves nos 9 or 114) in rather small amounts or scattered all over the burial chamber as in the case of grave no. 99. The quoted structure brings more interesting observations, hence after depositing the deceased in his "proper" position the body was covered with a thin layer of pure sand, then the sand was covered with another layer of red ochre, after that came quite numerous offerings and a mat, which was then poured over with liquid mud. Therefore, we deal here with the whole sequence of actions which were probably recognized as typical of a wealthy middle class funeral in the Protodynastic/Early Dynastic period but which are hardly ever so clearly registered.

With the example of grave no. 99 we come to the presence of pure sand in burial chambers. In most cases, sand is registered as a rather small amount of the material spread in the northern part of burials. It is known from Proto-/Early Dynastic graves nos 24, 98, 100 or 114, there is also a mention of a similar practice at Abusir (Bonnet 1928: 1). Inevitably, the sand was deposited below mats which covered the deceased and his/her offerings. In every case the material used was very fine-grained, clean and sunny yellow.

Another interesting element is the presence of mud on bottoms of burial chambers. The greasy, very humid and most probably liquid mud was poured into the richer graves over the deceased bodies and all of their offerings. This practice dates only to the oldest presently known group of burials from Tell el-Farkha, dated to Dynasty 0/1, and it was registered in graves nos 24, 98, 99, 100 and 114. The presence of mud is rather difficult to explain. It surely was a perfectly effective obstacle for eventual robbers – an example comes from grave no. 100 where an abandoned robbery shaft was recovered (Fig. 38). It should not be surprising, since digging into the mud is even presently very difficult and time-consuming. On the other hand, mud was responsible for higher humidity level within the protected burial chambers and

*Fig. 38. Unsuccessful robbery shaft in grave no. 100 at Tell el-Farkha*

*Fig. 39. Remains of a funerary feast in grave no. 86 at Tell el-Farkha*

thus, for highly advanced decomposition of all objects deposited inside, that is why the protective function of mud seems to be a side effect, rather than the main purpose. Mud was also attested in some pottery and stone jars which were offered to the deceased and, with the exception of mud, were usually empty. One such example comes from grave no. 91, where in a travertine cylinder vessel a bone spoon stuck in the mud was discovered. Taking into consideration that in much later times mud played a role of a fertility symbol, it is suggested that the main purpose of the material's presence was its cult importance, connected with the afterlife and rebirth conceptions.

Remains of funerary feasts are rather easily recognizable as they are usually preserved as animal bones thrown into a grave during the process of a structure closing. Grave no. 86 is a perfect example of a grand feast (Fig. 39). In a kind of shaft which was created by walls of a massive mud-bricked superstructure, upper layers of its filling were full of pottery pieces and hundreds of bones of numerous animals – cattle, goat/sheep, fish, birds, aurochs, dogs, cats, a hippopotamus, a donkey but mostly pigs (zooarcheological analyses by R. Abłamowicz), which were one of the basic diet elements of the people who settled in Tell el-Farkha. An interesting example comes also from grave no. 94 which consisted a kind of very deep shaft with many remains of cattle bones.

Apart from feasts, food was also considered to be a kind of grave offering. Two tombs (nos 94 and 99) preserved some interesting examples. Each of them was equipped with one basalt bowl with the inner surface clearly "consumed" by caustic chemical properties of a dissolving but, unfortunately, undefined kind of a meal which resembles porridge. A representation of food offerings were probably also granary models. In Tell el-Farkha there was a single set of five such objects registered in grave no. 50 (Kołodziejczyk 2009). These are pottery items of rather small height, not larger than 11cm, with characteristic holes made in their upper surface and in vertical walls close to the bottom. They were deposited in a planted layer of earth between the super- and substructure which comprised the construction (Fig. 25). Grave no. 50 is dated to the late Dynasty 1 and it fits well to the practice known from e.g. Abydos – from the tomb of Den (two objects presently at the Petrie Museum, inv. no. UC36721a and b) and graves nos 123 and 124 from the cemetery adjacent to royal enclosures (Petrie 1925, pl. XI, three objects presently at the Petrie Museum labelled UC16207), Helwan (Saad 1969, pl. XXIII) and Tarkhan (Petrie 1914: 4, pl. XV). There were also registered some larger scale analogies discussed in the chapter on model buildings.

Older Protodynastic graves from Tell el-Farkha like nos 91, 98 or 99 preserved pottery jars with wide mouths, broad shoulders and flat bottoms. Their form brings into mind the already mentioned granary models, and thus the pots are best described by the term 'granary jars' (Fig. 40). They are quite typical for settlements of the period and have some counterparts also at cemeteries such as Minshat Abu Omar (pottery type 1.A.7.1 – Kroeper and Wildung 1985, 48 and stone vessel from grave 192 (862) – Kroeper and Wildung 2000, 146), Turah (pottery types LIV, LV and LVI – Junker 1912, 38, taf. XXXVIIb) or Hierakonpolis (Adams 2000, fig. 17). The presence of 'granary jars' in offering sets of the Protodynastic graves from Tell el-Farkha seems to widen the above quoted practice of granary models offered as grave goods back to the end of Dynasty 0. The significance of cereals as an element of rebirth and the afterlife beliefs rather easily comes to mind and in later periods it is certified as an important part of burial practices.

One of the most disputable parts of early Egyptian funeral practices is the case of subsidiary burials, however, it was already discussed in a separate chapter. The same concerns also incomplete burials and an element which in later Egyptian history evolved into false door – an important part of funeral practices – were niches, also discussed above. And finally, structure no. 94 seems to be the actual usable floor space of the ancient Protodynastic cemetery. It was sloppy (repeating the original shape of the tell in the period) and covered with mineralized white substance, which probably comes from pressed organic material mixed with numerous fragments of pottery bread moulds and small pieces of animal and also human bones.

Moreover, the white layer was leaning against the lower part of superstructures which belonged to graves nos 63 and 114. Therefore, the observation may be interpreted as – on the one hand – another evidence that such structures were meant to be admired by the living on the ground surface, and – on the other hand – as a long lasting activity focused on the cemetery area, which must have been connected with remembering the deceased, most probably in a cult sense.

The facts presented above are nothing but a selection of numerous examples which illustrate some kinds of human activity best explained as ritually motivated. What needs to be stressed are the differences between graves of two older groups from the site of Tell el-Farkha, and that the change took place in the middle of Dynasty 1. The so-called Protodynastic cemetery was composed of numerous well equipped and carefully constructed tombs, which belonged to a wealthy society dominated by the affluent middle class. Its representatives paid a lot of attention to small details of almost each grave, which is shown by the presence of e.g. ochre, mud or sand within burial chambers. However, the people changed and the so-called Early Dynastic cemetery was used by a more structurally advanced and highly stratified community typical of the young Egyptian state and thus, burial traditions at the cemetery were already fixed and more strictly followed. The former diversity and quality of burial rituals seem to be replaced by quantity. The process is clear when the typical composition of pottery offerings is discussed, which in the period were based on multiplied bear jars, identical and rather badly fired. In the situation it should not be astonishing that similar simplification impoverished also burial rituals recorded in Early Dynastic graves at Tell el-Farkha. It was probably caused by new political circumstances of the settlement after unification and emergence of the state, but also by simple evolution of the Egyptian society and its beliefs. The author hopes that the juxtaposition of the above quoted data, which are rather infrequently registered at other sites, will help reconstruct some aspects of early Egyptian funeral practices, rituals and – to some extent – also beliefs.

*Fig. 40. "Granary jar" from grave no. 91 at Tell el-Farkha*

# 7. AFTERWORD

The above presented review of sepulchral material collected from the area of Northern Egypt and dated to the Pre-, Proto- and Early Dynastic periods demonstrates considerable variability within time and particular cultural units. Quite early, that is in the period of Dynasty 0, one can observe common standardization of rules concerning the way of posing the dead but also burial constructions and composition of grave goods offered to the deceased for their eternity. It appears then that rich burial furnishing, which was typical of younger periods in the Egyptian history, was introduced already in the early epoch. There are, of course, numerous unsatisfactorily explained issues, such as the presence of pottery pits, animal burials or loose human bones registered in settlements in regular habitation layers. But summing up the rich material and many issues which constitute the generally understood burial customs, attention should be drawn to their significant cognitive value. The structure of numerous necropolises reflects cultural rivalry of the native Lower Egyptian unit with the Naqada culture, coming from the South, and an evolving picture of the emerging Egyptian society. The material analysis reveals also political processes which occurred within the young state such as: independence of the Nile Delta during Dynasty 0 and the first half of Dynasty 1 or periods of the central authorities instability as was the case between the reigns of Aha and Den.

As it is obvious now, the study presents the wide issue of evolution of early Egyptian burial customs mainly from the point of view of architecture, distribution pattern of particular sites, number of graves attributed to a particular period or preferable positions of the deceased. The author understands – of course – that also detailed analyses of offering sets and pottery in particular as the main kind of burial goods and crucial dating factor is very informative for the subject, however, it forms such rich material that it would be enough for at least a few further works. Also the physical anthropological data were merely mentioned mainly because publications are insufficient and much more research has yet to be completed. But new excavation projects are in progress and information from Tell el-Farkha, Tell el-Murra, Tell el-Iswid, Abu Roash M or Helwan have the power to change our present knowledge in just a single season. Especially works at newly discovered sites, such as e.g. Tell el-Murra, seem to be promising as they fill in numerous white patches on the archeological map of Northern Egypt in the early period.

# 8. APPENDICES:

Appendix no. 1. List of all published burial related sites from Northern Egypt from Predynastic to Early Dynastic period

| Site | Other names | Date | Burial context | Burials number | Major publications |
|---|---|---|---|---|---|
| Abu Roash | Abu Roash 300 | end of Dynasty 0-beginning of Dynasty 1 (NIIIC1) | cemetery | 62 | Klasens 1958a; Lepsius 1897: 21; |
| | Abu Roash 400 | early Dynasty 1, reign of Aha (NIIIC1) | cemetery | 113 | Klasens 1959 |
| | Abu Roash 800 | late Dynasty 1-Dynasty 2 (NIIIC2-NIIID) | cemetery | 117 | Klasens 1960 |
| | Abu Roash 1957 | early Dynasty 1 (NIIIC1) | cemetery | 81 | Klasens 1957, 1958 |
| | Abu Roash M | Dynasty 1, reign of Den (NIIIC2) | elite cemetery | 21 main structures and at least 39 subsidiary burials | Joube 1938, 1946; Kanawaty 1981; Klasens 1960a; Montet 1938, 1946; Tristant 2008, 2008a; Tristant, Smythe 2011 |
| | Abu Roash North, Maktab al-Magaari | Dynasty 1, between reigns of Aha and Den (NIIIC1-NIIIC2) | cemetery | 3 | Hawass 1980 |
| Abusir | Abusir | late Dynasty 1-Dynasty 2 (NIIIC2-NIIID) | cemetery | over 68 | Bonnet 1928; Jeffreys, Tavares 1994: 149-150 |
| | Abusir North, Abu Ghurab | NIIIA-NIIID | elite cemetery | ca. 100 main structures (mainly unexcavated) and undefined number of subsidiary burials | Boessneck et al. 1992; Leclant, Clerc 1994a; Radwan 1991, 1995, 2000, 2003; van Wetering 2004: 1059 |
| Abusir el-Meleq | | NIID2-early NIIIB | cemetery | 851 (among them some of Hyksos, Dynasty 18 and Late Period) | Castillos 1982a; Möller 1906, 1907, 1926; Rubensohn 1905; Scharff 1926; Seeher 1999 |
| Batn el-Baqara | Old Cairo, Atar en-Nabi | Dynasty 1, around reign of Den (NIIIC2) | single discovery | 1 (reused in Ptolomeic Period) | Boghdady 1932 |
| Beni Amir | | NIID-NIIID | cemetery | 35 | el-Hagg Ragab 1992; Kroeper 1988: 18-19; Krzyżaniak 1989: 277; el-Moneim 1993a, 1993b, 1996a, 1996b |
| Buto | Tell el-Fara'in | Lower Egyptian culture, phase 2 (NIIC-NIID1) | settlement | 1 | von der Way 1997: 74-75 and Faltings 1998; Faltings et al. 2000; Faltings, Köhler 1996; Hartung 2003a; Hartung et al. 2003a; von der Way 1985, 1986a, 1986b, 1991, 1992, 1993, 1997 |
| Dimeh | | Early Dynastic to Old Kingdom | single discovery | 1 | Caton-Thompson, Gardiner 1934: 86 |
| Ezbet Kamel Sedqi el-Qebleyah | Helwan | Dynasty 1 (NIIIC-early NIIID) | cemetery | over 328 | el-Banna 1990 |
| Gerzeh | | Predynastic (NII) and | cemetery | 288 | Petrie et al. 1912; Stevenson 2006, 2009; Wenke 1999a: 316 |
| | | Dynasty 2 (NIIID) | | 9 | |
| Gezira Sangaha | Sagana, Tell Geniedyeh | Late Predynastic ? | cemetery ? | no data | Bietak 1975: 106, footnote 401; Fischer 1958: 86; Krzyżaniak 1989: 271 |
| Giza | Giza – "at the foot of the Great Pyramid" | Lower Egyptian culture, phase 1 or 2 (among NIIA-NIID1) | cemetery ? | a few ? | Kamal 1911: 116-117; Mortensen 1985; el-Sanussi, Jones 1997 |
| | Giza – Tramway | | | none | Mortensen 1985; Rizkana, Seeher 1987: 61; el-Sanussi, Jones 1997 |

| | Giza South, Nazlet Batran | Dynasty 1, around reign of Djet (late NIIIC1) – Dynasty 3 | elite cemetery | 39 main structures and 52 subsidiary burials | Covington 1905; Daressy 1905; Kromer 1991; Martin 1997; Petrie 1907 |
|---|---|---|---|---|---|
| Gurob | Kom Medinet el-Ghurab | Late Predynastic and Early Dynastic | 4 cemeteries | ca. 172 (ca. 50 excavated by Loat, ca. 50 at point O – excavated 16, 13 at point C and 59 at point C2 ) | Brunton, Engelbach 1927; Loat 1905 |
| Harageh | cemetery G | Lower Egyptian culture, phase 2 (NIIC-NIID1) or NIA ? | cemetery | 20 | Buchez, Midant-Reynes 2011; Castillos 1982; Engelbach 1923; Hendrickx, van den Brink 2002: 352, tabl. 23.1; Kaiser 1987a; Williams 1982 |
| | cemetery H | | | 27 | |
| | cemeteries D and S | | single discoveries | 3 | |
| Heliopolis | | Lower Egyptian culture, phase 1 (NIIA-NIIC) | cemetery | max. 200 – 56 published (45 human and 11 animal burials) | Debono 1950; Debono, Mortensen 1988; Kakosy 1077; Mortensen 1999a; Rizkana, Seeher 1990: 98 |
| Helwan | Ezbet el-Walda | NIIIA – Dynasty 3 (or even 4 ?) | cemetery | ca. 10500 (at least 10258 excavated by Saad and over 170 by Köhler) | Birrell 2000; Hikade 1999; Jeffreys 1999; Kaplony 1977; Köhler 1998, 1999, 2000-2001, 2001, 2003, 2004a, 2004b, 2004c, 2005, 2007, 2008, 2009; Köhler, van den Brink 2002; Köhler, Jones 2009; Saad 1942; 1943; 1947a; 1947b; 1951; 1965; Wilkinson 1996a; Wood 1987 |
| el-Huseiniya | Tell el-Fara'on, Tell Faraon Imet, Tell Bedawi, Tell Nebesheh | Lower Egyptian culture, phase 2 (NIIC-NIID) and Protodynastic-Early Dynastic (NIIIA-NIIIC) | cemetery | over 60 | Hendrickx, van den Brink 2002: 348, tabl. 23.1; Kroeper 1988: 18; Krzyżaniak 1989: 271; Mostafa 1988a, 1988b |
| Kafr Ghattati | | Dynasties 0 – 1 (NIIIB-early NIIID) | cemetery | 13 | Engels 1990 |
| Kafr Hassan Dawood | Tell Ezbet Hassan Dawud | NIIC/NIID-NIIIC1 (early Dynasty 1) | cemetery | 745 | Bakr et al. 1996; el-Hangary 1992; Hassan 2000a, 2000b; Hassan et al. 2003; el-Merghani 2003; Rowland, Hassan 2003; Tassie, van Wetering 2003; Tucker 2003 |
| Khelwet Abu Musallem | | Predynastic | cemetery | 2 | Leclant 1973: 396 |
| Kom el-Khilgan | | Lower Egyptian culture, phases 1-2 (NIIA-NIIC) | cemetery | 56 | Buchez, Midant-Reynes 2007, 2011; Midant-Reynes 2007; Midant-Reynes et al. 2003, 2004; Tristant et al. 2008 |
| | | Protodynastic-Dynasty 1(NIIIA-NIIIC/D) | | 34 | |
| | | Undefined | | 136 | |
| Kufur Nigm | Ezbet et-Tell, el-Khudariya, Tell Aga, Tell el-Faq'i | Dynasty 1 (NIIIC1-early NIIID) | cemetery | ca. 400 excavated | Bakr 1988, 1994, 2000, 2003; Kroeper 1988: 18; Tassie, van Wetering 2003: 505, footnote 3 |
| Lahun | Bashkatib | Predynastic | single discovery | 1 | Petrie et al. 1923 |
| | | Dynasties 1-3 (from NIIIC1) | cemetery | 112 | |
| | Dyke cemetery | | | a few | |
| | Kom el-Iswid | | single discovery | 1 | |
| Maadi | | Lower Egyptian culture, phase 1 (NIA/B-NIIC) | settlement | 55 (1 adult and 54 infant burials) | Caneva et al. 1989; Faltings 1998: 372-373; Hartung 2003; Klug, Beck 1985; Menghin, Amer 1936; Rizkana, |

| | | | | | |
|---|---|---|---|---|---|
| | | | | | Seeher 1987, 1989; Watrin 2003 |
| | Cemetery | Lower Egyptian culture, phase 1 (NIB) | cemetery | 76 (among them 1 dog burial) | Badawi 1987; Rizkana, Seeher 1990 |
| | Dynasty 1 cemetery | early Dynasty 1 (NIIIC1) | | over 19 | Brunton 1939 |
| Ma'asara | | Dynasty 2 – end rather (NIIID) | cemetery | 6 | Hughes 1941; Kessler 1980; Larsen 1940a, 1940b |
| Marsa Matruh – cemetery A | | Lower Egyptian culture, phase 2 (NIIC-NIID1) | cemetery | 5 | Bates 1915, 1927; Hendrick, van den Brink 2002: 348, tabl. 23.1 |
| Mendes | Tell el-Rub'a | Dynasty 1 or 2 (NIIIC1-NIIID) | cemetery ? | more than 3 | Brewer, Wenke 1992; Hansen 1965; 1967; Wenke 1999 |
| Merimde-Benisalame | | Merimde culture (ca. 5000/4900 - 4500/4400 BC) | settlement with/and cemetery | at least 134 (114 excavated by Junker, at least 20 by Eiwanger) | Badawi 1978; Castillios 1982c; Eiwanger 1978, 1979, 1980, 1982, 1984, 1988; 1992; Hawass et al.1988; Hassan 1985; Junker 1928, 1929, 1930a, 1930b, 1932, 1933, 1934, 1940; Patch 1997; Rizkana, Seeher 1987: 61 |
| | | Lower Egyptian culture, phase 2 (NIIA-NIID1) | cemetery | 6 | Badawi 1980; Eiwanger 1979: 27 |
| | | Early Dynastic | single discovery | 1 | Eiwanger 1979: 28 |
| Minshat Abu Omar | Tell es-Saaba Banat | Lower Egyptian culture, phases 2 and 3 (MAO I – NIIC-NIID | cemetery | 273 | Buchez, Midant-Reynes 2011; Kaiser 1987; Kroeper 1986/87, 1988, 1992, 1994a, 1994b, 1996, 1999, 2004; Kroeper, Krzyżaniak 1992; Mączyńska 2011; Wildung, Kroeper 1985, 1994, 2000 |
| | | ? MAO II (NIID-NIIIA) | | 8 | |
| | | Protodynastic (MAO III – NIIIA1-NIIIC1) | | 81 | |
| | | Early Dynastic (MAO IV – NIIIC1-early NIIID) | | 58 | |
| Minshat Ezzat | Tell el-Heglla | Late Predynastic (NIID) | cemetery | at least 10 late | Adly 2005; el-Baghdadi 1999, 2003; Leclant, Minault-Gout 1999 |
| | | Protodynastic–Dynasty 1, reign of Den (NIIIA-NIIIC2) | | at least 92 | |
| el-Omari | | Omari culture (ca. 4600-4400 BC) | settlement with/and cemetery | at least 77(43 – regions A and B, 31 – region F, singular in regions C, G and H) | Debono, Mortensen 1990; Mortensen 1992, 1999b |
| el-Qatta | | Early Dynastic | cemetery | ca. 650 (undefined number of early burials plus some innumerous Old Kingdom and Roman burials) | Junker 1928: 38-39; Leclant 1950, 1952, 1953, 1954 |
| es-Saff | | Lower Egyptian culture, phase 1 or 2 (NIIA-NIID1) | cemetery | 10 | Habachi, Kaiser 1985; Junker 1941: 54; Rizkana, Seeher 1990: 102 |
| Saqqara | Saqqara North | Dynasty 1, reign of Aha-Dynasty 3(from NIIIC1) | state elite cemetery | 348 (18 great mastabas with 98 subsidiary burials and 232 excavated by Quibell, of which undefined number belongs to Dynasty 3) | Emery 1938, 1939a, 1939b, 1949, 1954, 1958, 1966; Firth 1931; Kemp 1966; Leclant, Minault-Gout 1998; 2000; Leonard 2000; Morris 2007; O'Connor 2005; Quibell 1913, 1923; Tavares 1998, 1999; van Wetering 2004; Youssef 1996 |
| | Saqqara-Royal cemetery | Dynasty 2, reigns of Hatepsekhemwy and Raneb (NIIID) | royal cemetery | at least 2 | Barsanti 1901; 1902; Ćwiek 1995; Dodson 1996: 22; Hassan 1938; Jeffreys, Tavares 1994; Kaiser 1994; Maspero 1902; Munro 1983; |

| | | | | | |
|---|---|---|---|---|---|
| | | | | | 1993a; 1993b; Stadelmann 1985; van Walsem 2004; van Wetering 2004 |
| | Saqqara Serapeum, Saqqara West, Macramallah's rectangle | Dynasty 1, reign of Den (NIIIC2) | subsidiary cemetery ? | 231 | Castillos 1976; Kaiser 1985; Macramallah 1940; Morris 2007a; Swelim 1991; van Wetering 2004: 1058 |
| | Saqqara South | Dynasty 2 (NIIID) | elite cemetery | at least 2 | Raven et al. 2003a; 2003b; Regulski 2011; Regulski et al. 2010; van Walsem 2003; 2004 |
| Sedment | Cemetery J | Lower Egyptian culture, phase 2 (NIIC) | cache field ? | over 175 pottery pits | Petrie, Brunton 1924, 1924a; Williams 1982 |
| | Cemetery K | | | a few pottery pits | |
| | Sedment | Dynasties 1-2 (NIIIC-NIIID) | cemetery | 35 published, complete number unknown | Petrie, Brunton 1924, 1924a |
| | Mayana | | | | |
| Tarkhan | Kafr Tarkhan, Valley cemetery | NIIIA1-NIIIC2/early NIIID | cemetery | 1054 (among them 3 large mastabas and possibly 3 more) | Ellis 1992, 1996, 1999; Petrie 1912, 1914; Petrie et al. 1913; Seidlmayer 1988; Wilkinson 1996 |
| | Hill cemetery A | NIIIA1-early NIIID | elite cemetery | 305 (among them some dated to Dynasties 2-5) | |
| | Hill cemetery B | | cemetery | | |
| | Hill cemetery F | | | | |
| | Hill cemetery G | | | | |
| | Hill cemetery H | | | | |
| | Hill cemetery J | | | | |
| | Hill cemetery N | | | | |
| | Hill cemeteries E, L, M, O and Q | | single inhumations | | |
| Tell Basta | Bubastis | Early Dynastic | cemetery | no data – only 1 published as Early Dynastic | Bakr 1992; el-Sawi 1979 |
| Tell el-Daba'a el-Qanan | | Late Predynastic | cemetery | 100 | el-Baghdadi 2005; Chłodnicki 1988 |
| | | Early Dynastic | | 110 | |
| Tell el-Farkha | | NIIIA2/NIIIB1 | elite cemetery ? | 1 great mastaba | Abłamowicz 2008; Chłodnicki et al. 2012; Ciałowicz 2008b; Dębowska-Ludwin 2008, 2009, 2010, 2011a, 2011b; Jucha 2006, 2008, 2010a, 2010b |
| | | NIIIB-NIIIC1/2 | cemetery | 52 (among them 4 subsidiary burials) | |
| | | NIIIC2-NIIID | | 37 | |
| Tell el-Ginn | | Late Predynastic – Early Dynastic | cemetery ? | no data | Bietak 1975: 99, footnote 364a; Krzyżaniak 1989: 271 |
| Tell Ibrahim Awad | Umm 'agram | Dynasty 1 (NIIIC1-early NIIID) | cemetery | 6 published early graves | van den Brink 1988, 1992; Eigner 2003; van Haarlem 1993, 1996, 1997, 1998a, 1998b, 2000, 2001, 2003; Leclant, Minault-Gout 1999a; Zeist 1988 |
| Tell el-Iswid South | | NIIIC1-NIIID | cemetery | 18 | van den Brink 1988a, 1989; Midant-Reynes, Denoix 2011 |
| Tell el-Masha'la | | Lower Egyptian culture, phase 1/2 (NIIB/C ?) | settlement with/and cemetery | 7 | Rampersad 2003: 185, footnote 43 and 2006 |
| | | Dynasty 1 (NIIIC1-early NIIID) | cemetery | 2 | el-Hagg Ragab 1992 |
| Tell el-Murra | | Predynastic – Early Dynastic | cemetery | 7 | Jucha 2012; Kazimierczak 2012; Kozłowska 2012 |
| Tell es-Samara | | Late Dynasty 0/early Dynasty 1 – Dynasty 2 (NIIIB/C1-NIIID) | cemetery | 85 | el-Baghdadi 2005; el-Baghdadi, el-Said Nur 2002; Leclant, Minault-Gout 2001 |
| et-Tibbin | | Predynastic | cemetery | no data | Leclant 1973a |

| Turah | Turah | Dynasties 0-1 (NIIIB-NIIIC2) – Turah 1: reigns of Ka-Narmer, Turah 2: Narmer-Den, Turah 3: Den-Anjeeb/Semerkhet | cemetery | 582 | Castillos 1982b; Junker 1912; Śliwa 1980; Wilkinson 1996 |
|-------|-------|-------|-------|-------|-------|
|  | Turah el-Asmant | Dynasty 1 – reigns of Den-Anjeeb/Semerkhet (NIIIC2) | cemetery | over 200 | el-Khouli 1968; Leclant 1961, 1978; el-Sadeek, Murphy 1983; Yacoub 1981, 1983 |
|  | Turah Station | Lower Egyptian culture, phase 2 (NIIC-NIID1) | cemetery ? | No data | Hendrickx, van den Brink 2002: 350, tabl. 23.1; Junker 1912 and 1928: 872; Kaiser, Zaugg 1988; Mortensen 1999: 851; Scharff 1931: 122 |
| Wadi Digla | Maadi South | Lower Egyptian culture, phase 1 – WD I: NIB-NIC, WD II: NIIA-NIIC | Cemetery | 485 (among them 14 animal burials) | Amer, Rizkana 1953, 1953a; Klug, Beck 1985; Rizkana, Seeher 1990 |
| Wardan |  | Dynasty 2 (NIIID) | single discovery | 1 | Larsen 1956 |
| Zawiyet el-Arian |  | Dynasty 1(NIIIC1-early NIIID) | Cemetery | ca. 300 (only 72 published) | Dunham 1978 |

84

Appendix no. 2. Relative chronology of particular sites from the study (arranged according to their first use, then alphabetically)

| Site name | Period | | | | | | | | | | | | | | | | | | | | | |
|---|---|---|---|---|---|---|---|---|---|---|---|---|---|---|---|---|---|---|---|---|---|---|
| | Early Predynastic | NIA | NIB | NIC | NIIA | NIIB | NIIC | NIID1 | NIID2 | NIIIA1 | NIIIA2 | NIIIB | Late Dyn. 0 | Narmer | Aha | Djer | Djet | Den | Andjeeb | Semerkhet | Qa'a | Dyn. 2 |
| Merimde-Benisalame | X | | | | X | X | X | X | | | | X | X | X | X | X | X | X | X | X | X | X |
| el-Omari | X | | | | | | | | | | | | | | | | | | | | | |
| Maadi | | | X | X | X | X | X | | | | | | | | | | | | | | | |
| Maadi-cemetery | | | X | | | | | | | | | | | | | | | | | | | |
| Wadi Digla | | | X | X | X | X | X | | | | | | | | | | | | | | | |
| Heliopolis | | | | X | X | X | | | | | | | | | | | | | | | | |
| Gerzeh | | | | | X | X | X | X | X | | | | | | | | | | | | | X |
| Gezira Sangaha | | | | | X | X | X | X | X | X | X | | | | | | | | | | | |
| Gurob | | | | | X | X | X | X | X | X | X | X | X | X | X | X | X | X | X | X | X | X |
| Kom el-Khilgan | | | | | X | X | X | | X | X | X | X | X | X | X | X | X | X | X | | | |
| Khelwet Abu Musallam | | | | | X | X | X | X | X | X | X | | | | | | | | | | | |
| Tell el-Ginn | | | | | X | X | X | X | X | X | X | X | X | X | X | X | X | X | X | X | X | X |
| et-Tibbin | | | | | X | X | X | X | X | X | X | | | | | | | | | | | |
| Tell el-Masha'la | | | | | | X | X | | | | | | | X | X | X | X | X | X | X | X | |
| Buto | | | | | | | X | X | | | | | | | | | | | | | | |
| Giza-the Great Pyramid | | | | | | | X | X | | | | | | | | | | | | | | |
| Giza-tramway | | | | | | | X | X | | | | | | | | | | | | | | |
| Harageh G, H | | | | | | | X | X | | | | | | | | | | | | | | |
| el-Huseiniya | | | | | | | X | X | X | X | X | X | X | X | X | X | X | X | X | | | |
| Kafr Hassan Dawood | | | | | | | X | X | X | X | X | X | X | X | X | X | | | | | | |
| Marsa Matruh | | | | | | | X | X | | | | | | | | | | | | | | |
| Minshat Abu Omar | | | | | | | X | X | X | X | X | X | X | X | X | X | X | X | X | X | X | |
| Minshat Ezzat | | | | | | | X | X | X | X | X | X | X | X | X | X | X | X | | | | |
| es-Saff | | | | | | | X | X | | | | | | | | | | | | | | |
| Sedment J, K | | | | | | | X | | | | | | | X | X | X | X | X | X | X | X | X |
| Turah-station | | | | | | | X | X | | | | | | | | | | | | | | |
| Beni Amir | | | | | | | | X | X | X | X | X | X | X | X | X | X | X | X | X | X | X |
| Abusir el-Meleq | | | | | | | | X | X | X | X | | | | | | | | | | | |
| Lahun | | | | | | | | X | X | X | | | | X | X | X | X | X | X | X | X | X |
| Abusir North | | | | | | | | | X | X | X | X | X | X | X | X | X | X | X | X | X | X |
| Helwan | | | | | | | | | X | X | X | X | X | X | X | X | X | X | X | X | X | X |

| Site | 1 | 2 | 3 | 4 | 5 | 6 | 7 | 8 | 9 | 10 | 11 | 12 | 13 | 14 | 15 | 16 | 17 | 18 | 19 | 20 |
|---|---|---|---|---|---|---|---|---|---|---|---|---|---|---|---|---|---|---|---|---|
| Tarkhan | | | | | | | | X | X | X | X | X | X | X | X | X | X | X | X | |
| Tell el-Daba'a el Qanan | | | | | | | | X | X | X | X | X | X | X | X | X | X | X | X | X |
| Dimeh | | | | | | | | | | X | X | X | X | X | X | X | X | X | X | X |
| Kafr Ghattati | | | | | | | | | | X | X | X | X | X | X | X | X | X | X | |
| el-Qatta | | | | | | | | | | X | X | X | X | X | X | X | X | X | X | X |
| Tell el-Farkha | | | | | | | | | | X | X | X | X | X | X | X | X | X | X | X |
| Abu Roash 300 | | | | | | | | | | X | X | X | X | X | | | | | | |
| Tell Basta | | | | | | | | | | X | X | X | | | | | | | | |
| Tell el-Iswid South | | | | | | | | | | X | X | X | X | X | X | X | X | X | X | X |
| Tell el-Murra | | | | | | | | | | X | X | X | X | X | X | X | X | X | X | X |
| Tell es-Samara | | | | | | | | | | X | X | X | X | X | X | X | X | X | X | X |
| Turah | | | | | | | | | | X | X | X | X | X | X | X | X | | | |
| Abu Roash 1957 | | | | | | | | | | | X | X | X | X | | | | | | |
| Ezbet Kamel Sedqi el-Qebleyah | | | | | | | | | | | X | X | X | X | X | X | X | X | | |
| Kufur Nigm | | | | | | | | | | | X | X | X | X | X | X | X | X | | |
| Maadi-Dyn. 1 | | | | | | | | | | | X | X | X | X | | | | | | |
| Mendes | | | | | | | | | | | X | X | X | X | X | X | X | X | X | X |
| Tell Ibrahim Awad | | | | | | | | | | | X | X | X | X | X | X | X | X | | |
| Turah el-Asmant | | | | | | | | | | | X | X | X | X | X | X | X | | | |
| Zawiyet el-Arian | | | | | | | | | | | X | X | X | X | X | X | X | X | | |
| Abu Roash 400 | | | | | | | | | | | X | X | X | | | | | | | |
| Abu Roash North | | | | | | | | | | | X | X | X | X | | | | | | |
| Saqqara North | | | | | | | | | | | | | X | X | X | X | X | X | X | X |
| Giza South | | | | | | | | | | | | | | | X | X | X | X | X | X |
| Abu Roash M | | | | | | | | | | | | | | | | X | | | | |
| Abu Roash 800 | | | | | | | | | | | | | | | | X | X | X | X | X |
| Abusir | | | | | | | | | | | | | | | | X | X | X | X | X |
| Batn el-Baqara | | | | | | | | | | | | | | | | X | | | | |
| Saqqara-Serapeum | | | | | | | | | | | | | | | | X | | | | |
| Ma'asara | | | | | | | | | | | | | | | | | | | | X |
| Saqqara-Royal Cemetary | | | | | | | | | | | | | | | | | | | | X |
| Saqqara South | | | | | | | | | | | | | | | | | | | | X |
| Wardan | | | | | | | | | | | | | | | | | | | | X |

Appendix no. 3. Types of pit burials

| Site | Type of burial structure | | | | | | | | | | | | |
| --- | --- | --- | --- | --- | --- | --- | --- | --- | --- | --- | --- | --- | --- |
| | Simple pit burials | | | | | Pit burials with reinforced edges | | | | | | | |
| | Oval | Round | Oblong with rounded corners | Rectangular | Square | Mud plastered | Reinforced with stripes of mud | Inlayed with plaitings | Inlayed with wood | Reinforced with stones | Walls partially lined with mud-bricks | Bottom paved with mud-bricks | Roughly square with a mud-brick partition wall |
| Abu Roash 300 | | | | X | | | | | | X | X | | X |
| Abu Roash 400 | | | X | | | | | | | X | X | | X |
| Abu Roash 800 | X | | | | | | | | | X | X | | X |
| Abu Roash 1957 | X | X | X | X | | | | | | X | X | | X |
| Abu Roash M | | | | | | | | | | | X | | |
| Abu Roash North | | | | | | | | | | | | | |
| Abusir | | | | | | | | | | | | | |
| Abusir el-Meleq | X | X | | | | X | | X | X | | X | | |
| Abusir North | | | | | | | | | | | | | |
| Batn el-Baqara | | | | | | | | | | | | | |
| Beni Amir | | | X | | | | | | | | | | |
| Buto | X | | | | | | | | | | | | |
| Dimeh | | | X | | | | | | | | | | |
| Ezbet Kamel SeQ. | X | | | X | X | | | | | | | | |
| Gerza | X | | X | | | X | | | | | | | |
| Gezira Sangaha | | | | | | | | | | | | | |
| Giza South. | | | | | | | | | | | | | |
| Gurob | X | | | | | | | | | | | | |
| Harageh | X | | X | | | | | | | | | | |
| Heliopolis | X | X | | | | | | X | | | | | |
| Helwan | X | | X | | | | | | | | | | |
| el-Huseiniya | X | | | | | | | | | | | | |
| Kafr Ghattati | | | | | | | | | | | | | |
| Kafr Hassan D. | X | | | X | | X | | | | | | | |
| Kheluet Abu M. | X | | | | | | | | | | | | |
| Kom el-Khilgan | X | | X | | | X | | | | | | | |
| Kufur Nigm | | | | X | | | | | | | | | |
| Lahun | X | | | | | | | | | | | | X |
| Maadi-cemetary | X | | | | | | | | | | | | |
| Maadi-Dynasty 1 | | | | X | | X | | | | | | X | |
| Maadi-settlement | | | X | | | | | | | | | | |
| Ma'asara | | | | | | | | | | | | | |
| Marsa Matruh | X | | | | | | | | | | | | |
| Mendes | | | X | | | | | X | | | | X | |
| Merimde | X | | | | | | | | | | | | |
| Minshat Abu Omar | X | | | X | | X | | X | | | | X | |
| Minshat Ezzat | | | | | | | | X | X | | | | |
| el-Omari | X | | | | | | | | | | | | |
| el-Qatta | | | | | | | | | | | | | |
| es-Saff | X | | | | | | | | | | | | |
| Saqqara-Royal cemetery | | | | | | | | | | | | | |
| Saqqara North | | | | | | | | | | | | | |
| Saqqara-Serapeum | X | X | | X | X | X | | | | | | | |
| Saqqara South | | | | | | | | | | | | | |
| Sedment | X | | | X | | | | | | | | | |
| Tarkhan | X | | | X | | | | | X | | | | |
| Tell Basta | | | | | | | | | | | | | |
| Tell el-Daba'a el Qanan | | | | | | | X | | | | | | |

| | | | | | | | | | | | | | |
|---|---|---|---|---|---|---|---|---|---|---|---|---|---|
| Tell el-Farkha | X | | | X | | | | X | | | | X | |
| Tell el-Ginn | | | | | | | | | | | | | |
| Tell Ibrahim Awad | X | | | | | | | X | | | X | | |
| Tell el-Iswid South | X | | | | | | | X | | | | | |
| Tell el-Masha'la | X | | | | | | | | | | | | |
| Tell el-Murra | | | | | | | | | | | | | |
| Tell es-Samara | | | | | | | | | | | | | |
| et-Tibbin | | | X | | | | | | | | | | |
| Turah | X | X | | X | | X | | X | X | | X | | |
| Turah el-Asmant | X | | | X | | | | | | | | | |
| Wadi Digla | X | X | | | | | | | | | | | |
| Wardan | | | | | | | | | | | | | |
| Zawiyet el-Arian | X | | | X | | | | | X | | | | |

Appendix no. 4. Types of graves lined with mud bricks

| Site | oval: Single chambered | oval: Double chambered | Single chambered: With rounded corners | Single chambered: With barrel vaults | Single chambered: uwith storage pit | Double chambered: burials chamber and storage room at one short side | Three-chambered: One storage room at both short side | Three-chambered: 2 storage rooms at one short side | Three-chambered: 2 storage rooms at one short side but rough gable end | 2 burial chambers and one store room | Four-chambered: 2 small store rooms at one short side and 1 larger at the other one | Four-chambered: 2 small store rooms at one short side and 1 larger adjacent to the former ones | Four-chambered: 2 small store rooms at one short side and one along longer side | Five-chambered: Burial chamber 4 store rooms, 2 at both short sides | Five-chambered: Burial chamber 4 store rooms, 2 at both short sides but with rough gable end |
|---|---|---|---|---|---|---|---|---|---|---|---|---|---|---|---|
| Abu Roash 300 | | | X | X | | X | | X | | | | | | X | |
| Abu Roash 400 | | | X | | X | X | | | | | | | | | |
| Abu Roash 800 | | | | X | | X | X | | | | | | | | |
| Abu Roash 1957 | | | | X | | X | | X | | | | | | X | |
| Abu Roash M | | | | X | | X | X | X | | | | | | | |
| Abu Roash North | | | | | | | | | | | | | | | |
| Abusir | X | | | X | | | X | | | | | | | | |
| Abusir el-Meleq | | | | X | | X | | | | | | | | | |
| Abusir North | | | | | | | | | | | | | | | |
| Batn el-Baqara | | | | | | | | | | | | | | | |
| Beni Amir | X | X | | X | | X | X | X | | X | | | | | |
| Buto | | | | | | | | | | | | | | | |
| Dimeh | | | | | | | | | | | | | | | |
| Ezbet Kamel Sedqi el-Qebleya | | | | X | | X | X | X | | | X | | | X | |
| Gerza | | | | | | | | | | | | | | | |
| Gezira Sangaha | | | | | | | | | | | | | | | |
| Giza South | | | | | | | | | | | | | | | |
| Gurob | | | | | | | | | | | | | | | |
| Harageh | | | | | | | | | | | | | | | |
| Heliopolis | | | | | | | | | | | | | | | |
| Helwan | | | | X | | | | | | | | | | | |
| el-Huseiniya | | | | X | | | | | | | | | | | |
| Kafr Ghattati | | | | X | | | | | | | | | | | |
| Kafr Hassan Dawood | | | | | | | | | | | | | | | |
| Khelwet Abu Mussalem | | | | | | | | | | | | | | | |
| Kom el-Khilgan | | | | | | | | | | | | | | | |
| Kufur Nigm | | | | X | | X | | | | | | | | | |
| Lahun | | | | X | | X | | X | | | | | X | | |
| Maadi-cemetery | | | | | | | | | | | | | | | |
| Maadi-Dynasty 1 | | | | X | | X | | | | | | | | | |
| Maadi-settlement | | | | | | | | | | | | | | | |
| Ma'asara | | | | X | | | | | | | | | | | |
| Marsa Matruh | | | | | | | | | | | | | | | |
| Mendes | | | | | | | | | | | | | | | |
| Merimde | | | | X | | | | | | | | | | | |
| Minshat Abu Omar | | | | X | | X | X | | | | | | | | |
| Minshat Ezzat | | | | X | | | X | | | | | | | | |
| el-Omari | | | | | | | | | | | | | | | |
| el-Qatta | | | | X | | | | | | | | | | | |
| es-Saff | | | | | | | | | | | | | | | |
| Saqqara-Royal cemetery | | | | | | | | | | | | | | | |
| Saqqara North | | | | | | | | | | | | | | | |
| Saqqara Serapeum | | | | X | | | | | | | | | | | X |

| Site | 1 | 2 | 3 | 4 | 5 | 6 | 7 | 8 | 9 | 10 | 11 | 12 | 13 | 14 |
|---|---|---|---|---|---|---|---|---|---|---|---|---|---|---|
| Saqqara South | | | | | | | | | | | | | | |
| Sedment | | | | | | | | X | | | | | | |
| Tarkhan | | | X | | | | | | | | | | | |
| Tell Basta | | | | | | | | | | | | | | |
| Tell el-Daba'a el-Qanan | | | X | | X | X | | | | X | | | | |
| Tell el-Farkha | | | X | | X | | | | | | | | | |
| Tell el-Ginn | | | | | | | | | | | | | | |
| Tell Ibrahim Awad | | | | | | X | X | | | | | | | |
| Tell el-Iswid South | | | X | | | | | | | | | | | |
| Tell el-Masha'la | | | | | | | | | | | | | | |
| Tell el-Murra | | | | | X | | | | | | | | | |
| Tell es-Samara | | | X | | X | | | | | | | | | |
| et-Tibbin | | | | | | | | | | | | | | |
| Turah | | | X | X | X | X | X | X | | | X | | | |
| Turah el-Asmant | | | X | | X | | X | X | | | | | | |
| Wadi Digla | | | | | | | | | | | | | | |
| Wardan | | | X | | | | | | | | | | | |
| Zawiyet el-Arian | | X | | X | | | X | | | | | | | |

## Appendix no. 5. Remaining types of grave structures

| Site | Shaft and 1 burial chamber | Shaft and 2 burial chams | Shaft and 4 burial chams | 2 shafts and a broken line structure | Single steps | Straight staircase | L-shaped staircase | Graves with a shaft and stircase | Graves with a sloping corridor | Burial cham. and 3 stores | Burial cham. and 6 stores | Burial cham. and 7 stores | Burial cham. and 8 stores | Burial cham. and 9 stores | Alongated structures with numerous rooms | Tombs hewn in bedrock | Small mastabas | Great mastabas | In baskets | In bags | In pottery jars | 9in coffins |
|---|---|---|---|---|---|---|---|---|---|---|---|---|---|---|---|---|---|---|---|---|---|---|
| | Shaft graves | | | | Staircase graves | | | | | Multi-chamber tombs | | | | | | | | | Simple burials | | | |
| Abu Roash 300 | | | | | | | | | | | | | | | | | | | | | | |
| Abu Roash 400 | | | | | | | | | | | | | | | | | X | | | | | X |
| Abu Roash 800 | | | | | | | | | | | | | | | | | X | | | | | X |
| Abu Roash 1957 | | | | | | | | | | | | | | | | | | | | | X | X |
| Abu Roash M | | | | | | | | | | | | | | | | | | X | | | | X |
| Abu Roash North | | | | | | | | | | | | | | | | | | | | | | |
| Abusir | X | X | | | | X | | | | | | | | | | | | | | | | |
| Abusir el-Meleq | | | | | | | | | | | | | | | | | | | | | | |
| Abusir North | | | | | | | | | | | | | | | | | | X | | | | |
| Batn el-Baqara | | | | | | | | | | | | | | | | X | | | | | | |
| Beni Amir | | | | | | | | | | | | X | X | | | | | | | | | |
| Buto | | | | | | | | | | | | | | | | | | | | | | |
| Dimeh | | | | | | | | | | | | | | | | | | | | | | |
| Ezbet Kamel Sedqi el-Qebleyah | X | | | X | X | X | | | | | | | | | | | | | | | | |
| Gerzeh | | | | | | | | | | | | | | | | | | | | | | |
| Gezira Sangaha | | | | | | | | | | | | | | | | | | | | | | |
| Giza South | | | | | | | | | | | | | | | | | | X | | | | |
| Gurob | | | | | | | | | | | | | | | | | | | | | | |
| Harageh | | | | | | | | | | | | | | | | | | | | | | |
| Heliopolis | | | | | | | | | | | | | | | | | | | | | X | |
| Helwan | X | | | | | X | X | | | | | | | | X | X | X | | | | | |
| el-Huseiniya | | | | | | | | | | | | | | | | | | | | | | |
| Kafr Ghattati | | | | | | X | | | | | | | | | | | | | | | | |
| Kafr Hassan Dawood | | | | | | | | | | | | | | | | | | | | | | X |
| Khelwet Abu Mussalem | | | | | | | | | | | | | | | | | | | | | | |
| Kom el-Khilgan | | | | | | | | | | | | | | | | | | | | | X | X |
| Kufur Nigm | | | | | | | | | | | | | | | | | | | | | X | X |
| Lahun | X | X | X | | | X | | | X | | | | | | | | | | | | | X |
| Maadi-cemetery | | | | | | | | | | | | | | | | | | | | | | |
| Maadi-Dyn. 1 | | | | | | | | | | | | | | | | | | | X | | | X |
| Maadi-setlement | | | | | | | | | | | | | | | | | | | | | X | |
| Ma'asara | | | | | | | | | | | | | | | | | | | | | | |
| Marsa Matruh | | | | | | | | | | | | | | | | | | | | | | |
| Mendes | | | | | | | | | | | | | | | | | | | | | | |
| Merimde | | | | | | | | | | | | | | | | | | | | | | |

91

| Site | | | | | | | | | | | | | | | | | | | | | |
|---|---|---|---|---|---|---|---|---|---|---|---|---|---|---|---|---|---|---|---|---|---|
| Minshat Abu Omar | | | | | | | | | | | | | | | | | | | X | | |
| Minshat Ezzat | | | | | | | | | | | | | X | | | | | | | | |
| el-Omari | | | | | | | | | | | | | | | | | | X | X | | |
| el-Qatta | | | | | | | | | | | | | | | | | | | | | X |
| es-Saff | | | | | | | | | | | | | | | | | | | | | |
| Saqqara-Royal cemetery | | | | | | | | | | | | | | | X | | | | | | |
| Saqqara North | | | | | | | | | | | | | | | | | X | | | | X |
| Saqqara Serapeum | | | | | X | | | | | | | | | | | | | | | | X |
| Saqqara South | | | | | | | | | | | | | | | | | | | | | |
| Sedment | X | | | | | X | X | | | | | | | | | | | | | | |
| Tarkhan | X | | | | | X | | X | | | X | | | | | | X | X | | | |
| Tell Basta | | X | | | | | | | | | | | | | | | | | | | |
| Tell el-Daba el-Qanan | | | | | | | | | | | | | | | | | | | | | |
| Tell el-Farkha | | | | | | | | | | | | | | | | | X | X | | | |
| Tell el-Ginn | | | | | | | | | | | | | | | | | | | | | |
| Tell Ibrahim Awad | | | | | | | | | | X | | | | | | | X | | | | |
| Tell el-Iswid South | | | | | | | | | | | | | | | | | | | | | |
| Tell el-Masha'la | | | | | | | | | | | | | | | | | X | | | | |
| Tell el-Murra | | | | | | | | | | | | | | | | | | | | | X |
| Tell es-Samara | | | | | | | | | | | | | | | | | | | | | |
| et-Tibbin | | | | | | | | | | | | | | | | | | | | | X |
| Turah | X | | | | | | | X | | | | | | | | | | | | | X |
| Turah el-Asmant | X | | | | X | X | | | | | | | | | | | X | | | | |
| Wadi Digla | | | | | | | | | | | | | | | | | | | | | |
| Wardan | | | | | | | | | | | | | | | | | | | | | |
| Zawiyet el-Arian | | | | | | | | | | | | | | | | | | | | | X |

# 9. REFERENCES:

## ABBREVIATIONS:

*AnzAWW – Anzeiger der Akademie der Wissenschaften in Wien*
*ASAE – Annales du Service des Antiquités de l'Égypte*
*BACE – Bulletin of the Australian Centre for Egyptology*
*BCE – Bulletin de la Céramique Égyptienne*
*BIFAO – Bulletin de l'Institut Français d'Archeologie Orientale*
*CdE – Chronique d'Égypte*
*EA – Egyptian Archaeology*
*GM – Göttinger Miszellen*
*JARCE – Journal of the American Research Centre in Egypt*
*JEA – Journal of Egyptian Archaeology*
*JEOL – Jaarbericht van het Vooraziatisch-egyptisch Genootschap Ex Oriente Lux*
*JNES – Journal of Near Eastern Studies*
*JSSEA – Journal of the Society for the Study of Egyptian Antiquities*
*MDAIK – Mitteilungen des Deutschen Archäologischen Instituts, Abteilung Kairo*
*MDOG – Mitteilungen der Deutschen Orient-Gesellschaft*
*OMRO – Oudheidkundige Mededelingen uit het Rijksmuseum van Oudheden te Leiden*
*Or – Orientalia*
*PAM – Polish Archaeology in the Mediterranean*
*SAAC – Studies in Ancient Art and Civilization*


Abłamowicz R., 2002, Animal remains [in:] Chłodnicki M., Ciałowicz K.M. with contributions by Abłamowicz R., Herbich T., Jórdeczka M., Jucha M., Kabaciński J., Kubiak-Martens L. and Mączyńska A., Polish excavations at Tell el-Farkha (Ghazala) in the Nile Delta. Preliminary report 1998-2001, *Archeologia* LIII: 109-114.
- 2004, Animal Remains [in:] Chłodnicki M. and Ciałowicz K.M. with contributions by Abłamowicz R., Dębowska J., Jucha M., Kirkowski R. and Mączyńska A., Polish excavations at Tell el-Farkha (Ghazala) in the Nile Delta. Preliminary report 2002-2003, *Archeologia* LV: 70-74.
- 2006, Archeozoological research [in:] Chłodnicki M. and Ciałowicz K.M. with contributions by Abłamowicz R., Cichowski K., Dębowska-Ludwin J., Jucha M., Kabaciński J., Kaczmarek M., Pawlikowski M., Pryc G., Rewekant A., Skrzypczak M., Szejnoga P. and Wasilewski M., Polish excavations at Tell el-Farkha (Ghazala) in the Nile Delta. Preliminary report 2004-2005, *Archeologia* LVII : 109-114.
- 2008, Symbolic faunal remains from graves in Tell el-Farkha (Egypt), *PAM* XX: 373-378.

Adams B., 1990, An enigmatic sealing from Abydos, *Eretz-Israel* 21: 1-9.

- 1996, Elite tombs at Hierakonpolis [in:] Spencer A.J. (ed.), *Aspects of Early Egypt*, London: 1-15.
- 1999a, Early temples at Hierakonpolis and beyond [in:] *Centenary of Mediterranean Archaeology at the Jagiellonian University 1897-1997*, Kraków: 15-28.
- 1999b, Unprecedented discoveries at Hierakonpolis, *EA* 15: 29-31.
- 2000, *Excavations in the Locality 6 Cemetery at Hierakonpolis 1979-1985*, Oxford.
- 2002, Seeking the roots of ancient Egypt. A unique cemetery reveals monuments and rituals from before the pharaohs, *Archéo-Nil* 12: 11-28.

Adams B. and Ciałowicz K.M, 1997, *Protodynastic Egypt*, Princes Risborough.

Adly E., 2005, Minshat Ezzat, *Bulletin of the Institute of Archaeology* XXX:100.

Amer M. and Rizkana I., 1953a, Excavations in Wadi Digla: first season's report (1951-1952), *Bulletin of the Faculty of Arts* XV, 97-100.
- 1953b, Excavations in Wadi Digla. Second season report (1953), *Bulletin of the Faculty of Arts* XV, 201-205.

Ayrton E.R., Currely C.T. and Weingall A.E.P., 1904, *Abydos, Part III*, London.

Badawi F.A., 1978, Die Grabung der ägyptischen Altertümerverwaltung in Merimde-Benisalame im Oktober/November 1976, *MDAIK* 34 (1978): 43-51.
- 1980, Beigabengräber aus Merimde [in:] Eiwanger J., Dritter Vorbericht über die Wierderaufnahme der Grabungen in der neolithischen Siedlung Merimde-Benisalame, *MDAIK* 36, 70-76.
- 1987, Kurzbericht über die neuen ägyptischen Ausgrabungen in Ma'adi (Prädynastisch), *Mitteilungsblatt der Archaeologia Venatoria* e.V. 12.
- 2003, Preliminary report on the 1984-1986 excavations at Maadi-West, *MDAIK* 59: 1-10.

Baghdadi S.G. el-, 1999, La palete decorée de Minshat Ezzat (delta), *Archéo-Nil* 9: 9-11.
- 2003, Proto- and Early Dynastic necropolis of Minshat Ezzat, Dakahlia province, Northeast Delta, *Archéo-Nil* 13: 143-152.
- 2005, The Proto-Dynastic and Early Dynastic necropolis of Tell el-Daba'a (El-Qanan) and Tell el-Samarah (El Dakahlia province, Northeast Delta) [in:] Midant-Reynes B., Tristan Y. et al. (eds), *Predynastic and Early Dynastic Egypt. Origin of State, Toulouse (France) – 5-8 Sept. 2005, Abstracts of Papers*, Toulose: 95-96.

Baghdadi S.G. el- and el-Said Nur N.M., 2002, The Late Predynastic-Early Dynastic cemeteries of Minshat Ezzat and Tell el-Samarah (el-Daqahliya governorate), Northeastern Delta [in:] Ciałowicz K.M., Chłodnicki M. and Hendrickx S. (eds),

*Abstracts of Papers, Origin of the State. Predynastic and Early Dynastic Egypt, International Conference, Cracow 28th August – 1st September 2002*, Kraków: 31-32.

Bakr M.I., 1988, The new excavations at Ezbet El-Tell, Kufur Nigm; the first season 1984 [in:] van den Brink E.C.M. (ed.), *The Archaeology of the Nile Delta. Problems and Priorities*, Amsterdam: 49-62.
- 1992, *Tombs and Burial Custom at Bubastis. The Area of the so-called Western Cemetery*, Cairo.
- 1994, Excavations of Kufur Nigm, *Bibliothèque d'Étude* 106/4: 9-17.
- 2000, Recent excavations at Ezbet et-Tell [in:] Hawass Z. and Milward Jones A. (eds), *Eighth International Congress of Egyptologists. Cairo, 28 March - 3 April 2000. Abstracts of Papers*, Cairo: 25-26.
- 2003, Excavations at Ezbet al-Tel, Kufur Nigm: the third and fourth season (1988-1990) [in:] Hawass Z. (ed.), *Egyptology at the Dawn of the Twenty-first Century. Proceedings of the Eighth International Congress of Egyptologists, Cairo 2000. Vol. 1, Archaeology*, Cairo-New York: 30-43.

Bakr M.I., el-Moneim M.A.A. and Selim M.O.M., 1996, Protodynastic excavations at Tell Hassan Dawud (Eastern Delta) [in:] Krzyżaniak L., Kroeper K. and Kobusiewicz M. (eds), *Interregional Contacts in the Later Prehistory of Northeastern Africa*, Poznań: 277-278.

Banna E. el-, 1990, Une nécropole inedité d'époque archaique decouvertée près de Helouan, au sud du Caire, *GM* 117/118: 7-27.

Bard K.A., 1987, The geography of excavated Predynastic sites and the rise of complex society, *JARCE* 24: 81-94.

Barsanti A., 1901, Rapports de M. Alexandre Barsanti sur les déblaiements opérés autour de la pyramide d'Ounas pendant les années 1899-1901, *ASAE* II: 244-257.
- 1902, Fouilles autour de la pyramide d'Ounas. (1901-1902), *ASAE* III: 182-184.

Bates O., 1915, Archaic burials at Marsa Matruh, *Ancient Egypt*: 158-165.
- 1927, Excavations at Marsa Matruh, *Harvard African Studies* 8: 123-198.

Baud M., 2005, La nécropole d'élite de la Ière dynastie á Abou Rawach: essai cartographique, *Archéo-Nil* 15: 11-16.

Baumgartel E.M., 1960, *The Cultures of Prehistoric Egypt II*, London.

Beckerath J. von, 1984, *Handbuch der ägyptischen Königsnamen*, Munich-Berlin.

Bestock L., 2008, The evolution of royal ideology: new discoveries from the reign of Aha [in:] Midant-Reynes B. and Tristant Y. (eds), Rowland J. and Hendrickx S. (coll.), *Egypt at its origins 2. Proceedings of the international conference 'Origin of the State. Predynastic and Early Dynastic Egypt', Toulouse (France), 5th–8th September 2005*, Leuven-Paris: 1091-1106.

Bietak M., 1975, *Tell el Dab'a II. Der Fundort im Rahmen einer archäologisch-geographischen Untersuchung über das ägyptische Ostdelta*, Wien.

Birrell M., 2000, Portcullis stones: tomb security during the Early Dynastic period, *BACE* 11: 17-28.

Boessneck J. and von den Driesch A., 1990, [Animal Remains] [in:] Dreyer G., Umm el-Qaab. Nachuntersuchungen im frühzeitlichen Königsfriedhof. 3./4. Vorbericht, *MDAIK* 46: 53-90.

Boessneck J., von den Driesch A. and Eissa A., 1992, Eine Eselsbestattung der 1. Dynastie in Abusir, *MDAIK* 48: 1-10.

Boghdady F., 1932, An Archaic tomb at Old Cairo, *ASAE* 32: 153-160.

Bonnet H., 1928, *Ein frühgeschichtliches Gräberfeld bei Abusir*, Leipzig.

Borchardt L., 1898, Das Grab des Menes, *Zeitschrift zur Äegyptische Sprache* 36: 87-105.

Brewer D.J., 2006, *Ancient Egypt. Foundations of a Civilization*, Edinburgh.

Brewer D.J. and Wenke R.J., 1992, Transitional Late Predynastic – Early Dynastic occupations at Mendes: a preliminary report [in:] van den Brink E.C.M. (ed.), *The Nile Delta in Transition: 4th-3rd Millennium B.C.*, Tel Aviv: 191-197.

Brink E.C.M. van den, 1988a, The Amsterdam University survey expedition to the Northeastern Nile Delta (1984-1986), [in:] van den Brink E.C.M. (ed.), *The Archaeology of the Nile Delta. Problems and Priorities*, Amsterdam: 65-114.
- 1988b, Survey, Sharqiya province, *BCE* XII, 4-7.
- 1989, A transitional Late Predynastic – Early Dynastic settlement site in the Northeastern Nile Delta, Egypt, *MDAIK* 45, 55-108.
- 1992a, Preliminary report on the excavations at Tell Ibrahim Awad, seasons 1988-1990 [in:] van den Brink E.C.M. (ed.), *The Nile Delta in Transition: 4th-3rd Millennium B.C.*, Tel Aviv: 43-57.
- 1992b, Preface and short introduction [in:] van den Brink E.C.M. (ed.), *The Nile Delta in Transition: 4th-3rd Millennium B.C.*, Tel Aviv: vi-viii.
- 1993, Settlement patterns in the Northeastern Nile Delta during the forth-second millennia B.C. [in:] Krzyżaniak L., Kobusiewicz M. and Alexander J. (eds), *Environmental Change and Human Culture in*

*the Nile Basin and Northern Africa until the Second Millennium B.C.*, Poznań: 279-303.

Brunton G., 1939, A First Dynasty cemetery at Maadi, *ASAE* XXXIX: 419-424.
- 1948, *Matmar*, London.

Brunton G. and Engelbach R., 1927, *Gurob*, London.

Buchez N. and Midant-Reynes B., 2007, Le site prédynastique de Kom el-Khilgan (Delta oriental). Données nouvelles sur le processus d'unification culturelle au IVe millénaire [in:] *Objects for Eternity. Egyptian Antiquities from the W. Arnold Meijer Collection, BIFAO* 107: 43-70.
- 2011, A tale of two funerary traditions: the Predynastic cemetery at Kom el-Khilgan (Eastern Delta) [in:] Friedman R.F. and Fiske P.N (eds) *Egypt at its Origins 3. Proceedings of the Third International Conference "Origin of the State. Predynastic and Early Dynastic Egypt", London, 27th July – 1st August 2008*, Leuven: 831-858.

Caneva I., Frangipane M. and Palmieri A., 1989, Recent excavations at Maadi (Egypt) [in:] Krzyżaniak L. and Kobusiewicz M. (eds), *Late Prehistory of the Nile Basin and the Sahara*, Poznań: 287-293.

Capart J., 1905, *Primitive Art in Egypt*, London.

Case H. and Payne J.C., 1962, Tomb 100: the decorated tomb at Hierakonpolis, *JEA* 48: 5-18.

Castillos J.J., 1976, An analysis of the tombs in a Ist Dynasty cemetery at Sakkara, *JSSEA* 6, 4: 1-12.
- 1982a, An analysis of the Predynastic cemeteries G and H at Harageh [in:] Castillos J.J., *A Reappraisal of the Published Evidence on Egyptian Predynastic and Early Dynastic Cemeteries*, Toronto: 149-152.
- 1982b, An analysis of the tombs in the Protodynastic cemetery at Abusir-el-Meleq [in:] Castillos J.J., *A Reappraisal of the Published Evidence on Egyptian Predynastic and Early Dynastic Cemeteries*, Toronto: 153-158.
- 1982c, An analysis of the tombs in the Protodynastic cemeteries at Turah [in:] Castillos J.J., *A Reappraisal of the Published Evidence on Egyptian Predynastic and Early Dynastic Cemeteries*, Toronto: 165-170.
- 1982d, An analysis of the tombs in the Early Predynastic cemetery at Merimde Beni Salame [in:] Castillos J.J., *A Reappraisal of the Published Evidence on Egyptian Predynastic and Early Dynastic Cemeteries*, Toronto: 171-172.
- 1983, *A Study of the Spatial Distribution of Large and Richly Endowed Tombs in Egyptian Predynastic and Early Dynastic Cemeteries*, Toronto.

Caton-Thompson G. and Gardiner E.W., 1934, *The Desert Fayum*, London.

Chłodnicki M., 1988, Pottery from the archaeological survey of the Eastern Nile Delta, Egypt – interim report, *BCE* 13: 22-26.
- 2010, Excavations at the Central Kom [in:] Chłodnicki M. and Ciałowicz K.M. with contribution by Abłamowicz R., Dębowska-Ludwin J., Jucha M.A., Mączyńska A., Pryc G., Rozwadowski M. and Sobas M., Polish excavations at Tell el-Farkha (Ghazala) in the Nile Delta. Preliminary report 2006-2007, *Archeologia* LVIII (2008): 105-109.
- 2011, The Central kom of Tell el-Farkha: 1000 years of history (c. 3600-2600 BC) [in:] Friedman R.F. and Fiske P.N. (eds), *Egypt at its Origins 3. Proceedings of the Third International Conference "Origin of the State. Predynastic and Early Dynastic Egypt", London, 27th July – 1st August 2008*, Leuven: 41-57.

Chłodnicki M. and Ciałowicz K.M. with contributions by Abłamowicz R., Herbich T., Jórdeczka M., Jucha M., Kabaciński J. and Mączyńska A., 2002a, Tell el-Farkha seasons 1998-1999. Preliminary report, *MDAIK* 58: 89-117.

Chłodnicki M. and Ciałowicz K.M. with contributions by Abłamowicz R., Herbich T., Jórdeczka M., Jucha M., Kabaciński J., Kubiak-Martens L. and Mączyńska A., 2002b, Polish excavations at Tell el-Farkha (Ghazala) in the Nile Delta. Preliminary report 1998-2001, *Archeologia* LIII: 63-119.

Chłodnicki M. and Ciałowicz K.M. with contributions by Abłamowicz R., Dębowska J., Jucha M., Kirkowski R. and Mączyńska A., 2004, Polish excavations at Tell el-Farkha (Ghazala) in the Nile Delta. Preliminary report 2002-2003, *Archeologia* LV: 47-74.

Chłodnicki M. and Ciałowicz K.M. with contributions by Abłamowicz R., Cichowski K., Dębowska-Ludwin J., Jucha M., Kabaciński J., Kaczmarek M., Pawlikowski M., Pryc G., Rewekant A., Skrzypczak M., Szejnoga P. and Wasilewski M., 2006, Polish excavations at Tell el-Farkha (Ghazala) in the Nile Delta. Preliminary report 2004-2005, *Archeologia* LVII :71-128.

Chłodnicki M., Ciałowicz K.M and Mączyńska A. (eds), 2012, *Tell el-Farkha I*, Poznań-Kraków.

Chłodnicki M. and Geming M.M., 2012, Lower Egyptian settlement on the Central Kom [in:] Chłodnicki M., Ciałowicz K.M. and Mączyńska A. (eds), 2012, *Tell el-Farkha I*, Poznań-Kraków: 89-104.

Ciałowicz K.M., 1987, *Les tête de massues des périodes prédynastique at archaïque dans la vallée du Nil*, Warszawa-Kraków.
- 1991, *Les palettes égyptiennes aux motifs zoomorphes et sans décoration*, Kraków.
- 1993, *Symbolika przedstawień władcy egipskiego w okresie predynastycznym*, Kraków.

*Early Burial Customs in Northern Egypt*

- 1996, La Dynastie 0. Conquérants ou administrateurs ?, *SAAC* 7: 7-23.
- 1998, The King and his retinue. The origins of archaic accompanied burials, *African Reports* I: 23-32.
- 1999, *Początki cywilizacji egipskiej*, Warszawa-Kraków.
- 2001, *La naissance d'un royaume. L' Égypte dès la période prédynastique à la fin de la I^{ère} Dynastie*, Kraków.
- 2008a, The nature of the relation between Lower and Upper Egypt in the Protodynastic period. A view from Tell el-Farkha [in:] Midant-Reynes B. and Tristant Y. (eds), Rowland J. and Hendrickx S. (coll.), *Egypt at its origins 2. Proceedings of the international conference 'Origin of the State. Predynastic and Early Dynastic Egypt', Toulouse (France), 5th–8th September 2005*, Leuven-Paris: 501–513.
- 2008b, Enigmatic building from Tell el-Farkha. Preliminary study, *PAM* XX: 399-411.
- 2012a, Lower Egyptian settlement on the Western Kom [in:] Chłodnicki M., Ciałowicz K.M. and Mączyńska A. (eds), *Tell el-Farkha I*, Poznań-Kraków: 149-162.
- 2012b, Protodynastic and Early Dynastic settlement bon the Western Kom [in:] Chłodnicki M., Ciałowicz K.M. and Mączyńska A. (eds), *Tell el-Farkha I*, Poznań-Kraków: 163-180.

Cichowski K., 2001, Konstrukcje osadnicze kultury dolnoegipskiej (ok. 3800-3200 p.n.e.) w Tell el-Farcha, Kraków. (unpublished master thesis)
- 2006, Excavations at the Western Kom [in:] Chłodnicki M. and Ciałowicz K.M. with contribution by Abłamowicz R., Cichowski K., Dębowska-Ludwin J., Jucha M., Kabaciński J., Kaczmarek M., Pawlikowski M., Pryc G., Rewekant A., Skrzypczak M., Szejnoga P. and Wasilewski M., Polish excavations at Tell el-Farkha (Ghazala) in the Nile Delta. Preliminary report 2004-2005, *Archeologia* LVII: 72-77.
- 2008, The brewery complex from Tell el-Farkha. Archaeological aspects of the discovery [in:] Midant-Reynes B. and Tristant Y. (eds), Rowland J. and Hendrickx S. (coll.), *Egypt at its origins 2. Proceedings of the international conference 'Origin of the State. Predynastic and Early Dynastic Egypt', Toulouse (France), 5th–8th September 2005*, Leuven-Paris: 33-40.

Covington D., 1905, Mastaba Mount excavations, *ASAE* VI: 193-218.

Crubézy E. and Midant-Reynes B., 2000, Les sacrifices humains á l'époque prédynastique: l'apport de la nécropole d'Adaima, *Archéo-Nil* 10: 21-40.

Czarnowicz M., 2009, Tell el-Farkha 2006. Oval-shaped pottery from grave no. 9, *SAAC* 13: 43-49.

Ćwiek A., 1995, Gisr el-Mudir and the early royal necropolis at Saqqara [in:] Eyre J. (ed.), *Seventh International Congress of Egyptologists, Cambridge 1995. Abstracts of Papers*, Oxford: 41-42.

Daressy G., 1905, Un edifice archaique a Nezlet Batran, *ASAE* VI: 99-106.

Davis W.M., 1983, Cemetery T at Naqada, *MDAIK* 39: 17-29.

Debono F., 1950, Héliopolis. Trouvailles prédynastiques, *CdE* 25: 233-237.

Debono F. and Mortensen B., 1988, *The Predynastic Cemetery at Heliopolis*, Mainz am Rhein.
- 1990, *El-Omari. A Neolithic Settlement and Other Sites in the Vicinity of Wadi Hof, Helwan*, Mainz am Rhein.

Dębowska-Ludwin J., 2008, Political and economic transformation as reflected by burial rites observed at the Protodynastic part of cemetery in Tell el-Farkha, *PAM* XX, Research 2008: 457-466.
- 2009, The catalogue of graves from Tell el-Farkha, *Recherches Archéologiques NS* 1: 457–486.
- 2010, Multiple and disordered burials as special funerary practices in early Egypt – examples from Tell el-Farkha, *Folia Orientalia* 47: 371-378.
- 2011a, Sepulchral architecture in detail: new data from Tell el-Farkha [in:] Friedman R.F. and Fiske P.N. (eds) *Egypt at its Origins 3. Proceedings of the Third International Conference "Origin of the State. Predynastic and Early Dynastic Egypt", London, 27th July – 1st August 2008*, Leuven: 257-268.
- 2011b, The necropolis at Tell el-Farkha reconsidered, *Recherches Archéologiques NS* 2: 4-20.
- 2012, The cemetery [in:] Chłodnicki M., Ciałowicz K. M. and Mączyńska A. (eds), *Tell el-Farkha I*, Poznań-Kraków: 53-75.

Dębowska-Ludwin J., Jucha M., Kołodziejczyk P. and Pryc G., 2010, Tell el-Farkha (2009 season): grave no. 100, *SAAC* 14, 23-42.

Dodson A., 1996, The mysterious Second Dynasty, *KMT* 7,2: 19-31.

Dougherty S. and Friedman R., Sacred or mundane: scalping and decapitation at Predynastic Hierakonpolis [in:] Midant-Reynes B. and Tristant Y. (eds), Rowland J. and Hendrickx S. (coll.), *Egypt at its origins 2. Proceedings of the international conference 'Origin of the State. Predynastic and Early Dynastic Egypt', Toulouse (France), 5th–8th September 2005*, Leuven-Paris: 311-338.

Dreyer G., 1998, *Umm el-Qaab. Das prädynastische Königsgrab U-j und seine frühen Schriftzeugnisse*, Mainz.

- 2007, Ein unterirdisches Labyrinth: das Grab des Königs Ninetjer in Sakkara [in:] Dreyer G. and Polz D. (eds), *Begegnung mit der Vergangenheit: 100 Jahre in Ägypten: Deutsches Archäologisches Institut Kairo 1907-2007*, Mainz am Rhein: 130-138.

Dreyer G. with contributions by Boessneck J., von den Driesch A. and Klug S., 1990, Umm el-Qaab. Nachuntersuchungen im frühzeitlichen Königsfriedhof. 3./4. Vorbericht, *MDAIK* 46: 53-90.

Dreyer G., Hartung U. and Pumpenmeier F., 1993, Umm el-Qaab. Nachuntersuchungen im frühzeitlichen Königsfriedhof. 5/6 Vorbericht, *MDAIK* 49: 23-62.

Dreyer G., Engel E-M., Hartung U., Hikade T., Köhler E. Ch. and Pumpenmeier F., 1996, Umm el-Qaab. Nachuntersuchungen im frühzeitlichen Königsfriedhof. 7/8 Vorbericht, *MDAIK* 52: 11-81.

Dreyer G., Hartung U., Hikade T., Köhler E. Ch., Müller V. and Pumpenmeier F., 1998, Umm el-Qaab. Nachuntersuchungen im frühzeitlichen Königsfriedhof. 9/10 Vorbericht, *MDAIK* 54: 77-167.

Dunham D., 1978, *Zawiyet el-Aryan. The Cemeteries Adjacent to the Layer Pyramid*, Boston.

Eigner D., 2003, Tell Ibrahim Awad: a sequence of temple buildings from Dynasty 0 to the Middle Kingdom [in:] Hawass Z. (ed.), *Egyptology at the Dawn of the Twenty-first Century. Proceedings of the Eighth International Congress of Egyptologists, Cairo 2000. Vol. 1, Archaeology*, Cairo-New York: 162-170.

Eiwanger J., 1978, Erster Vorbericht über die Wiederaufnahme der Grabungen in der neolitischen Siedlung Merimde-Benisalame, *MDAIK* 34: 33-42.
- 1979, Zweiter Vorbericht über die Wiederaufnahme der Grabungen in der neolithischen Siedlung Merimde-Benisalame, *MDAIK* 35: 23-57.
- 1980, Dritter Vorbericht über die Wiederaufnahme der Grabungen in der neolithischen Siedlung Merimde-Benisalame, *MDAIK* 36: 61-76.
- 1982, Die neolithische Siedlung von Merimde-Benisalame: Vierter Bericht, *MDAIK* 38: 67-82.
- 1984, *Merimde-Benisalame I. Die Funde der Urschicht*, Mainz am Rhein.
- 1988, *Merimde-Benisalame II. Die Funde der mittleren Merimdekultur*, Mainz am Rhein.
- 1992, *Merimde-Benisalame III. Die Funde der jungeren Merimdekultur*, Mainz am Rhein.

Ellis Ch., 1992, A statistical analysis of the Protodynastic burials in the "Valley" cemetery of Kafr Tarkhan [in:] van den Brink E.C.M. (ed.), *The Nile Delta in Transition: 4th. - 3rd. Millennium B.C.*, Tel Aviv: 241-258.
- 1996, Expressions of social status: a statistical approach to the Late Predynastic/Early Dynastic cemeteries of Kafr Tarkhan [in:] Krzyżaniak L., Kroeper K. and Kobusiewicz M. (eds), *Interregional Contacts in the Later Prehistory of Northeastern Africa*, Poznań: 151-164.
- 1999, Kafr Tarkhan (Kafr Ammar) [in:] Bard K.A. (ed.), *Encyclopedia of the Archaeology of Ancient Egypt*, London-New York: 389-390.

Emery W.B., 1938, *The Tomb of Hemaka*, Cairo.
- 1939a, *Hor-Aha*, Cairo.
- 1939b, A Preliminary Report on the First Dynasty Copper Treasure from North Saqqara, *ASAE* XXXIX: 427-437.
- 1949, *Great Tombs of the First Dynasty I*, Cairo.
- 1954, *Great Tombs of the First Dynasty II*, London.
- 1958, *Great Tombs of the First Dynasty III*, London.
- 1961, *Archaic Egypt*, Edinburgh.
- 1966, Preliminary Report on the Excavations at North Saqqara, 1965-6, *JEA* 52: 3-8.

Engel E.-M., 1996, Grabkomplex des Qa'a [in:] Dreyer G., Engel E.-M., Hartung U., Hikade T., Köhler E. Ch. and Pumpenmeier F., Umm el-Qaab. Nachuntersuchungen im frühzeitlichen Königsfriedhof. 7/8 Vorbericht, *MDAIK* 52: 57-71.

Engelbach R., 1923, *Harageh*, London.

Engles D.R., 1990, An Early Dynastic cemetery at Kafr Ghattati, *JARCE* XXVII: 71-87.

Faltings D., 1998, Recent excavations in Tell el-Fara'in/Buto: new finds and their chronological implications [in:] Eyre C.J. (ed.), *Proceedings of the Seventh International Congress of Egyptologists*, Leuven: 365-375.
- 2002 , The chronological frame and social structure of Buto in the Fourth Millenium BC [in:] van den Brink E.C.M. and Levy T.E. (eds), *Egypt and the Levant. Interrelations from the 4th through the Early 3rd Millenium BCE*, London-New York: 165-170.

Faltings D., Ballet P., Forster F., French P., Ihde C., Sahlmann H., Thomalsky J., Thumshirn C. and Wodzińska A., 2000, Zweiter Vorbericht über die Arbeiten in Buto von 1996 bis 1999, *MDAIK* 56: 131-143.

Faltings D. and Köhler Ch., 1996, Vorbericht über die Ausgrabungen des DAI in Tell el-Fara'in/Buto 1993 bis 1995, *MDAIK* 52: 87-114.

Firth C.M., 1931, Excavations of the Departament of Antiquities at Saqqara, 1930-1931, *ASAE* XXXI: 46-8.

Fischer H.G., 1958, A fragment of Late Predynastic Egyptian relief from the Eastern Delta, *Artibus Asiae* XXI: 64-88.

Friedman R.F., 1996, The ceremonial centre at Hierakonpolis Locality HK29A [in:] Spencer A.J. (ed.), *Aspects of Early Egypt*, London: 16-35.

- 2008, Excavating Egypt's early kings: recent discoveries in the elite cemetery at Hierakonpolis [in:] Midant-Reynes B. and Tristant Y. (eds), Rowland J. and Hendrickx S. (coll.), *Egypt at its origins 2. Proceedings of the international conference 'Origin of the State. Predynastic and Early Dynastic Egypt', Toulouse (France), 5th–8th September 2005*, Leuven-Paris: 1157–1194.
- 2009, Hierakonpolis locality HK29A: the Predynastic ceremonial center revisited, *JARCE* 45: 79-103.

Friedman R., van Neer W. and Linseele V., 2011, The elite predynastic cemetery at Hierakonpolis: 2009-2010 update [in:] Friedman R. F. and Fiske P. N. (eds), *Egypt at its Origins 3. Proceedings of the Third International Conference "Origin of the State. Predynastic and Early Dynastic Egypt", London, 27th July – 1st August 2008*, Leuven: 157-191.

Friedman R., Watrall E., Jones J., Fahmy A.G., van Neer W. and Linseele V., 2002, Excavations at Hierakonpolis, *Archéo-Nil* 12: 55-68.

Garstang J., 1903, *Mahâsna and Bêt Khallaf*, London.
- 1905, The so-called Tomb of Mena at Nagadeh in Upper Egypt [in:] *British Association for the Advancement of Science, Report of the 74th Meeting, Cambridge 1904*, London: 711-712.

Ginter B., Kozłowski J.K., Pawlikowski M. and Śliwa J., 1982, El-Tarif und Qasr el-Sagha, Forschungen zur Siedlungsgeschichte des Neolithikums, der Frühpredynastischen Epoche und des Mittleren Reiches, *MDAIK* 38: 97-129.

Ginter B., Kozłowski J.K., Pawlikowski M., Śliwa J. and Kemmerer-Grothaus H., 1998, *Frühe Keramik und Kleinfund aus El-Târif*, Mainz.

Haarlem W.M. van, 1993, Additions and corrections to the publication of a First Dynasty tomb from Tell Ibrahim Awad (Eastern Nile Delta), *GM* 133: 37-41.
- 1996, A tomb of the First Dynasty at Tell Ibrahim Awad, *OMRO* 76: 7-34.
- 1997, Imitations in pottery of stone vessels in a Protodynastic tomb from Tell Ibrahim Awad, *Archéo-Nil* 7: 145-150.
- 1998a, The excavations at Tell Ibrahim Awad (Eastern Nile Delta): recent results, [in:] Eyre C.J. (ed.), *Proceedings of the 7th International Congress of Egyptology, Cambridge 1995*, Leuven: 509-513.
- 1998b, Les fouilles à Tell Ibrahim Awad (delta oriental du Nil): Resultats recents, *Bulletin de la Société Française d'Égyptologie* 141: 8-19.
- 2000, An introduction to the site of Tell Ibrahim Awad, *Ägypten und Levante* 10: 13-16.
- 2001, Tell Ibrahim Awad, *EA* 18: 33-35.
- 2003, The excavations at Tell Ibrahim Awad (Sharqiya province), seasons 1995-2000 [in:] Hawass Z. (ed.), *Egyptology at the Dawn of the Twenty-first Century. Proceedings of the Eighth International Congress of Egyptologists, Cairo 2000. Vol. 1, Archaeology*, Cairo-New York: 536-540.

Habachi L. and Kaiser W., 1985, Ein Friedhof der Maadikultur bei es-Saff, *MDAIK* 41: 43-46.

Hagg Ragab M.A. el-, 1992, A report on the excavations of the Egyptian Antiquities Organization (E.A.O.) at Beni Amir and el-Masha'la in the Eastern Nile Delta [in:] van den Brink E.C.M. (ed.), *The Nile Delta in Transition: 4th-3rd Millennium B.C.*, Tel Aviv: 207-213.

Hangary M.S. el-, 1992, The excavations of the Egyptian Antiquities Organization at Ezbet Hassan Dawud (Wadi Tumilat), season 1990 [in:] van den Brink E.C.M. (ed.), *The Nile Delta in Transition: 4th-3rd Millennium B.C.*, Tel Aviv: 215-216.

Hansen D.P., 1965, Mendes 1964, *JARCE* 4: 31-37.
- 1967, Mendes 1965 and 1966. I. The excavations at Tell el Rub'a, *JARCE* 6: 5-16.

Hartung U., 1998, Friedhof U [in:] Dreyer G., Hartung U., Hikade T. and Köhler E.Ch., Umm el-Qaab. Nachuntersuchungen im frühzeitlichen Königsfriedhof 9./10. Vorbericht, *MDAIK* 54: 79-100.
- 2003a, Maadi, fouille de souvetage aux confines du Caire, *Archéo-Nil* 13: 29-35.
- 2003b, Bouto, fouille d'habitat dans le Delta du Nil, *Archéo-Nil* 13: 73-76.
- 2004, Rescue excavations in the Predynastic settlement of Maadi [in:] Hendrickx S., Friedman R.F., Ciałowcz K.M. and Chłodnicki M. (eds), *Egypt and its Origins. Studies in Memory of B. Adams*, Leuven: 337-356.

Hartung U., Abd el-Gelil M., von den Driesch A., Fares G., Hartmann R. and Hikade T., 2003a, Vorbericht über neue Untersuchungen in der prädynastischen Siedlung von Maadi, *MDAIK* 59: 149-198.

Hartung U., Ballet P., Beguin F., Bourriau J., French P., Herbich T., Kopp P., Lecuyot G. and Schmitt A., 2003b, Tell el-Fara'in – Buto , 8. Vorbericht, *MDAIK* 59: 199-267.

Hassan S.A., 1938, Excavations at Saqqara 1937-1938. IV. Underground cemetery of the IInd Dynasty, *ASAE* 38: 521.

Hassan F.A., 1985, Radiocarbon chronology of Neolithic and Predynastic sites in Upper Egypt and the Delta, *African Archaeological Review* 3: 95-116.
- 2000a, Kafr Hassan Dawood, *EA* 16: 37-39.
- 2000b, Kafr Hassan Dawood, preliminary results of the SCA-UCL archaeological investigations 1995-1999 [in:] Hawass Z. and Milward Jones A. (eds), *Eighth International Congress of Egyptologists. Cairo, 28 March - 3 April 2000. Abstracts of Papers*, Cairo: 81-82.

Hassan F.A., Tassie G.J., Tucker T.L., Rowland J.M. and van Wetering J., 2003, Social dynamics at the Late Predynastic to Early Dynastic site of Kafr Hassan Dawood, East Delta, Egypt, *Archéo-Nil* 13: 37-46.

Hawass Z., 1980, Archaic graves recently found at North Abu Roash, *MDAIK* 36: 229-244.

Hawass Z., Hassan F.A. and Gautier A., 1988, Chronology, sediments, and subsistence at Merimda Beni Salama, *JEA* 74: 31-38.

Helck W., 1987, *Untersuchungen zur Thinitenzeit*, Wiesbaden.

Hendrickx S., 1995, Vase decorated with hunting scene. Vase decorated with victory scene [in:] Phillips T. (ed.), *Africa. The Art of a Continent*, London : 59-60.
- 1996, The relative chronology of the Naqada culture: problems and possibilities [in:] Spencer A.J. (ed.), *Aspects of Early Egypt*, London: 36-69.
- 2002, Checklist of Predynastic "Decorated" pottery with human figures, *Cahiers Caribéens d'Egyptologie* 3/4: 29-50.
- 2006, Predynastic – Early Dynastic chronology [in:] Hornung E., Krauss R. and Warburton D.A. (eds), *Ancient Egyptian Chronology*, Leiden-Boston: 55-93.

Hendrickx S. and van den Brink E.C.M., 2002, Inventory of Predynastic and Early Dynastic cemerety and settlement sites in the Egyptian Nile Valley [in:] van den Brink E.C.M. and Levy T.E (eds), *Egypt and the Levant. Interrelations from the 4th through the Early 3rd Millenium BCE*, London-New York: 346-399.

Hikade T., 1999, An Early Dynastic flint workshop at Helwan, Egypt, *BACE* 10: 47-57.

Hoffman M.A., 1982, *The Predynastic of Hierakonpolis. An interim report*, Cairo, Illinois.
- 1983, Where nations began, *Science* 83,4: 42-51.
- 1987, *A Final Report to the National Endowment for the Humanities on Predynastic Research at Hierakonpolis 1985-86*, Columbia.
- 1991, *Egypt before the Pharaohs*, London, 2nd ed.

Hoffman M.A., Hamroush H.A. and Allen R.O., 1986, A model of urban development for the Hierakonpolis region from Predynastic through Old Kingdom times, *JARCE* 23: 175-188.

Holmes D.L., 1989, *The Predynastic Lithic Industries of Upper Egypt. A comparative Study of the Lithic Traditions of Badari, Naqada and Hierakonpolis*, Oxford.

Hughes G.R., 1941, The Oriental Institute archaeological reports on Near East, 1941, *American Journal of Semitic Languages and Literatures* 58: 406.

Jeffreys D., 1999, Helwan [in:] Bard K.A. (ed.), *Encyclopedia of the Archaeology of Ancient Egypt*, London-New York: 367-368.

Jeffreys D. and Tavares A., 1994, The historic landscape of Early Dynastic Memphis, *MDAIK* 50: 143-156.

Jones J., 2002, Funerary textiles of the rich and poor, *Nekhen News* 14: 13.

Joube G.R., 1938, Catalogue de l'outillage lithique provenant des tombes d'Abou-Roach, *KÊMI* 7: 71-113.
- 1946, Note additionnelle sur les objets Nos 8 et 9 d'Abou-Roach, *KÊMI* 8: 127-155.

Jucha M., 2006, Pottery from the graves [in:] Chłodnicki M., Ciałowicz K.M. et al., Polish excavations at Tell el-Farkha (Ghazala) in the Nile Delta. Preliminary report 2004-2005, *Archeologia* 57: 97-101.
- 2008, The corpus of "potmarks" from the graves at Tell el-Farkha [in:] Midant-Reynes B. and Tristant Y. (eds), *Egypt at its origin 2. Proceedings of the International Conference "Origin of the State. Predynastic and Early Dynastic Egypt" Toulouse (France), 5th-8th September 2005*, Leuven-Paris: 133-149.
- 2010a, The early Egyptian rulers in the Nile Delta. A view from the necropolis at Tell el-Farkha [in:] Hudec A. and Petrik M. (eds), *Commerce and Economy in Ancient Egypt. Proceedings of the Third International Congress for Young Egyptologists held in Budapest in September 2009*, Budapest : 81-97.
- 2010b, Pottery from the graves [in:] Chłodnicki M., Ciałowicz K.M. et al., Polish excavations at Tell el-Farkha (Ghazala) in the Nile Delta. Preliminary report 2006-2007, *Archeologia* 58: 132-135.
- 2012, The resent results of research in the North-Eastern Nile Delta: a view from Tell el-Murra [in:] Jucha M.A., Dębowska-Ludwin J. and Kołodziejczyk P. (eds), *VIth Central European Conference of Egyptologists. Egypt 2012: Perspective of Research. Programme and Abstracts*, Krakow: 18.

Jucha M.A. and Mączyńska A., 2011, Settlement sites in the Nile Delta, *Archéo-Nil* 21: 33-50.

Junker H., 1912, *Bericht über die Grabungen auf dem Friedhof in Turah. Winter 1909-10*, Wien.
- 1928, *Bericht uber die von der Akademie der Wissenschaften in Wien nach dem Westdelta entsendete Expedition*, Wien-Leipzig.
- 1929, Vorläufiger Bericht über die erste Grabung der Akademie der Wissenschaften in Wien auf der vorgeschichtlichen Siedlung Merimde-Benisalâme in 1929, *AnzAWW*, XVI-XVIII: 156-249.
- 1930a, Vorläufiger Bericht über die zweite Grabung der Akademie der Wissenschaften in Wien auf der vorgeschichtlichen Siedlung Merimde-Benisalâme

vom 7. Februar bis 8. April 1930, *AnzAWW*, V-XIII: 21-83.

- 1930b, Bericht uber die vom Deutschen Institut fur Ägyptische Altertumskunde nach dem Ostdelta-Rand unternommene Erkundungsfahrt, *MDAIK* 1: 3-37.
- 1932, Vorbericht über die dritte von der Akademie der Wissenschaften in Wien in Verbindung mit dem Egyptiska Museet in Stockholm unternommene Grabung auf der neolithischen Siedelung von Merimde-Benisalâme vom 6. November 1931 bis 20. Jänner 1932, *AnzAWW*, I-IV: 36-97.
- 1933, Vorläufiger Bericht über die vierte von der Akademie der Wissenschaften in Wien in Verbindung mit dem Egyptiska Museet in Stockholm unternommenen Grabungen auf der neolithischen Siedlung von Merimde-Benisalâme vom 2. Jänner bis 20. Februar 1933, *AnzAWW*, XVI-XXVII: 54-97.
- 1934, Vorläufiger Bericht über die fünfte von der Akademie der Wissenschaften in Wien in Verbindung mit dem Egyptiska Museet in Stockholm unternommenen Grabungen auf der neolithischen Siedlung von Merimde-Benisalâme in 1934, *AnzAWW*, X: 118-132.
- 1940, Vorbericht über die siebente Grabung der Akademie der Wissenschaften in Wien auf der vorgeschichtlichen Siedlung von Merimde-Benisalâme vom 25. Januar bis 4. April 1939, *AnzAWW*, I-V: 3-25.
- 1941, *Die politische Lehre von Memphis,* Abhandlungen der Preussischen Akademie der Wissenschaften, philosophisch-historische Klasse 6: 1-77.

Kabaciński J., 2003, Lithic industry at Tell el-Farkha (Eastern Delta) [in:] Krzyżaniak L., Kroeper K. and Kobusiewicz M. (eds), *Cultural Markers in the Late Prehistory of Northeastern Africa*, Poznań: 201-212.

Kahl J., 2006, Dynasties 0 – 3 [in:] Hornung E., Krauss R. and Warburton D.A. (eds), *Ancient Egyptian Chronology*, Leiden-Boston: 94-115.

Kaiser W., 1961, Bericht über eine archäologische-geologische Felduntersuchung in Ober- und Mittelägypten, *MDAIK* 17: 1-53.
- 1969, Zu den königlichen Talbezirken der 1. und 2. Dynastie in Abydos und zur Baugeschichte des Djoser-Grabmals, *MDAIK* 25: 1-21.
- 1985a, Ein Kultbezirk des Königs Den in Sakkara, *MDAIK* 41: 47-60.
- 1985b Kaiser W., Zur Südausdehnung der vorgeschichtlichen Deltakulturen und zur frühen Entwicklung Oberägyptens, *MDAIK* 41: 61-87.
- 1987a, Zum Friedhof der Naqada-kultur von Minshat Abu Omar, *ASAE* 71: 119-126.
- 1987b, Vier vorgeschichtliche Gefässe von Haraga, *MDAIK* 43: 121-122.
- 1990, Zur Entstehung des gesamtägyptischen Staates, *MDAIK* 46: 287-299.

- 1991, Zur Nennung von Sened und Peribsen in Sakkara B3, *GM* 122: 49-55.
- 1994, Zu den Königsgrabern der 2. Dynastie in Sakkara und Abydos [in:] Bryan B.M. and Lorton D. (eds), *Essays in Honour of Hans Goedicke*, San Antonio: 113-123.

Kaiser W. and Dreyer G., 1982, Umm el-Qaab. Nachuntersuchen im frühzeitlichen Königsfriedhof. 2. Vorbericht, *MDAIK* 38: 211-269.

Kaiser W. and Zaugg A., 1988, Zum Fundplatz der Maadikultur bei Tura, *MDAIK* 44: 121-124.

Kákosy L., 1977, Heliopolis [in:] Helck W. and Otto E. (eds), *Lexikon der Ägyptologie*, Wiesbaden, vol. 2: 1111-1113.

Kanawaty M., 1981, Mobilier funéraire de la nécropole M d'Abou Roach. Epoque thinite [in:] Desroches-Noblecourt C. and Vercoutter J. (eds), *Un Siècle de Fouilles Françaises en Égypte 1880-1980*, Paris : 28-43.

Kamal A.B., 1911, (Gisa), *ASAE* X: 116-121.

Kaplony P., 1977, Heluan [in:] Helck W. and Otto E. (eds), *Lexikon der Ägyptologie*, Wiesbaden, vol. 2: 1115.

Kazimierczak M., 2012, The pottery from Tell el-Murra graves (seasons 2011-2012) [in:] Jucha M.A., Dębowska-Ludwin J. and Kołodziejczyk P. (eds) *Egypt 2012: Perspective of Research. Programme and Abstracts*, Krakow: 41.

Kemp B., 1966, Abydos and the royal tombs of the First Dynasty, *JEA* 52: 13-22.
- 1968, Merimda and the theory of house burial in Prehistoric Egypt, *CdE* 43, 85: 22-33.
- 1989, *Ancient Egypt: Anatomy of Civilization*, London-New York.

Kessler D., 1980, Ma'sara II [in:] Helck W. and Otto E. (eds), *Lexikon der Ägyptologie*, Wiesbaden, t. 3: 1196.

Khouli A. el-, 1968, A preliminary report on the excavations at Tura, 1963-64, *ASAE* 60.1: 73-76.

Klasens A., 1957, The excavations of the Leiden Museum of Antiquities at Abu-Roash. Report of the first season: 1957, part I, *OMRO* 38: 58-68.
- 1958a, The excavations of the Leiden Museum of Antiquities at Abu-Roash. Report of the first season: 1957, part II, *OMRO* 39: 20-31.
- 1958b, The excavations of the Leiden Museum of Antiquities at Abu-Roash. Report of the second season: 1958, part I, *OMRO* 39: 32-55.
- 1959, The excavations of the Leiden Museum of Antiquities at Abu-Roash. Report of the second season: 1958, part II, *OMRO* 40: 41-61.

- 1960a, The excavations of the Leiden Museum of Antiquities at Abu-Roash. Report of the third season: 1959, part I, *OMRO* 41: 69-94.
- 1960b, The excavations of the Leiden Museum of Antiquities at Abu-Roash. Report of the third season: 1959, part II, *OMRO* 41: 108-128.

Klug S. and Beck K.-G., 1985, Preliminary report on the human skeletal remains from Maadi and Wadi Digla, *MDAIK* 41: 99-107.

Kołodziejczyk P., 2009, Tell el-Farkha 2006. Granary models, *SAAC* 13: 49-54.
- 2012, Tokens and seals [in:] Chłodnicki M., Ciałowicz K.M. and Mączyńska A. (eds), *Tell el-Farkha I. Excavations 1998-2011*, Poznań-Kraków: 267-277.

Kozłowska A., 2012, A preliminary report of anthropological resaerch from Tell el-Murra site – difficulties, challenges and perspectives [in:] Jucha M. A., Dębowska-Ludwin J. and Kołodziejczyk P. (eds) *Egypt 2012: Perspective of Research. Programme and Abstracts*, Krakow: 41.

Köhler E.Ch., 1998, Excavations at Helwan – new insights into Early Dynastic masonry, *BACE* 9: 65-72.
- 1999, Re-assessment of a cylinder seal from Helwan, *GM* 168: 49-56.
- 2000, Excavations in the Early Dynastic cemetery at Helwan. A preliminary report of the 1998/1999 and 1999/2000 seasons, *BACE* 11: 83-92.
- 2000-2001, Preliminary report on the 2nd excavation season of the Australian Centre for Egyptology, Maquarie University Sydney at the Cemetery of Helwan/Ezbet el-Walda, *ASAE* LXXVI: 23-29.
- 2001, Excavations at Helwan, *EA* 18: 38-40.
- 2003, The new excavations in the Early Dynastic necropolis at Helwan, *Archéo-Nil* 13: 17-27.
- 2004a, On the origins of Memphis – the new excavations in the Early Dynastic necropolis at Helwan [in:] Hendrickx S., Friedman R.F., Ciałowcz K.M. and Chłodnicki M. (eds), *Egypt and its Origins. Studies in Memory of B. Adams*, Leuven: 295-315.
- 2004b, Seven years of excavations at Helwan, Egypt, *BACE* 15: 79-88.
- 2004c, *The Cairo Museum Collection of Artefacts from Zaki Saad's Excavations at Helwan*, Armidale.
- 2005, *Helwan I. Excavations in the Early Dynastic Cemetery. Seasons 1997/1998* (with contributions by Birell M., Casey I., Hikade T., Smythe J. and St.Clair B.), Heidelberg.
- 2007, Final report on the 9th season of excavations in the Early Dynastic cemetery at Helwan/Ezbet el-Walda, *ASAE* 81: 191-215.
- 2008a, Final report on the tenth season of excavations in the Early Dynastic cemetery at Helwan/Ezbet el-Walda, *ASAE* 82: 171-181.
- 2008b, Early Dynastic society at Memphis [in:] Engel E.M., Müller V. and Hartung U. (eds),

*Zeichen aus dem Sand: Streiflichter aus Ägyptens Geschichte zu Ehren von Günter Dreyer*, Wiesbaden: 381-399.
- 2008c, The interaction between the roles of Upper and Lower Egypt in the formation of the Egyptian state. Another view [in:] Midant-Reynes B. and Tristant Y. (eds), *Egypt at its origin 2. Proceedings of the International Conference "Origin of the State. Predynastic and Early Dynastic Egypt" Toulouse (France), 5th-8th September 2005*, Leuven-Paris: 515-543.
- 2009, Final report on the 11th season of excavations in the Early Dynastic cemetery at Helwan/Ezbet el-Walda by the Australian Centre for Egyptology, Macquarie University, Sydney, *ASAE* 83: 279-293.
- 2011, Neolithic in the Nile Valley (Fayum A, Merimde, el-Omari, Badarian), *Archéo-Nil* 21, 17-20.

Köhler Ch. and van den Brink, E.C.M., 2002, Four jars with incised serekh-signs from Helwan recently retrieved from the Cairo Museum, *GM* 187: 59-75.

Köhler E. Ch. and Jones J., 2009, *Helwan II. The Early Dynastic and Old Kingdom Funerary Relief Slabs*, Rahden.

Kroeper K., 1986/87, The ceramic of the Pre/Early Dynastic cemetery of Minshat Abu Omar, *Bulletin of the Egyptological Seminar* 8: 73-94.
- 1988, The excavations of the Münich East-Delta Expedition in Minshat Abu Omar [in:] van den Brink E.C.M. (ed.) *The Archaeology of the Nile Delta, Egypt. Problems and Priorities*, Amsterdam: 11-19.
- 1992, Tombs of the elite in Minshat Abu Omar [in:] van den Brink E.C.M. (ed.), *The Nile Delta in Transition: 4th-3rd Millennium B.C.*, Tel Aviv: 127-150.
- 1994a, Minshat Abu Omar, *BCE* 18: 19-32.
- 1994b, Minshat Abu Omar. Pot burials occurring in the Dynastic cemetery, *BCE* 18: 19-32.
- 1996, Minshat Abu Omar – burials with palettes [in:] Spencer A.J. (ed.), *Aspects of Early Egypt*, London: 70-92.
- 1999, Minshat Abu Omar [in:] Bard K.A. (ed.), *Encyclopedia of the Archaeology of Ancient Egypt*, London-New York: 529-531.
- 2004, Minshat Abu Omar. Aspects of the analysis of cemetery [in:] Hendrickx S., Friedman R.F., Ciałowcz K.M. and Chłodnicki M., (eds) *Egypt and its Origins. Studies in Memory of B. Adams*, Leuven: 859-880.

Kroeper K. and Krzyżaniak L., 1992, Two ivory boxes from Early Dynastic graves in Minshat Abu Omar [in:] Friedman R. and Adams B. (eds), *The Followers of Horus. Studies dedicated to Michael Allan Hoffman, 1944-1990*, Oxford: 207-214.

*Early Burial Customs in Northern Egypt*

Kroeper K. and Wildung D., 1985, *Minshat Abu Omar. Münchner Ostdelta Expedition. Vorbericht 1978-1984*, München.
- 1994, *Minshat Abu Omar I. Ein vor- und frühgeschichtlicher Friedhof im Nildelta*, Mainz.
- 2000, *Minshat Abu Omar II. Ein vor- und frühgeschichtlicher Friedhof im Nildelta*, Mainz.

Kromer K., 1991, *Nezlet Batran: eine Mastaba aus dem Alten Reich bei Gisen (Ägypten), Österreichische Ausgrabungen 1981-1983*, Vienna.

Krzyżaniak L., 1989, Recent archaeological evidence on the earliest settlement in the eastern Nile Delta [in:] Krzyżaniak L. and Kobusiewicz M. (eds), *Late Prehistory of the Nile Basin and the Sahara*, Poznań: 267-285.
- 1992, *Schyłek pradziejów w środkowym Sudanie*, Poznań.

Kubiak-Martens L. and Langer J.J., 2008, Predynastic beer brewing as suggested by botanical and physicochemical evidence from Tell el-Farkha, eastern Delta [in:] Midant-Reynes B. and Tristant Y. (eds), *Egypt at its origin 2. Proceedings of the International Conference "Origin of the State. Predynastic and Early Dynastic Egypt" Toulouse (France), 5th-8th September 2005*, Leuven-Paris: 427-441.

Lacher C.M., 2011, The tomb of king Ninetjer at Saqqara [in:] Friedman R.F. and Fiske P.N (eds), *Egypt at its Origins 3. Proceedings of the Third International Conference "Origin of the State. Predynastic and Early Dynastic Egypt", London, 27th July – 1st August 2008*, Leuven: 213-231.

La Loggia A.S., 2011, Egyptian engineering in the Early Dynastic period: the sites of Saqqara and Helwan [in:] Friedman R. F. and Fiske P. N. (eds), *Egypt at its Origins 3. Proceedings of the Third International Conference "Origin of the State. Predynastic and Early Dynastic Egypt", London, 27th July – 1st August 2008*, Leuven: 233-256.

Larsen H., 1940a, Tomb six at Maasara: an Egyptian Second Dynasty tomb, *Acta Archaeologica* 11: 103-124.
- 1940b, Three shaft tombs at Maasara, Egypt, *Acta Archaeologica* 11: 161-206.
- 1956, A Second Dynasty grave at Wardan, Northern Egypt, *Orientalia Suecana* V: 3-11.

Leclant J., 1950, Compte rendu des fouilles et travaux menés en Égypte, 1948-50. Qatta, *Or* 19: 494-5.
- 1952, Fouilles et travaux en Égypte, 1950-51. Qatta, *Or* 21: 247.
- 1953, Fouilles et travaux en Égypte, 1951-52. Qatta, *Or* 22: 98-99.
- 1954, Fouilles et travaux en Égypte, 1952-53. Qatta, *Or* 23: 74.
- 1961, Fouilles et travaux en Égypte, 1959-60. Tourah, *Or* 30: 104.

- 1973a, Fouilles et travaux en Égypte et ou Soudan, 1971-72. Khelwet Abou Musallem, *Or* 42: 396.
- 1973b, Fouilles et travaux en Égypte et ou Soudan, 1971-72. Tibbin, *Or* 42: 404.
- 1978, Fouilles et travaux en Égypte et ou Soudan, 1976-77, Tourah, *Or* 47: 274.

Leclant J. and Clerc G., 1994a, Fouilles et travaux en Égypte et au Soudan, 1992-1993. Abousir, *Or* 63: 376-377.
- 1994b, Fouilles et travaux en Égypte et au Soudan, 1992-1993. Edfou, *Or* 63: 427.

Leclant J. and Minault-Gout A., 1998, Fouilles et travaux en Égypte et au Soudan, 1998-1999. Saqqara, *Or* 67: 347.
- 1999a, Fouilles et travaux en Égypte et ou Soudan. 1997-98. Minschat Ezzat, *Or* 68: 332-333.
- 1999b, Fouilles et travaux en Égypte et ou Soudan. 1997-98. Tell Ibrahim Awad, *Or* 68: 334.
- 2000, Fouilles et travaux en Égypte et au Soudan, 1998-1999. Saqqara. c), *Or* 69: 236-237.
- 2001, Fouilles et travaux en Égypte et ou Soudan. 1999-2000. Tell es-Samara, *Or* 70: 366.

Legrain G., 1903, Notes d'inspection. VI. La nécropole archaïque du Gebel Silsileh, *ASAE* IV: 218-220.

Leonard A., 2000, Food for thought: Saqqara tomb 3477 revisited, *Near Eastern Archaeology* 63,3: 177-179.

Lepsius K.R., 1897, *Denkmäler aus Ägypten und Äthiopien*, Tekst, I, Berlin.

Lindemann J., 1988, Prähistorische Siedlungsreste nördlich des Satettempels [in:] Kaiser W. et al., Stadt und Tempel von Elephantine. 15./16. Grabungsbericht, *MDAIK* 44: 141-144.

Loat W.L.S, 1905, *Gurob*, London.

Macramallah R., 1940, *Un cimetière archaïque de la classe moyenne du peuple à Saqqarah*, le Caire.

Martin G.T., 1997, "Covington's tomb" and related early monuments at Giza [in:] Berger C. and Mathieu B. (ed.), *Études sur l'Ancien Empire et la nécropole de Saqqara dedieé à Jean-Philippe Lauer*, Montpellier: 279-288.

Maspero M.G., 1902, Note sur les objects recuellis sous la pyramide d'Ounas, *ASAE* 3: 185-190.

Mathieson I., Bettles E., Clarke J., Duhig C., Ikram S., Maguire L., Quie S., and Tavares A., 1997, The National Museum of Scotland Saqqara survey project 1993-95, *JEA* 83: 17-53.

Matson F.R., 1969, Some aspects of ceramic technology, [in:] Brothwell D. and Higgs E. (eds), *Science in Archaeology*, Bristol: 592-602.

Mączyńska A., 2004, Społeczności delty Nilu w okresie predynastycznym (3800-3300/3200 BC) oraz ich kontakty z Palestyną, Poznań. (unpublished doctoral thesis)

- 2011, The Lower Egyptian-Naqada transition: a view from Tell el-Farkha [in:] Friedman R.F. and Fiske P.N (eds), *Egypt at its Origins 3. Proceedings of the Third International Conference "Origin of the State. Predynastic and Early Dynastic Egypt", London, 27*[th] *July – 1*[st] *August 2008*, Leuven: 879-910.

Menghin O. and Amer M., 1936, *The Excavations of the Egyptian University in the Neolithic Site at Maadi. Second Preliminary Report Season 1932*, Cairo.

Merghani S. el-, 2003, How studies of botanical remains and animal bones contribute to the re-writing of the history of the Delta over time [in:] Hawass Z. (ed.), *Egyptology at the Dawn of the Twenty-first Century. Proceedings of the Eighth International Congress of Egyptologists, Cairo 2000. Vol. 1, Archaeology*, Cairo-New York: 339-344.

Midant-Reynes B., 2000, *The Prehistory of Egypt. From the First Egyptians to the First Pharaohs*, Oxford.
- 2003, *Aux origines de l'Égypte. Du Néolothique à l'émergence de l'Etat*, Fayard.
- 2007, Kôm el-Khilgan (Delta du Nil). Premiers résultats après 4 ans de fouille (2002-2005), *Archéo-Nil* 12: 1-11.

Midant-Reynes B. and Denoix S., 2011, 1. Le delta du Nil au IVe millénaire, Tell al-Iswid [in: ] Midant-Reynes B. and Denoix S., *Rapport d'activité 2010-2011(IFAO), Axe 1. Milieux et peuplement*: 3-10.

Midant-Reynes B., Buchez N., Crubézy E. and Janin T., 1996, The Predynastic site of Adaima: settlement and cemetery [in:] Spencer A.J. (ed.), *Aspects of Early Egypt*, London: 93-97.

Midant-Reynes B., Briois F., Buchez N., Crubézy E., De Dapper M., Duschesne S., Fabry B., Hochstrasser-Petit Ch., Staniaszek L. and Tristant Y., 2003, Kom el-Khilgan: un nouveau site predynastique dans le Delta, *Archéo-Nil* 13: 55-64.

Midant-Reynes B., Briois F., Buchez N., De Dapper M., Duchesne S., Fabry B., Hochstrasser-Petit Ch., Staniaszek L. and Tristant Y., 2004, Kom el-Khilgan. A New Site of the Predynastic Period in Lower Egypt. The 2002 Campaign [in:] Hendrickx S., Friedman R.F., Ciałowcz K.M. and Chłodnicki M., (eds), *Egypt and its Origins. Studies in Memory of B. Adams*, Leuven: 465-486.

Möller G., 1906, Ausgrabung der Deutschen Orient-Gesellschaft auf dem vorgeschichtlichen Friedhofe bei Abusir el-Meleq im Sommer 1905, *MDOG* 30: 1-28.
- 1907, 2. Ausgrabung bei Abûsir el-Meleq 1906, *MDOG* 34: 2-13.

- 1926, *Die Archäologische Ergebnisse des Vorgeschichtlichen Gräberfeldes von Abusir el-Meleq*, Osnabrück.

el-Moneim M.A.M.A. el-, 1993a, Der spätvordynastische-frühdynastische Tell von Beni 'Amir (Östl. Delta), *Journal of Historical and Archaeological Researches* 1: 1-29.
- 1993b, Late Predynastic-Early Dynastic Cemetery of Beni Amir (Eastern Delta), *Journal of Historical and Archaeological Researches* 1: 78-95.
- 1996a, Late Predynastic - Early Dynastic Cemetery of Beni Amir (Eastern Delta) [in:] Krzyżaniak L., Kroeper K. and Kobusiewicz M. (eds), *Interregional Contacts in the Later Prehistory of Northeastern Africa*, Poznań: 241-251.
- 1996b, Late Predynastic - Early Dynastic mound of Beni Amir (Eastern Delta) [in:] Krzyżaniak L., Kroeper K. and Kobusiewicz M. (eds), *Interregional Contacts in the Later Prehistory of Northeastern Africa*, Poznań: 253-275.

Monnet-Saleh J., 1987, Remarques sur les representations de la peinture d'Hierakonpolis (Tombe no. 100), *JEA* 73: 51-58.

Montet P., 1938, Tombeaux de la I[ere] et de la IV[e] dynasties à Abou-Roach, *KÊMI* 7: 11-69.
- 1946, Tombeaux de la I[ere] et de la IV[e] dynasties à Abou-Roach. Deuxiéme partie: inventaire des objets, *KÊMI* 8: 157-227.

Morgan H. de, 1984, Archaeological research in the Nile Valley between Esna and Gebel el-Silsila (1908) [in:] Needler W. (ed.), *Predynastic and Archaic Egypt in the Brooklyn Museum*, Brooklyn: 50-66.

Morgan J. de, 1897, *Recherches sur les origines de l'Égypte. II. Ethnographie préhistorique et tombeau royal de Negedah*, Paris.

Morris E.F., 2007a, On the ownership of the Saqqara mastabas and allotment of political and ideological power at the dawn of the state [in:] Hawass Z., Richards J. (eds), *The Archaeology and Art of Ancient Egypt. Essays in Honour of David B. O'Connor*, vol. II, Cairo: 171-190.
- 2007b, Sacrifice for the state: First Dynasty royal funerals and the rites at Macramallah's Rectangle [in:] Laneri N. (ed.), *Performing death. Social analyses of funerary traditions in the ancient Near East and Mediterranean*, Chicago: 2-37.

Mortensen B., 1985, Four jars from the Maadi Culture found in Giza, *MDAIK* 41: 145-147.
- 1992, Carbon-14 Dates from El Omari, [in:] Friedman R.F. and Adams B. (eds), *The Followers of Horus*, Oxford: 173-174.
- 1999a, Tura, predynastic cemeteries [in:] Bard K.A. (ed.), *Encyclopedia of the Archaeology of Ancient Egypt*, London-New York: 851-852.

*Early Burial Customs in Northern Egypt*

- 1999b, Heliopolis. The predynastic cemetery [in:] Bard K.A. (ed.), *Encyclopedia of the Archaeology of Ancient Egypt*, London-New York: 366-367.
- 1999c, El-Omari [in:] Bard K.A. (ed.), *Encyclopedia of the Archaeology of Ancient Egypt*, London-New York: 592-594.

Mostafa I.A., 1988a, A preliminary report on the excavation of the E.A.O. at Tell Fara'on "Imet", season 1985-1986 [in:] van den Brink E.C.M. (ed.), *The Archaeology of the Nile Delta. Problems and Priorities*, Amsterdam: 141-149.
- 1988b, Some objects dating from the Archaic Period found at Tell Faraon Imet, *GM* 102: 73-84.

Munro P., 1983, Einige Bemerkungen zum Unas-Friedhof in Sakkara. 3. Vorbericht uber die Arbeiten der Gruppe Hannover im Herbst 1978 und im Fruhjar 1980, *Studien zur Altägyptischen Kultur* 10: 277-295.
- 1993a, Zur Topographie des Unas-Friedhofes [in:] Munro P., *Der Unas-Friedhof nord-west. I. Topographisch-histirische Einleitung. Das Doppelgrab der Konniginnen*, Mainz: 1-8.
- 1993b, Report on the work of the Joint Archaeological Mission Free University of Berlin / University of Hannover during their 12th campaign (15th March until 14th May, 1992) at Saqqâra, *Discussions in Egyptology* 26: 47-58.

Needler W. (ed.), 1984, *Predynastic and Archaic Egypt in the Brooklyn Museum*, Brooklyn.

Nowak M.M., 2011, Results of preliminary analysis of Lower Egyptian settlement discovered on the Central Kom in Tell el-Farkha, *SAAC* 15: 49-63.

Nørdström, H.Å., 1972, *Neolithic and A-Group Sites. The Scandinavian Joint Expedition to Sudanese Nubia III*, Stockholm.

O'Connor D., 1989, New funerary enclosures (Talbezirke) of the Early Dynastic period at Abydos, *JARCE* 26: 51-86.
- 1991, Boat graves and pyramid origins, *Expedition* 33, 3: 5-17.
- 2005, The ownership of elite tombs at Saqqara in the First Dynasty [in:] Daoud Kh., Bedier Sh. and Abd El-Fatah S., *Studies in Honor of Ali Radwan*, vol. II, Cairo: 223-231.

Oren E.D., 1989, Early Bronze age settlement in Northern Sinai: a model for Egypto-Canaanite interconnections [in:] de Miroschedji P.R. (ed.), *L'urbanisation de la Palestine à l'âge du bronze ancien*, Oxford: 389-405.

Pawlikowski M. and Dębowska-Ludwin J., 2011, Bone material and mineralogical processes of its destruction at the site of Tell el-Farkha, *SAAC* 15: 37-47.

Payne J.C., 1993, *Catalogue of the Predynastic Egyptian Collection in the Ashmolean Museum*, Oxford.

Patch D.C., 1997, Merimde, [in:] Meyers E.M. (ed.) *The Oxford Encyclopaedia of Archaeology in the Near East*, New York-Oxford vol. 3: 471-472.

Peet T.E., 1914, *The Cemeteries of Abydos. Part II. 1911-1912*, London.

Petrie W.M.F., 1900, *Royal Tombs of the First Dynasty I*, London.
- 1901a, *Royal Tombs of the First Dynasty II*, London.
- 1901b, *Diospolis Parva. The Cemeteries of Abadiyeh and Hu. 1898-1899*, London.
- 1902, *Abydos I*, London.
- 1903, *Abydos II*, London.
- 1907, *Gizeh and Rifeh*, London.
- 1912, A cemetery of the earliest dynasties, *Man* 12: 137-138.
- 1914, *Tarkhan II*, London.
- 1921, *Corpus of Prehistoric Pottery and Palettes*, London.

Petrie W.M.F. and Brunton G., 1924a, *Sedment I*, London.
- 1924b, *Sedment II*, London.

Petrie W.M.F., Brunton G. and Murray M.A., 1923, *Lahun*, London.

Petrie W.M.F., Wainwright G.A. and Gardiner A.H., 1913, *Tarkhan I and Memphis V*, London.

Petrie W.M.F., Wainwright G.A. and Mackay E., 1912, *The Labyrinth, Gerzeh, and Mazghuneh*, London.

Petrie W.M.F. and Quibell J.E., 1896, *Naqada and Ballas*, London.

Pryc G., 2007, Stone vessels from Tell el-Farkha site. Season 2007, *SAAC* 13: 55–65.

Quibell J.E., 1913, *Excavations at Saqqara (1911-1912). The Tomb of Hesy*, Cairo.
- 1923, *Excavations at Saqqara (1912-1914). Archaic Mastabas*, Cairo.

Quibell J.E. and Green F.W., 1902, *Hierakonpolis II*, London.

Radwan A., 1991, Ein Treppengrab der 1. Dynastie aus Abusir, *MDAIK* 47: 305-308.
- 1995, Recent excavations of the Cairo University at Abusir „A cemetery of the 1st Dynasty" [in:] Kessler D. and Schulz R. (eds), *Gedenkschrift für Winfried Barta*, Frankfurt: 311-314.
- 2000, Mastaba XVII at Abusir (First Dynasty) preliminary results and general remarks [in:] Batra M. and Krejci J. (eds), *Abusir and Saqqara in the Year 2000*, Praha: 509-514.

- 2003, Some remarks concerning the superstructure of some mastabas at Abusir [in:] Hawass Z. (ed.), *Egyptology at the Dawn of the Twenty-first Century. Proceedings of the Eighth International Congress of Egyptologists, Cairo 2000, Vol. 1, Archaeology*, Cairo-New York: 377-379.

Rampersad S., 2003, Report of the first field season at Tell el-Masha`la, Egypt 2002, *JARCE* 40: 171-186.
- 2006,Tell el-Masha`la: a Predynastic/Early Dynastic site in the Eastern Nile Delta [in:] Kroeper K., Chłodnicki M. and Kobusiewicz M. (eds), *Archaeology of Early Northeastern Africa: In Memory of Lech Krzyżaniak*, Poznań: 789-816.

Randal-MacIver D. and Mace A.C., 1902, *El Amrah and Abydos*, London.

Raven M.J., van Walsem R., Aston B.G. and Strouhal E., 2003a, Preliminary report on the Leiden excavations at Saqqara, eeasons 2001: the tomb of Meryneith, *JEOL* 37: 71-89.
- 2003b, Preliminary report on the Leiden excavations at Saqqara, seasons 2002: the tomb of Meryneith, *JEOL* 37: 91-109.

Regulski I., 2011, Investigating a new necropolis of Dynasty 2 at Saqqara [in:] Friedman R.F. and Fiske P.N (eds) *Egypt at its Origins 3. Proceedings of the Third International Conference "Origin of the State. Predynastic and Early Dynastic Egypt"*, London, 27th July – 1st August 2008, Leuven: 293-311.

Regulski I., Lacher C. and Hood A., 2010, Preliminary report on the excavations in the Second Dynasty necropolis at Saqqara, season 2009, *JEOL* 42: 25-53.

Reisner G.A., 1936, *The Development of the Egyptian Tomb down to the Accession of Cheops*, Cambridge, Massachusetts.

Rizkana I. and Seeher J., 1987, *Maadi I. The Pottery of the Predynastic Settlement*, Mainz am Rhein.
- 1988, *Maadi II. The Lithic Industries of the Predynastic Settlement*, Mainz am Rhein.
- 1989, *Maadi III. The Non-Lithic Small Finds and the Structural Remains of the Predynastic Settlement*, Mainz am Rhein.
- 1990, *Maadi IV. The Predynastic Cemeteries of Maadi and Wadi Digla*, Mainz am Rhein.

Rowland J.M. and Hassan F.A., 2003, The computerized database and potential for a geographic information system at Karf Hassan Dawood [in:] Hawass Z. (ed.), *Egyptology at the Dawn of the Twenty-first Century. Proceedings of the Eighth International Congress of Egyptologists, Cairo 2000. Vol. 1, Archaeology*, Cairo-New York: 416-423.

Rubensohn O., 1905, Ausgrabungen in Abusir-el-Mäläq, *Bulletin de la Société Archéologique d'Alexandrie* 8: 20-24.

Ryholt K., 2008, King Seneferka in the kind-list and his position in the Early Dynastic period, *Journal of Egyptian History* 1: 159-173.

Saad Z.Y., 1942, Preliminary report on the royal excavations at Helwan (1942), *ASAE* XLI: 405-409.
- 1943, Preliminary report on the royal excavations at Helwan (1942) (Plan), *ASAE* 42: 357.
- 1947a, Preliminary report on the royal excavations at Saqqara 1941-1942 [in:] Saad Z.Y., *Royal excavations at Saqqara and Helwan (1941-1945)*, Cairo: 105-112.
- 1947b, Preliminary report on the royal excavations at Saqqara 1944-1945 [in:] Saad Z.Y., *Royal excavations at Saqqara and Helwan (1941-1945)*, Cairo: 161-178.
- 1951, *Royal excavations at Helwan (1945-1947)*, Cairo.
- 1969, *The Excavations at Helwan. Art and Civilization in the First and Second Dynasties*, Oklahoma.

Sadeek W.T. el- and Murphy J.M., 1983, A mud sealing with Seth vanquished (?), *MDAIK* 39: 159-175.

Sanussi A. el- and Jones M., 1997, A site of the Maadi culture near the Giza Pyramids, *MDAIK* 53: 241-253.

Sawi A. el-, 1979, *Excavations at Tell Basta. Report on Seasons 1967-1971 and Catalogue of Finds*, Praag.

Scharff A., 1926, *Das Vorgeschichtliche Gräberfeld von Abusir el-Meleq*, Leipzig.
- 1931, *Die Altertümer der Vor- und Früzeit*, Berlin.

Schmandt-Besserat D., 1992, *Before Writing*, Austin.

Schmidt K., 1992a, Tell el-Fara'in/Buto and Tell el-Iswid (south): the lithic industries from the Chalcolithic to the early Old Kingdom [in:] van den Brink E.C.M. (ed.), *The Nile Delta in Transition: 4th. - 3rd. Millennium B.C.*, Tel Aviv: 31-42.
- 1992b, Tell Ibrahim Awad: a preliminary report on the lithic industries [in:] van den Brink E.C.M. (ed.), *The Nile Delta in Transition: 4th. - 3rd. Millennium B.C.*, Tel Aviv: 76-96.
- 1993, Comments on the lithic industry of the Buto-Maadi culture in Lower Egypt [in:] Krzyżaniak L., Kobusiewicz M. and Alexander J. (eds), *Environmental Change and Human Culture in the Nile Basin and Northern Africa until the Second Millennium B.C.*, Poznań: 267-277.

Seeher J., 1990, Maadi - eine prädynastische Kulturgruppe zwischen Oberägypten und Palästina, *Prähistorische Zeitschrift* 65: 123-156.
- 1999, Abusir el-Meleq, [in:] Bard K.A. (ed.), *Encyclopedia of the Archaeology of Ancient Egypt*, London: 91-93.

Seidlmayer S.J., 1988, Funerarer Aufwand und soziale Ungleichheit. Eine methodische Anmerkung zum

*Early Burial Customs in Northern Egypt*

Problem der Rekonstruktion der gesellschaftlichen Gliederung aus Friedhofsfunden, *GM* 104: 25-51.

Śliwa J., 1980, *Pottery from Turah in the collection of the Archaeological Museum in Cracow*, Warszawa-Kraków.
- 1998, Keramik der Naqada-Kultur und der archaischen Zeit [in:] Ginter B., Kozłowski J.K., Pawlikowski M., Śliwa J. and Kemmerer-Grothaus H., *Frühe Keramik und Kleinfund aus El-Târif*, Mainz: 45-58.

Spencer A.J., 1979, *Brick Architecture in Ancient Egypt*, Warmister.

Stadelmann R., 1985, Die Oberbauten der königsgraber der 2. Dynastie in Sakkara [in:] Posener-Krieger P. (ed.), *Mélanges Gamal Eddin Mokhtar*, Cairo, vol. II: 295-307.

Stevenson A., 2006, *Gerzeh, A Cemetery Shortly Before History*, London.
- 2009, *The Predynastic Egyptian Cemetery of el-Gerzeh. Social Indentities and Mortuary Practices*, Leuven-Paris-Walpole MA.

Swelim N., 1991, Some remarks on the great rectangular monuments of middle Saqqara, *MDAIK* 47: 389-402.

Tassie G.J. and van Wetering J., 2003, Early cemeteries of the East Delta: Kafr Hassan Dawood, Minshat Abu Omar and Tell Ibrahim Awad [in:] Hawass Z. (ed.), *Egyptology at the Dawn of the Twenty-first Century. Proceedings of the Eighth International Congress of Egyptologists, Cairo 2000. Vol. 1, Archaeology*, Cairo-New York: 499-507.

Tavares A., 1998, The Saqqara Survey Project [in:] Eyre C.J. (ed.) *Proceedings of the Seventh International Congress of Egyptologists*, Leuven: 1135-1142.
- 1999, Saqqara North, Early Dynastic tombs [in:] Bard K.A. (ed.), *Encyclopedia of the Archaeology of Ancient Egypt*, London-New York: 700-704.

Tristant Y., 2005, L'occupation humaine dans le delta du Nil aux 5e et 4e millénaire. Approche géoarchéologique à partir de la région de Samara (delta oriental), Toulouse. (unpublished doctoral thesis)
- 2008a, Deux grands tombeaux du cimetière M d'Abou Rowach (I$^{re}$ dynastie), *Archéo-Nil* 18: 131-147.
- 2008b, Les tombes des premières dynasties à Abou Roach, *BIFAO* 108: 325-370.

Tristant Y., De Dapper M. and Midant-Reynes B., 2008, Human occupation of the Nile Delta during Pre- and Early Dynastic times. A view from Kom el-Khilgan [in:] Midant-Reynes B. and Tristant Y. (eds), Rowland J. and Hendrickx S. (coll.), *Egypt at its origins 2. Proceedings of the international conference 'Origin of the State. Predynastic and Early Dynastic Egypt', Toulouse (France), 5th–8th September 2005*, Leuven-Paris: 463-482.

Tristant Y. and Midant-Reynes B., 2011, The predynastic cultures of the Nile Delta [in:] Teeter E. (ed.), *Before the Pyramids. The Origins of Egyptian Civilization*, Chicago: 45-54.

Tristant Y. and Smythe J., 2011, New Excavations for an old cemetery: preliminary results of the Abu Rowash project on the M cemetery (Dynasty 1) [in:] Friedman R. F. and Fiske P. N. (eds), *Egypt at its Origins 3. Proceedings of the Third International Conference "Origin of the State. Predynastic and Early Dynastic Egypt", London, 27th July – 1st August 2008*, Leuven: 313-332.

Tucker T.L., 2003, Bioarchaeology of Kafr Hassan Dawood: preliminary investigations [in:] Hawass Z. (ed.), *Egyptology at the Dawn of the Twenty-first Century. Proceedings of the Eighth International Congress of Egyptologists, Cairo 2000. Vol. 1, Archaeology*, Cairo-New York: 530-535.

Vandier J., 1952, *Manuel d'archéologie égyptienne. I. Les époques de formation. 1. La préhistoire*, Paris.

Walsem R. van, 2003, Une tombe royale de la deuxième dynastie à Saqqara sous la tombe Nouvel Empire de Meryneith, Campagne de fouille 2001-2002, *Archéo-Nil* 13: 6-15.
- 2004, The tomb of Merneith at Saqqara. Results of the Dutch mission 2001-2003, *BACE* 14: 117-134.

Watrin L., 2003, Lower-Upper Egyptian interaction during the Pre-Naqada period: from initial trade contacts to the ascendancy of Southern chiefdoms [in:] Hawass Z. (ed.), *Egyptology at the Dawn of the Twenty-first Century. Proceedings of the Eighth International Congress of Egyptologists, Cairo 2000. Vol. 2, History, Religion*, Cairo-New York: 566-581.

Watrin L. and Blin O., 2003, The Nile's early stone architecture: new data from Ma'adi West [in:] Hawass Z. (ed.), *Egyptology at the Dawn of the Twenty-first Century. Proceedings of the Eighth International Congress of Egyptologists, Cairo 2000. Vol. 1, Archaeology*, Cairo-New York: 557-567.

Way T. von der, 1985, Bericht über den Fortgang der Untersuchungen im Raum Tell el-Fara'in – Buto, *MDAIK* 41: 269-291.
- 1986a, Tell el-Fara'in – Buto. 1. Bericht, *MDAIK* 42: 191-212.
- 1986b, Tell el-Fara'in – Buto. 2. Bericht, *MDAIK* 43: 241-257.
- 1991, Die Grabungen in Buto und die Reichseinigung, *MDAIK* 47: 419-424.
- 1992, Excavations at Tell el-Fara'in/Buto in 1987-1989 [in:] van den Brink E.C.M. (ed.), *The Nile*

*Delta in Transition: 4th. - 3rd. Millennium B.C.*, Tel Aviv: 1-10.

- 1993, *Untersuchungen zur Spätvor- und Frühgeschichte Unterägyptens*, Heidelberg.
- 1997, *Tell el-Fara'in - Buto I. Ergebnisse zum Frühen Kontext. Kampagnen der Jahre 1983-1989*, Mainz.

Wengrow D., 2006, *The Archaeology of Early Egypt. Social Transformations in North–East Africa, 10,000–2,650 BC.*, Cambridge.

Wenke R.J., 1999a, Mendes [in:] Bard K.A. (ed.), *Encyclopedia of the Archaeology of Ancient Egypt*, London-New York: 499-501.
- 1999b, Fayum, Neolithic and Predynastic sites [in:] Bard K.A. (ed.), *Encyclopedia of the Archaeology of Ancient Egypt*, London-New York: 313-316.

Wetering J. van, 2004, The royal cemetery of the Early Dynastic period at Saqqara and the Second Dynasty royal tombs [in:] Hendrickx S., Friedman R.F., Ciałowcz K.M. and Chłodnicki M. (eds), *Egypt and its Origins. Studies in Memory of B. Adams*, Leuven: 1055-1080.

Wilkinson T.A.H., 1996a, *State Formation in Egypt: Chronology and Society*, Oxford.
- 1996b, A re-examination of the Early Dynastic necropolis at Helwan, *MDAIK* 52: 337-354.
- 1999, *Early Dynastic Egypt*, London/New York.

Williams B., 1982, Notes on Prehistoric cache fields of Lower Egyptian tradition at Sedment, *JNES* 41/3, 213-221.

Williams B.B and Logan T.J., 1987, The Metropolitan Museum knife handle and aspects of pharaonic imagery before Narmer, *JNES* 46: 245-286.

Wilson P. and Gilbert G., 2003, The Prehistoric Period at Saïs (Sa el-Hagar), *Archéo-Nil* 13: 65-72.

Wodzińska A., 2009a, *A Manual of Egyptian Pottery, Volume 1: Fayum – Lower Egyptian Culture*, Boston.
- 2009b, *A Manual of Egyptian Pottery, Volume 2: Naqada III – Middle Kingdom*, Boston.

Wood W., 1987, The Archaic stone tombs at Helwan, *JEA* 73: 59-70.

Yacoub F., 1981, The Archaic tombs at Tura el-Asmant, *ASAE* LXIV: 159-161.
- 1983, Excavations at Tûra el-Asmant, *JSSEA* 13,2: 103-106.

Youssef M., 1996, A preliminary report on a new Archaic mastaba at Saqqara, *GM* 152: 105-108.

Zeist W., 1988, Plant remains from a First Dynasty burial at Tell Ibrahim Awad [in:] van den Brink E.M.C. (ed.), *The Archaeology of the Nile Delta: Problems and Priorities*, Amsterdam: 111-114.